מאורות

ArtScroll Judaiscope Series®

Torah

Collected from the pages of
The Jewish Observer
by

Rabbi Nisson Wolpin
Editor

Lives

A Treasury of Biographical Sketches

Published by

Mesorah Publications, ltd

in conjunction with

Agudath Israel of America

FIRST EDITION
First impression ... October 1995

Published and Distributed by
MESORAH PUBLICATIONS, Ltd.
Brooklyn, N.Y. 11232

Distributed in Israel by
SIFRIATI / A. GITLER
4 Bilu Street / P.O.B. 14075 / Tel Aviv 61140

Distributed in Europe by
J. LEHMANN HEBREW BOOKSELLERS
20 Cambridge Terrace / Gateshead
Tyne and Wear / England NE8 1RP

Distributed in Australia and New Zealand by
GOLDS BOOK & GIFT CO.
36 William Street / Balaclava 3183, Vic., Australia

Distributed in South Africa by
KOLLEL BOOKSHOP
22 Muller Street / Yeoville 2198, Johannesburg, South Africa

ARTSCROLL JUDAISCOPE SERIES / TORAH LIVES
© Copyright 1995
by MESORAH PUBLICATIONS, Ltd.
4401 Second Avenue / Brooklyn, N.Y. 11232 / (718) 921-9000

ISBN
0-89906-319-5 (hard cover)
0-89906-320-9 (paperback)

Typography by CompuScribe at ArtScroll Studios, Ltd.
4401 Second Avenue / Brooklyn, N.Y. 11232 / (718) 921-9000

Printed in the United States of America by Noble Book Press Corp.
Custom bound by Sefercraft, Inc., Brooklyn, N.Y. 11232

Table of Contents

✒ Pioneers on the American Scene

The biographical sketches in this book first appeared
as articles in The Jewish Observer,
a monthly journal of thought and opinon
published by Agudath Israel of America.
Dr. Ernst L. Bodenheimer, Chairman, Editorial Board.

The following biographical sketches appear in *The Torah Personality* of the ArtScroll Judaiscope Series (in order of appearance): Rabbi Chaim Brisker (Soloveitchik); Rabbi Yisroel Meir HaKohen (*Chofetz Chaim*); Rabbi Avraham Yeshaya Karelitz (*Chazon Ish*); Moreinu Yaakov Rosenheim; Rabbi Yechiel Yaakov Weinberg (*Seride Esh*); Rabbi Meir Simcha HaKohen (*Or Same'ach*); Rabbi Yosef Rosen (Rogatchover *Gaon*); Rabbi Chaim Ozer Grodzensky; Rabbi Aaron Yoseif (Reb Archik) Baksht; Rabbi Yoseif Kahaneman (Ponevezher *Rav*); Rabbi Michael Ber Weissmandl; Rabbi Chaim Meir Hager (Vizhnitzer *Rebbe*); Rabbi Yisroel Alter (Gerer *Rebbe*); Rabbi Nochum Mordechai Perlow (Novominsker *Rebbe*); Rabbi Yoel Teitelbaum (Satmar *Rav*); Rabbi Moshe Yitzchok (Reb Itzikel) Gewirczman; Chacham Yoseif Chaim (*Ben Ish Chai*); Rabbi Yaakov Culi (*MeAm Loez*); Rabbi Raphael Chaim Yitzchok Karigal; Chazan Gershom Mendes Seixas; Rabbi Abraham Joseph Rice; Rabbi Yissachar Dov Illowy; Chazan Samuel Myer Isaacs; Rabbi Jacob Joseph; Rabbi Dr. Hillel Klien; Reb Elimelech Gavriel (Mike) Tress; Rabbi Yoseif Eliyahu Henkin; Rabbi and Mrs. Baruch Shapiro.

The following biographical sketches appear in *The Torah World* of the ArtScroll Judaiscope Series (in order of appearance): Rabbi Jacob Ettlinger (*Aroch LeNeir*); Reb Shraga and Golda Frank; Rabbi Pesach Pruskin (Kobrin); Rabbi Boruch Ber Lebowitz (Kaminetz); Rabbi Elchonon Wasserman (Baranovich); Rabbi Meir Shapiro (Lublin); Rabbi Menachem Ziemba (Warsaw); Rabbi Yosef Yitzchok Schneerson (Lubavitch); Rabbi Dov Ber Weidenfeld (Tshebin); Rabbi Yerucham Levovitz (Mir); Rabbi Yisrael Yaakov Lubchansky (Baranovich); Rabbi Dovid Kronglas (Baltimore); Rabbi Moshe Schwab (Gateshead); Sarah Schenirer; Dr. Leo Deutschlander (Bais Yaakov Movement); Rabbi Aharon Kotler (Kletzk — Lakewood); Rabbi Reuvain Grozovsky (Kaminetz — Monsey); Rabbi Joseph Breuer (Frankfurt — Washington Heights); Rabbi Avraham Kalmanowitz (Mir — Brooklyn); Rabbbi Chaim Leb Shmulevitz (Mir — Jerusalem); Rabbi Eliyahu Meir Bloch (Telshe — Cleveland); Rabbi Raphael Baruch Sorotzkin (Telshe — Cleveland); Rabbi Gedalia Schorr (Yeshiva Torah Vodaas); Rabbi Yitzchok Hutner (Yeshiva Rabbi Chaim Berlin — Brooklyn).

The following biographical sketches appear in *The Torah Profile* of the ArtScroll Judaiscope Series (in order of appearance): Rabbi Yisroel Salanter; Rabbi Yechiel Michel Epstein (*Aruch HaShulchan*); Rabbi Malkiel Tenenbaum (Lomza); Rabbi Yechiel Mordechai Gordon (Lomza-Petach Tikvah); Rabbi Yehoshua Tzvi Michel (Reb Hirsch Michel) Shapiro; Rabbi Yaakov Yisroel Kanievsky (Steipler *Gaon*); Rabbi Ezra Attiah (Yeshiva Porat Yosef); Rabbi Yitzchok Abohav (*Menoras Hamaor*); Ribi Ya'akov Abu-Hasira; Hacham Yishak Hai Tayeb (Tunis); Reb Shraga Feivel Mendlowitz (Yeshiva Torah Vodaath); Rabbi Yaakov Kamenetsky (Yeshiva Torah Vodaas); Rabbi Moshe Feinstein (Mesivtha Tifereth Jerusalem); Rabbi Yaakov Yitzchok Ruderman (Ner Israel, Baltimore); Rabbi Shneur Kotler (Lakewood); Rabbi Meir Shapiro (Lublin); Rabbi Moshe Yechiel Epstein (Ozerover *Rebbe*); Rabbi Eliezer Zisya Portugal (Skullener *Rebbe*); Schwester Selma Mayer; Rebbetzin Chana Perel Kotler; Rebbetzin Sarah Yaffen; Rebbetzin Vichna Kaplan.

The following biographical sketches appear in *Torah Luminaries* of the ArtScroll Judaiscope Series (in order of appearance): Rabbi Zelig Reuven Bengis (Yerushalayim); Rabbi Yisroel Zev Gustman; Rabbi Nochum Partzovitz (Mir); Rabbi Binyamin Beinush Finkel (Mir); Rabbi Simcha Wasserman; Rabbi Shaul Yedidyah Elazar Taub (Modzitzer *Rebbe*); Rabbi Dovid Yitzchok Isaac Rabinowitz (Skolye *Rebbe*); Rabbi Avrohom Yehoshua Hesh'l Twersky (Machnovke *Rebbe*); Rabbi Yisroel Spira (Bluzhever *Rebbe*); Rabbi Simcha Bunim Alter (Gerrer *Rebbe*); Rabbi Dovid Leibowitz (Yeshivah Chofetz Chaim); Rabbi Meir Chodosh; Rabbi Eliezer Levin (Detroit); Rabbi Yehudah Zev Segal (Manchester); Rabbi Pinchos Dovid Horowitz (Bostoner *Rebbe*); Rabbi Zalman Yaakov Friederman; Rabbi Moshe Zvi Aryeh Bick; Rabbi Dovid Lifshitz; Rabbi Shlomo Freifeld (Shor Yoshuv); Rabbi Mordechai Weinberg; Rabbi Yitzchok Kirzner; Mrs. Necha Golding; Mrs. Renee Reichman; Rebbetzin Feige Wasserman; Rebbetzin Sima Feinstein.

Contributors to this volume:

Mr. Berl Belsky, one of the first talmidim of Yeshivah Torah Vodaath, spent two years in Radin, from after Succos in 1931 (5632) through September 1933, when the Chofetz Chaim passed away.

Mrs. Lynn M. Berkowitz, of Southfield, Michigan, is working on a novel about Jews and the Civil War.

Rabbi Yaakov Feitman, a well-known author and lecturer, is *Rav* of the Young Israel of Beachwood, in Cleveland.

Rabbi Shimon Finkelman, a *rebbi* in Yeshivah Darchei Torah, Far Rockaway, N.Y., is a frequent contributor to *The Jewish Observer.* He is the author of several works published by ArtScroll/Mesorah, most recently, *Shabbos Stories* and *Chofetz Chaim: A Lesson A Day,* which he co-authored.

Rabbi Binyomin Forst is the author of *Laws of B'rachos* and *Laws of Kashrus,* published by ArtScroll/Mesorah. He lives in Far Rockaway, New York.

Rabbi Yerachmiel D. Fried, who serves as *Rosh Kollel* in Dallas, Texas, is the author of the *sefer Yom Tov Sheini K'hilchoso* as well as *Kuntress Tziuniim L'Ramban al HaTorah,* and *Sefer Minchas Erev Al Arvei Pesachim.*

Mr. Josef Friedenson is the founding editor of *Dos Yiddishe Vort,* Agudath Israel of America's Yiddish-language monthly journal of thought and opinion. This article is excerpted from a larger treatment of this subject that appeared in that journal. He is the author of several books on World War II Hatzalah efforts, most recently, *Dateline: Istanbul* about Dr. Jacob Griffel, published by Artscroll/Mesorah.

Mr. Sidney Greenwald, Chairman of the International Board of Directors of Sanz Medical Center/Laniado Hospital, is an independent consultant to health care services. He resides in Monsey, N.Y.

Rabbi Eliyahu Meir Klugman grew up in Washington Heights, where he enjoyed a close relationship with Rabbi Shimon Schwab, the subject of his article. He currently lives in Jerusalem where he is a *maggid shiur* in a *yeshivah gedolah.* His biography on Rabbi S.R. Hirsch is soon to be released by ArtScroll/Mesorah.

Dr. Gershon Kranzler, educator, author of a number of children's classes on Jewish themes, as well as *Williamsburg — A Sociological Study,* was an active member in Zeirei Agudath Israel in the late 30's and early

40's. He is currently a professor of sociology at Towson State College and Johns Hopkins University in Baltimore, Maryland.

Rabbi Alexander Linchner was among the seventy-five to one hundred American young men who studied in European yeshivos during the 1930's.

Mrs. Miriam Margoshes, who lives in Brooklyn, is a teacher in the Beth Jacob High School, as well as a free-lance writer, translator and editor. This article is based in part on an essay by Rabbi Moshe Yaakov Kanner, which appeared in *Dos Yiddishe Vort.*

Mr. Yonason Rosenblum, who lives in Jerusalem, is a regular contributor to *The Jewish Observer.* He is the author and translator of many works, including the recent *They Called Him Mike,* a biography of the legendary Reb Elimelech "Mike" Tress published by ArtScroll/Mesorah.

Mrs. Miriam Samsonowitz, a published writer, lives in Jerusalem.

Rabbi Chaim Shapiro, currently a Baltimore resident, is a frequent contributor to *The Jewish Observer.* His autobiographical account of his experiences in World War II, *Go, My Son,* was published by Feldheim.

Mrs. Sarah Shapiro, a published author who lives in Jerusalem, is a frequent contributor to *The Jewish Observer.* She has edited several authologies, including *Of Home and Heart* in the Judaiscope Series.

Mr. Martin H. Stern lives in London. The original Yiddish manuscript on which this book is based was never published.

Mrs. Gitti Weissmandl, a direct descendent of Rabbi Aszod, lives in Monsey, NY.

Rabbi Nisson Wolpin, editor of *The Jewish Observer* as well as this volume.

Rabbi Charles Wengrov, who lives in Jerusalem, is responsible for rendering into English such books as *Sefer Hachinuch, The Chofetz Chaim on the Siddur* and *A Tzaddik in Our Time.* He has been called "the dean of the translators."

Daas Torah:
Tapping the Source of Eternal Wisdom

*Is this a recently proclaimed phenomenon,
or has it always existed?
Who are the people endowed with it?*

◄§ Gedolim: A Timeless Concept

One of the most important quests in our lives is recognizing our true leaders. Just knowing to whom to turn on the sensitive and important issues, both individually and collectively, provides a measure of tranquility when facing the vicissitudes of life.

We are fortunate in that we know with certainty that in every generation there will be leaders who can be and must be followed in the same way as earlier generations were endowed with their own leaders:

"And you will come to the Kohanim, the Levi'im who will live in those days ...and you shall follow and adhere to all that they teach you" (Devarim 17,9).

In an oft-quoted passage, the Talmud asks: "Could one then consider going to the leaders of other generations?" This comes to teach us, says the *Gemara*, that the leaders of every generation are the appropriate ones for that generation.[1] There must, therefore, be *Gedolim* in every era, and we must be loyal to their teachings. The Torah here acknowledges the natural tendency to reject one's leadership when compared with that of previous generations. Many an age and era has bemoaned the seemingly precipitous fall of its Torah leadership from former grandeur and splendor. However, what each epoch must accept and come to terms with is that it is given the guiding lights — the *Gedolim* — that it requires. The question is not one of greater or lesser, but of need. These *Gedolim* are of their era, yet are able to tap eternal wells. It is their judgments that embody the timeless word of the Torah for their time,

---

1. *Rosh Hashanah* 25b; see *Torah Temimah* to *Devarim* 17,9.

and it is their guidance which is DAAS TORAH.

But, far from an answer, that is where the questions must begin:

Is Daas Torah something old or is it a recent innovation? ... Who has it or personifies it? ... How does one obtain Daas Torah? ... Can we know for sure who they are? ...

✒ Antagonism to Daas Torah

While the concept of *Daas Torah* as a source of authority is a fundamental Jewish teaching, some find it troubling. For, although many of us live by this principle and make the most important decisions of our lives based upon it, we are hard-pressed to identify its mechanism or even define its criteria.

But before quoting any specific response to those who oppose *Daas Torah*, it is worth taking note of a teaching of our sages: *"Avda b'hefkeira nicha lai* — A slave prefers a state of freedom without restraints"; the most primitive instinct of man is to rebel against authority to give himself free rein (see *Gittin* 13a). "No one is going to tell me what to do," can be rationalized as an expression of free will, but it is actually the natural retrogression into childlike defiance of parents and teachers, even when their inherent claim to authority should be obvious. One of the most subtle yet pernicious manifestations of this phenomenon is the often emotional, occasionally outright illogical hostility to the concept of *Daas Torah*.

One of the major criticisms against *Daas Torah* results from the impression that the phrase is of rather recent vintage. (As we shall note, there is some truth to this.) The opponents of the very concept of *Daas Torah* delight in pointing out that although the term may be found in the Talmud,[2] *Rishonim*[3] and *Acharonim*,[4] it was never before taken to mean (as a contemporary scholar has described its most common current application) "the authority of Torah sages to rule on matters which are not only in the sphere of religion but also upon issues which are inherently political, economical or social in nature."[5]

---

2. *Chullin* 90b.
3. *Rambam, Moreh Nevuchim*, p. 209; Responsa *Rashba* (attributed to *Ramban*) 2:33, 3:25.
4. See Introduction of *Netziv* to *Haamek Davar* to *Shemos*.
5. Dr. Gershon Bacon, *Daas Torah V'chevlei Moshiach, Tarbitz*, § 52, 1983. I am indebted to Rabbi Moshe Kolodny, Director of the Agudath Israel Archives, for providing me with this source.

The contention of these critics is that "the term *Daas Torah* in its current ideological sense seems to originate in the latter part of the nineteenth and in the first part of the twentieth century among heads of the Eastern European Yeshivot who were associated with Agudat Israel (e.g., the Haffetz Hayyim and R. Elkhanan Wasserman z.t.l.) as a response to the challenge to and breakdown of traditional rabbinic authority. It is a well-known phenomenon that when an institution has lost real power it makes extreme and excessive theoretical claims on its behalf."[6]

These writers go on to try to analyze the "need" for *Daas Torah* in sociological terms and even to compare it (*lehavdil elef havdalos*) to the "development of the doctrine of papal infallibility when the authority of the pope was waning."[7]

In other words, to further their own political (Agudath Israel?), religious (waning power?), or other agendas, these sages, it is alleged, created a new and halachically unwarranted hierarchy and authority, with themselves at the top of this new spiritual ladder.

Although the Chofetz Chaim and Reb Elchonon's accusers dutifully add the זצ״ל to these *Gedolim's* names, in reality they are imputing to them a crime of monstrous proportions. Could it be that these paragons of piety and virtue, the Chofetz Chaim, who was the "father of *Klal Yisrael*," and Reb Elchonon, who gave his life for his people and Torah, would crassly and blatantly distort Torah tradition simply to achieve some power for themselves or their successors? Not only our intuition about these sages, but even basic logic, dictates that this does not make sense.

Even more bizarrely, one of the critics of these *Gedolim* notes that since he has no problem with innovations in Judaism, he would in principle be able to accept the "new" doctrine of *Daas Torah*, but finds it strange that "the group that subscribes to the notion of *Daas Torah*" be the one that rejects any new ideas and incursions into tradition.[8]

---

6. Lawrence Kaplan, *Tradition*, Fall, 1980, p. 248, note 5.
7. Bacon, p. 302, note 26.
8. Kaplan, ibid.

◆§ An Ancient Concept with a New Name

Unfortunately, the confusing of semantics with substance here has resulted in a fundamental and extremely dangerous error. Yes, it is true that the current use of the term *Daas Torah* originated with the early leaders of Agudath Israel.[9] In fact, it was Reb Elchonon Wasserman who said of the Chofetz Chaim, "His ideas constitute 100% pure *Daas Torah*."[10] And yes, as we shall see, the imperative to coin a new phrase did flow from the exigencies of the era. But, most importantly, neither the Chofetz Chaim nor Reb Elchonon Wasserman contrived to devise a new form of rabbinic authority. As the critics of *Daas Torah* themselves perceive in moments of candor and honesty, it is ludicrous to impute major corruptions of ancient tradition to those whose lives are defined by being repositories of that tradition. So while they are correct in not finding the phrase in the writings of earlier generations, they missed the fact that, in truth, the concept is not new; through the use of the term, a time-honored tenet had simply been reaffirmed.

For what many of us, living in a century polluted by the sputterings of politicians, academics and "experts" of every type, have forgotten, is that for all our history until every recently, it was the Torah leadership, and it alone, that was the spokesman for the people of Israel. It has always been unthinkable for any major decision affecting the nation to be made by someone other than a Torah sage. And so, the term *Daas Torah* was superfluous because everyone knew that *Daas* with any other suffix was an oxymoron. Listening to *Gedolim* was as natural to the nation of Israel as breathing itself, and therefore we breathed in their wisdom and guidance with the same lack of self-consciousness as inhaling fresh air. To change the metaphor, for most of the saga of our nation, the Torah leadership was looked to as the "eyes of the congregation"[11] of Israel; no other perspective would have been considered for a moment.

---

9. See, for instance, the Hebrew version of the speeches of *Moreinu Reb Yaakov Rosenheim,* vol. I, p. 105, where as noted by Bacon, the Hebrew term דעת תורה is used.
10. See Aaron Sorasky, *Ohr Elchonon,* vol. 2, p. 94.
11. *Shir HaShirim Rabbah* 1,63.

Although this fact about our history should be, and to many is, self-evident, let us briefly review the generational chain, just in case there is any lingering doubt. No one needs to explain that *Moshe Rabbeinu's* entire persona as a leader flowed from the beloved *"Rabbeinu"* in his title. By virtue of his direct contact with the Giver of the Torah ("Mouth to mouth do I speak to him" - *Bamidbar* 12,8), he was the very quintessence of Torah.[12] As for the prophets, the *Rambam*[13] refers to each of the leaders of the generations from *Moshe Rabbeinu* until the close of the Talmud as "David and his *Beis Din* ... Yeshaya and his *Beis Din* .. Nachman and his *Beis Din*" etc. Clearly, the head of each generation was the leader because he was the outstanding Torah scholar of his time, the head of the rabbinic court, the voice of ... *Daas Torah*. Prophesy was the highest rung on a scale of spiritual accomplishment which included as a *sine qua non* greatness in Torah. Every prophet was a giant of Torah, and prophesy was the crown of years of toil to achieve ever-growing levels of holiness.

◄§ Millennia in a Moment: A Trip Through Time

In the time of the Talmud, when the nation of Israel needed representation to deal with the gentile governments, who went? Politicians? Diplomats? Ph.Ds in international relations? Not quite. It was Rabban Yochanan ben Zakkai, who dealt with Vespasian (*Gitten* 56a, *Eichah Rabbah* 115, No. 31) ... Rabban Gamliel who went to Domitian (*Ediyos* 7:7, *Sanhedrin* 11a, *Yerushalmi Sanhedrin* 7:19)... Rabbi Chanina and Rabbi Yehoshua ben Levi who traveled to the ruler in Ceasarea (*Yerushalmi Berachos* 5:1, *Bereishis Rabbah* 78:5). Indeed, the Talmud is replete with stories about how the *Tannaim* and *Amoraim* deliberated, decided and acted, in the most natural and expected of manner, on behalf of the entire nation. The absence of these facts in secular history books proves nothing at all. Just as Arnold Toynbee tried to write the Jewish people out of world history, so have the secular historians tried to eliminate the Torah leadership from their textbooks. Even Josephus, no friend of the Rabbis, was forced to admit that the sages were respected "even

---

12. For a halachic explanation of this concept, see *Margaliyos Ha'Yam* to *Sanhedrin* 82a, No. 29 and *Tzofnas Pa'ane'ach* to *Shemos* 19,19 and 25,10.
13. Introduction to *Mishneh Torah*.

against the king and the high priest... for the people hearken to every word which comes from their mouth."[14]

In the time of the *Gaonim*, it was the *Gaon* and his disciples alone who made the communal decisions for all of *Klal Yisrael* (with notable exceptions when the *Resh Galusa* was out of step with the *Gaon*, similar to errant kings who defied the prophets, as recounted in *Tanach*). Here, even the secular historians report that "beside managing the Academy, the work of the *Gaon* included all Jewish affairs in Eretz Israel ... The *Gaonim* were recognized by the foreign ruler as the representatives of the Jewish community in Eretz Israel...In case of emergency, they traveled [to Baghdad and Egypt] in order personally to negotiate in the court of the rulers."[15]

From the period of the *Rishonim*, we have *teshuvos* that document how the *Rambam*, the *Rashba*, Rashi, *Rabbeinu Tam* and the other great commentators of the Talmud were the sole arbiters of right and wrong for our people on all issues — not just the obviously halachic, but what would today appear to be questions of a social, political or economic nature.

◆§ After Chmielnicki's Massacres

Even in the difficult period following the Chmielnicki massacres, in the midst of the seventeenth century, autonomous Jewish communities turned to their *poskim* and *Gedolim* for guidance in virtually all matters of life. The *Bach* in Cracow, the *Taz* in Levov, the *Shach* in Vilna, the *P'nai Yehoshua* in Frankfurt, the *Magen Avraham* in Kallish, all dealt with issues affecting the nation and were the acknowledged decisors for the people of Israel, as is apparent from their many recorded responsa.

A striking example of the all-encompassing power and influence of Torah sages at this time is the *Vaad Arba Aratzos*, the Council of the Four Lands, which was the central institution of Jewish self-government in Poland and Lithuania from the middle of the sixteenth century until 1764.[16] The authority of the Council

---

14. Josephus, *Antiquities*, XII, 10,5.
15. *Encyclopedia Judaica*, "Gaonim," p. 322.
16. There were actually two separate bodies, the *Vaad Arba Aratzos*, which controlled the affairs of Polish Jewry, and the *Vaad Medinas Lita*, which was the sister organization for the Lithuanian grand duchy, which was associated with the Polish Crown.

was described by a contemporary as that of "the Sanhedrin of the *Lishkas Hagazis* [in the Temple],...they had the authority to dispense justice to all Israel in the kingdom of Poland, to safeguard the law, to frame ordinances, and to inflict punishment as they saw fit."[17]

Who were the leaders of this body, which was recognized by kings and governments? In the Lithuanian division, the highest position traditionally belonged to the *Av Beis Din* (Head of the Rabbinic Court) of the city of Brest-Litovsk, known in the Torah world as Brisk. The list of signatories to communal legislation of the time is indistinguishable from a list of the Torah giants of that era: the *Maharsha*, the *Kli Yaakov*, the *Maharam* of Lublin, the *Shelah*.

⋘ On the Threshold of Modern Times

The late eighteenth and nineteenth centuries introduced the post-Mendelssohn era, when counterfeit alternatives to Torah leadership were being openly promulgated. Facing the onslaught of alien philosophies and spiritual dangers, the Gaon of Vilna, Rabbi Akiva Eiger in Posen, the *Chasam Sofer* in Pressburg, Rabbi Yonasan Eyebeshutz in Prague, all continued to lead the people of Israel by the light of ancient Torah principles and the force of their Torah-permeated personalities.

The voluminous responsa of these sages is eloquent testimony to their involvement in all matters relating to Jewish life. They were consulted, they ruled and they were obeyed in politics, monetary matters, social issues and the entire range of problems to which human beings are heir. And they fought the attempts to relegate the rabbis exclusively to the realm of ritual and ceremony.

In the later years of the nineteenth century, Rabbi Naftali Tzvi Yehudah Berlin of Volozhin, Rabbi Yitzchak Elchanan Spector of Kovno, Rabbi Samson Raphael Hirsch of Frankfurt, the *Sefas Emes* of Gur, the *Avnei Tzedek* of Lubavitch, all added a link in the great chain of Torah-guided leadership, as is recorded in the annals of history.

The giants of the tragic but noble generation of the early twentieth century — the *Chofetz Chaim* and the Gerrer *Rebbe*, Reb

---

17. Rabbi Nathan Nata Hannover (passed away in 1683), quoted in *Encyclopedia Judaica*, vol. 5, p. 1004.

Chaim Ozer Grodzensky and the *Chazon Ish* — continued the battle and recognized the need for Torah interpretation of swiftly
moving events; it was then that the *Gedolei Torah* began to talk of
Daas Torah.[18]

How ludicrous it is to speak of them as having improvised a
new authoritarian structure! From every word they wrote, from
everything that we know of their lives, each of them was engaged
in the holy task of saving not only their generation, but *Knesses
Yisrael* for all future generations. The institution that they chose to
strengthen and revitalize was the time-honored one of *"Emunas
Chachamim"* — trust in and reverence for the acknowledged Torah
leadership of the day. This was not a self-aggrandizing decision,
nor an insignificant one. With the challenges arising from social
and political revolutions, the concept that "only a Torah interpretation of *Klal Yisrael's* destiny has validity" required a new lexicon,
and called for the re-emphasis on ancient tradition — how to
define *hashkafah* questions, how to pose them and to whom, and
how to heed the answers.

If, then, *Daas Torah* is actually part of a venerable tradition,
what are the elements that connect the *Daas Torah* of Rabbi Akiva
to that of Rabbi Aharon Kotler, the Vilna Gaon to the *Chazon Ish*?
What is the thread that can be drawn unbroken through the generations?

⋙ Beginning with Basics

Let us begin with the basic question: Why should Torah sages,
immersed as they are in the seemingly other-wordly universe of
the Torah, be able to render judgments on the complex issues of a
world so apparently alien to their own? Are they, so to speak, competent concerning the "real world"?

To answer this, we need first to remind ourselves where the
world itself came from: אסתכל באורייתא וברא עלמא, "G-d looked
into the Torah and created the world."[19]

---

18. See *Chofetz Chaim al Torah* (ed. by Rabbi Greineman), p. 30; *Ohr Elchonon*, vol. 2, pp. 97-
98; Rabbi Elchonon Wasserman, *Kovetz Maamarim*, pp. 102:24, 140; and Rabbi Chaim Ozer
Grodzensky, *Collected Letters*, vol. 1, p. 291, etc.
19. *Zohar, Terumah*, 161a; see also beginning of *Bereishis Rabbah*.

Thinking of all the professionals we usually seek out to build a house, would one hire an architect who doesn't know a blueprint from a bluebird? Who better, then, to consult about problems with the house than the greatest expert on the blueprint?

One must conclude that it is only Torah sages who can truly understand the world. Not only is the Torah the sole lens through which to view the world around us accurately, but even the granting of the Torah to mortal man is predicated upon its role as the practical guide to every aspect of life. When *Moshe Rabbeinu* went up to receive the Torah, the angels attempted to dissuade G-d from giving it to such spiritually fragile creatures as mere mortals. Our saving quality, however, was our obvious synergy with the Torah itself. It is only man who can honor his parents, eat properly, wind *tefillin* on his arm, rest on *Shabbos,* and raise a family in the Torah way.[20]

Moshe Rabbeinu's triumphant argument was clearly that the Torah was meant for those who live, who engage in all the normative requirements of human life; eating, sleeping, family life, and so on. It is obvious that *life* implies social relationships, as well. If the Torah was meant for creatures who form societies, interact with each other as individuals and collectively, then it is a given that the Torah must provide direction for these activities. Otherwise, *Moshe Rabbeinu's* position would have been strangely limited only to a small area of mankind's activities, a poor argument, indeed, if it were so. But *Moshe Rabbeinu's* victory had to have been based upon the principle that the totality of Man's activities — not just limited segments — is meant to be governed by Torah. There must therefore be an ongoing mechanism for discovering what the Torah teaches concerning every area of human endeavor.

Thus, it should be most natural and far from surprising that the one most engaged in Torah should have gained the wisdom required to navigate through the byways of this world. Even more importantly, there are many ways of obtaining data and forming conclusions. But when the source of that knowledge is in the original design, it is that much closer to the essence of truth itself.

The story is told of Rabbi Meir Simchah Hakohein of Dvinsk (the Ohr Same'ach) who was informed during World War I that surrounding

---

20. See *Shabbos* 88b-89a.

communities were hiding the bulk of their Sifrei Torah in a centralized place far behind the lines, deep in Russia, in fear of the advancing German troops. Reb Meir Simchah refused to follow suit. Eventually, when the Bolsheviks took over Russia, the Torah scrolls from the other cities were discovered in the storage house, and destroyed. When asked how he knew what to do, he replied, "Learn Parshas Vayishlach and you, too, will understand. There, the Torah teaches us not to put all that is most precious to us together in one depository" (Bereishis 30:8-9).

In our own day, Rabbi Moshe Feinstein "justified" his own halachic decision-making process and value system in difficult areas by declaring: "My entire *outlook* stems solely from Torah knowledge with no mixture of extraneous influences whatsoever."[21]

❧ The "Torah Lishmah" Factor

If we search for a source documenting that Torah study yields proficiency in seemingly disparate areas of knowledge, we need look no further than *Pirkei Avos:*

"One who involves himself in Torah study lishmah — for its own sake — is granted many things...and people benefit from him counsel and sound wisdom" (Avos 6,1).

The *Maharal* of Prague explains that one who studies Torah for its own sake becomes one with the Torah, and the power of Torah becomes his power. But one who studies the Torah for ulterior motives remains separate from the Torah and so gains none of the characteristics of the Torah itself. Indeed, one of the most dramatic personifications of *Daas Torah* in our time — the *Chazon Ish* ז"צל — whose advise on medical, personal and national matters was known to be almost miraculously unerring — had decided on his Bar Mitzvah day to henceforth study Torah solely *lishmah*, for its own sake.[22]

By its very definition, *Daas Torah* emerges when Torah knowledge is pursued *lishmah*. The authority that comes with *Daas Torah* is the reward and the result, never the goal. Thus, immersion in Torah for decades eventually achieves that metamorphosis of the mere scholar, erudite though he might have been, into the "ever-flowing spring" described later in the above passage in *Avos*.

---

21. *Igros Moshe, Even Ha'Ezer,* vol. 2, no. II. See also the statement by the Chofetz Chaim in footnote 7 above.
22. See *Pe'er Hador,* vol. I, p. 165.

◆§ Constantly Preoccupied with Torah

The idea that one should constantly be preoccupied with Torah study never withheld Torah leaders from being activists as well. It simply meant that no matter what else one was doing, the mind was to be occupied by "thinking in learning," where feasible. This teaching was transmitted to the family of Rabbi Chaim Soloveitchik of Brisk in an interesting pedagogic way. Reb Chaim would assign his sons specific tasks to be carried out which required their moving about, speaking to people and involving themselves in apparently run-of-the-mill activities. At the same time, he would give them a Torah problem to consider while they were performing their duties, which they needed to report on immediately after their mission was complete. In this way, Reb Chaim trained his children how to keep the mind constantly involved in Torah, no matter what else was happening around them.[23]

Although much has been written about this absolute immersion in Torah study as the hallmark of the *Daas Torah* personality, this immersion must be accompanied by an additional element:

Rabbi Mordechai Gifter, *Rosh Hayeshivah* of Telshe, points out that *Daas Torah* is measured not so much by the amount of knowledge gained from Torah as by the on-going yearning, striving and effort to uncover ever more of what he calls "the mystery of the Torah." That mystery, explains Rabbi Gifter, is not Kabbalah or esoteric wisdom, but the constant process of uncovering and revealing more of what one has not yet understood.[24]

In other words, a *Daas Torah* in stagnation is not *Daas Torah* at all. It is not merely a function of accumulated facts and figures or even once-attained spiritual levels. It flows directly from perpetual renewal in the refreshing well of Torah study. Rabbi Yaakov Yisrael Kanievsky, the Steipler Rav צ"ל, was once asked a question which he deemed to require a *Daas Torah* perspective. "Go to Rabbi Shlomo Zalman Auerbach," he suggested, "for he learns much and can

---

23. Rabbi Shlomo Wolbe, *Alei Shur*, vol. I, p. 235.
24. Rabbi Mordechai Gifter, *Torah Perspectives*, p. 20.

decide through the power of his Torah. Because of my weakness, I can no longer learn more than a few hours a day and so cannot decide this matter." He also suggested going to Rabbi Elazar Shach, *Rosh Hayeshivah* of Ponevezh, adding similarly that "he learns much and can decide this."[25] Interestingly, the *Chazon Ish* sharply rebuked someone for not hearkening to *Daas Torah*, referring to the *Gedolim* who have this authority as חכמי התורה והוגיה יומם ולילה, "the sages of the Torah and those who engage in her study day and night."[26]

To understand what *Daas Torah* really is, to comprehend its singular process and outlook, one would need to live on that rarified spiritual plane. As Rabbi Eliyahu Dessler זצ"ל described it, speaking of the Chofetz Chaim, Rabbi Chaim Soloveitchik and Rabbi Chaim Ozer Grodzensky, "I can tell you with certainty that even given the little that we understand of their greatness and comprehend of their wisdom, their discernment and sagacity were utterly astonishing. Their intellects literally plumbed the depths of the unfathomable, and certainly people like us could not comprehend their system of thinking and reasoning.[27]

◄§ The Total Personality

Many people became highly accomplished Torah scholars, but never were recognized as *Gedolim*. To achieve this distinction, one must also be exceptional in his refinement of personality. Thus, it has been axiomatic throughout our history that each Torah leader, every *Gadol* worthy of the title, was also worthy of having stories told about his exceptional personality and character traits. The twenty-four-thousand disciples of Rabbi Akiva who died for a sin of interpersonal behavior[28] are the most eloquent testimony to the irrevocable bond between Torah study and personal deportment. Their greatness in Torah study *per se* is undisputed. But their failing in the realm of personality perfection left them unfit to transmit Torah to the following generation and to be considered leaders of Israel. As Rabbi Shlomo Wolbe[29] points out, G-d's own trait of

---

25. Rabbi Horowitz, *Orchos Rabbeinu*, p. 213.
26. *Pe'er Hador*, vol. 5, p. 53.
27. *Michtav M'Eliyahu*, vol. I, p. 75.
28. See *Yevamos* 62b.
29. *Alei Shur*, vol. 2, p. 62.

"greatness" is defined by the *middah* of goodness — את גדלך זו מדת טובך, and therefore one cannot achieve the status of a *Gadol* without being a paradigm of goodness, as well. The thrust of all of *Pirkei Avos*, as seen throughout the centuries by all of its commentators, is that one cannot mine the riches of the Torah's gold without the indispensable development of sterling character as a prerequisite.

◆§ Secrets for the G-d-Fearing

The vast Torah knowledge and exemplary character and conduct of the true Torah leader must be built on the foundation of *yiras Shamayim*, which is so much a part of him that it radiates from his mere presence. Rabbi Shlomo Wolbe[30] illustrates that fear of G-d is the medium through which the Torah becomes part of a person, to rearrange the molecules of a soul, to create a utensil for pouring out G-d's wisdom and teachings. Thus, the leitmotif of Torah leaders has always been *"Sod Hashem liyerei'av* — The secret of G-d is for those who fear Him, and His covenant is to let them know," the process by which the complete Torah personality becomes the source for advice, inspiration and direction.[31]

◆§ Achrayus: the Sense of Responsibility

When describing the Chofetz Chaim, Rabbi Chaim Ozer Grodzensky and Rabbi Chaim Soloveitchik in their deliberations, Rabbi Dessler alerts us to another criterion which is distinct from the intellectual and even the spiritual loftiness we associate with *Gedolim*. "It was awe inspiring to witness, " he relates, "the profound sense of responsibility that was written on their faces. As they went about their discussions with the utmost gravity, it was obvious that the *Shechinah* rested on their work. Indeed, whoever was not fortunate enough to see their response to *achrayus* has never truly seen this magnificent trait."[32]

Thus another tool, delicate though it surely is, for detecting the true voice of *Daas Torah* is the sense that here is a person who thinks, speaks and acts for the good of *Klal Yisrael*. No ego, no wish

---

30. Ibid. p. 490.
31. See *Tehillim* 25,14 and commentaries. For a study of this concept, see Rabbi Nisson Wolpin's introduction to *The Torah Profile*.
32. *Michtav M'Eliyahu*, vol. I, p. 75.

or need for publicity, certainly no narcissistic self-promotion.

Using this standard on a practical basis brings to mind the Kotzker *Rebbe's* pithy answer to an apposite question. The *Rebbe* was asked: Our sages teach regarding the verse, "For the lips of the *Kohein* preserve wisdom and Torah should be sought from his mouth" (*Malachi* 2,4): If the *Rav* may be likened to a heavenly angel, seek Torah from his mouth; if he is not, do not.[33]

Asked a Kotzker *Chassid*, "But *Rebbe*, I have never seen an angel, so how can I know if the *Rav* is similar to one?" Said the *Rebbe* crisply, "You may not be able to recognize an angel when you see one, but you will surely know who is not an angel."

It may be difficult to measure the level of someone else's absolute devotion to *Am Yisrael*. But often in our history we are granted opportunities to witness one person's absolute selflessness in attending to the needs of *Klal Yisrael*, while someone else is clearly fulfilling his own personal agenda. Despite the latter's brilliance, oratory or influence, the sense of the nation is almost always that the former emerges as the repository of *Daas Torah* of his generation.

❧ The Community of Prophets — The Fellowship of Gedolim

Another way to know the sources of *Daas Torah* is even more simple, yet at times elusive. The model for all revealed and intuitive Torah knowledge is prophecy. To be sure, we are no longer privileged to experience it, yet the prophetic phenomenon can teach us much about the giants to whom we should turn today. The *Gemara* cites an opinion that a prophet who does not reveal his prophecy receives *malkos* (lashes). "But who is there to warn him?" asks the *Gemara*. The answer, says Abaye, is "his fellow prophets." Still, persists the *Gemara*, how do they know? Answers Abaye, "G-d does not do something unless he reveals the secret to his servants, the prophets."[34]

Prophecy, sadly to say, is no longer with us, so there is no reason for anyone to be able to recognize a prophet. But the *Gedolim* do know and recognize each other; it is one of the Creator's gifts to us that in every generation there is a sense of transmission, where the sages symbolically lay their hands upon the leaders of the next era

33. *Moed Kattan* 17a.
34. *Sanhedrin* 90b.

Once, when the Chofetz Chaim and the Chazon Ish were in the home of Rabbi Chaim Ozer Grodzensky, the Chofetz Chaim turned to the young Chazon Ish and directed him to begin "assuming the burden of leading Klal Yisrael."[35] *In 5668 (1908), when Rabbi Aharon Kotler was sixteen years old, he met the great Gaon, Rabbi Meir Simchah of Dvinsk* זצ"ל, *the author of the Ohr Same'ach, who was visiting Kovno. After speaking with the young scholar, the Ohr Same'ach declared, "He will be the Rabbi Akiva Eiger of his generation."*[36]

This scenario is repeated countless times in our history, each time serving a dual purpose. It is the most foolproof method for *Klal Yisrael* to obtain the correct address for *Daas Torah,* and it also serves the continuum of Jewish history with that formal link of the *Mesorah* process.

Ever since Sinai, continuity has been the watchword of the Torah leadership process. When explaining the relationship of the *Gaonim* to their predecessors, the *Rishonim* write, "...for they sat in the yeshivah of Rav Ashi and in his synagogue they prayed."[37] Just being in the yeshivah of the *Amoraim,* praying in the same halls where the rabbis of the Talmud flourished, gave the *Gaonim* a measure of their Torah authority. Torah scholars who sat for decades at the feet and in the yeshivos of the *Gedolim* of the previous era have always had priority in being considered the *Daas Torah* of the new generation. As *Rabbeinu Yonah* writes, "This is the process which is described at the beginning of *Pirkei Avos*...and continues unbroken until this very day."

◄§ Torah Authority in Every Generation

One point constantly raised by those who do not wish to submit to any *Daas Torah* authority is that we no longer have established bodies of rabbinic authority, such as the Great *Sanhedrin,* which can impose their will on the nation as a whole. Here, too, a mistake has been made concerning the source of Torah authority. The fact is that although we pray thrice daily for the return of the great formal systems of jurisprudence, nevertheless, the jurisdic-

---

35. Rabbi Y.Z. Diskin of Pardes Chanah, quoted by Rabbi A. Wolf, *Rabboseinu,* p. 100.
36. *Marbitzei Torah Umussar,* vol. 3, p. 220.
37. See *Ramban, "Milchamos,"* end of *Rosh Hashanah; Rosh* to *Rosh Hashanah* 4:13; *Maharit, Yoreh De'ah* 11.

tion of *Daas Torah* continues unabated throughout the ages.

Rabbi Moses Feinstein, in a major address delivered at a convention of the Agudas Harabbanim and later published in a Torah journal,[38] declared that the *poskim* and *Daas Torah* representatives of every generation "have the same decision-making power in regard to *psak* and *takanos* (halachic decision and ordinances) as the Great *Beis Din* that sat in the *Lishkas Hagazis.*"

✦§ When Giants Disagree

Can there be a disagreement among *Gedolim*, each of whom would individually be considered *Daas Torah*?

One can say with certainty that the concept "these and those are the word of the Living G-d" applies to all disagreements between Torah giants, for that is an integral part of the Torah transmission through the ages. The *Ritva*, one of the major Talmudical commentators among the *Rishonim*, explains, "When Moshe went up to receive the Torah, he was shown forty-nine approaches to forbid and forty-nine approaches to permit each questionable issue. When he asked G-d about this, he was told that it would be up to the sages of each generation to make a determination as to which of these heavenly-validated methods to apply."[39]

It is therefore not surprising to discover disagreement on many issues among sages of equally great standing. But, of course, one does not always have the luxury to say, "You're both right," since quite often one must take a stand or follow a specific path.

Here a practice has been sanctified by time, rooted in basic *halachah* itself, and taught by our *Gedolim* even when it meant submitting to an opinion they themselves did not espouse. During the Third Knessia Gedolah in Marienbad, in 1937, the *Moetzes Gedolei HaTorah* debated the issue of the partition of Palestine. Rabbi Elchonon Wasserman and Rabbi Aharon Kotler opposed endorsing the Peel Commission's plan for partition, while the Gerrer *Rebbe*, the *Imrei Emes*, felt that since, in his opinion, partition was inevitable, it should be accepted; all that could be done to enhance

---

38. *HaPardes Anthology,* 1939; Rav Moshe's words proved to be a timely defense of *Daas Torah* and the need to recognize its authority in all ages.
39. *Chiddushei HaRitva* to *Eruvin* 13b. See also *Maharsha* to *Yevamos* 12a, *Derashos HaRan,* 5 and 12 and *Maharshal,* introduction to *Yam Shel Shlomo.*

the religious quality of the future state should be done.

Eventually, when the prospect of partition became an immediate issue, the *Moetzes* voted formally not to oppose the emerging state, in effect following the position of the Gerrer *Rebbe*.

The Brisker *Rav*, Rabbi Yitzchak Zev Soloveitchik, was not a member of the *Moetzes* and had not participated in its deliberations. Nevertheless, it was well known that he took the same position as Rabbi Elchonon Wasserman and Rabbi Aharon Kotler. When the *Moetzes* voted, the Brisker *Rav's* silence surprised his children. They asked him about this, and he taught them a lesson which is actually for all time.

"The *Moetzes Gedolei HaTorah* is the *Beis Din* of *Klal Yisrael*. Once the body has spoken, *Hashem imo* — G-d is with it. After G-d gives His consent to the *Beis Din's* decision, no individual has the right to voice any contrary sentiment." The Brisker *Rav* then brought an original proof to his words from *Tanach*, showing that when *Daas Torah* is in conflict, one must follow the majority if it has ruled in a body such as the *Moetzes Gedolei HaTorah*.[40]

❧ Beyond Personal Involvement

With all this in mind, the query arises: Why is there such antagonism to *Daas Torah?* If it is actually so obvious as to who the purveyors of *Daas Torah* are, and even how to resolve conflicting opinions, why doesn't everyone see it? Again, we turn to that embodiment of *Daas Torah*, the *Chazon Ish:*

...There is another spiritual malady which the Evil Inclination has concocted to sway people from אמונת חבמים *(trust in Torah scholars), and that is the canard that they are not objective.*[41]

The *Chazon Ish* goes on to explain that the true Torah scholar's judgment (*Daas Torah*) will not be clouded by personal involvement. The fact that a judge who is a relative or is personally involved cannot serve on a *Beis Din* is a *chok*, a statute that supersedes reason and logic. Imagine, says the *Chazon Ish*, a poor *talmid chacham* who owns but one cow, and his entire livelihood is dependent upon her. Yet, if he must judge whether she was slaughtered

---

40. Rabbi Moshe Shmuel Shapiro, *The Jewish Observer*, December, 1981, p. 30.
41. *Chazon Ish al Emunah Ubitachon*, 3:30. See also the explanation of these words in *Pachad Yitzchak* on *Shavuos, Maamar* 44:6.

properly or not, he is permitted to do so. Only in a *Beis Din* situation, with two litigants is there a *gezeirus hakasuv* (Scriptural decree) that invalidates him, but this has nothing to do with his ability to remain impartial under all circumstances.

The Chofetz Chaim[42], too, speaks of the *yeitzer hara's* special efforts to convince us that the *Gedolim* are no longer great enough to be listened to or that we simply don't know who they are. The Evil Inclination's prodigious efforts in this area should alert us to the importance of being vigilant in this matter. For, as the *Chazon Ish* concludes, if we listen to those who deny the existence of *Daas Torah*, "the entire generation becomes orphaned and there is no room for judgment at all."

If, however, we accept *Daas Torah* as our link to eternal truth, we will drink of the purest stream in the universe, one unsullied even by the sands of time, for it flows pristine and undefiled, providing all who are thirsty with the living waters of Torah itself.

---

42. *Chofetz Chaim, Hilchos Issurei Lashon Hara, 8:4.*

Torah Lives

Recent Losses from the Torah World

Men of spirit and dedication who changed the world we live in

The Late Sanz-Klausenberger Rav
Rabbi Yekusiel Yehudah Halberstam
זכר צדיק לברכה

The Rebbe arose from personal tragedy and irreplaceable loss to serve as both spiritual giant and creative communal builder for his people

≈§ The Dichotomy

The late Klausenberger *Rav*, Rabbi Yekusiel Yehudah Halberstam, **זצוק"ל**, was a direct descendant of the *Divrei Chaim*, Rabbi Chaim Halberstam, the Sanzer *Rav*, and many aspects of his personal and public life reflected the ways of this saintly great-grandfather.

> *So totally immersed in Torah and intense service to G-d was the Sanzer Rav, that material possessions had no function to him other than as a means to help alleviate the plight of the poor, the suffering and the abandoned. "How can a person waste his time worrying about the vanities of this world," he was wont to say, "when it is all emptiness, through and through!"*
>
> *The Klausenberger Rav, for his part, often spoke admiringly of one his grandmothers, the Gorlitzer Rebbetzin, who prayed that*

her children be poor in earthly assets, but that they earn greatness as Rabbanim and poskim.

The Klausenberger *Rav* not only recounted the events and the *minhagim* of the Sanzer *Rebbe's* court in great detail, as if he himself had been present, he was equally meticulous in all the customs, rituals, modes of dress and specific expressions of Sanz. He even repeated the words of his *"Sanzer Zaida"* as if he had heard them directly from him. The only way to ensure complete adherence to the ways of his holy ancestors, he maintained, was by segregating oneself and ghettoizing the community, remaining free of any secular, mundane or profane influence. In fact, the first thirty-six years of the life of the Klausenberger *Rav* were carried out under these ideal conditions. His approach, however, was not unique in those pre-War days when he was *Rav* of Klausenberg; he was one of many hundreds of *Rabbanim* in that region of Eastern Europe who were followers of the *Chasam Sofer*, or the great Chassidic masters, who led their communities in complete separation from outside influences.

Yet he was quite alone at the onset of the *Churban* (Holocaust), during the deportations, in the concentration camps, and the D.P. (displaced persons) camps after the liberation, when he was thrust into unknown surroundings, with people from the widest range of backgrounds. How did a man whose earlier years were so sheltered come to deal with realities that required him to engage himself with devastated souls of a type unencountered in Rudnik, Klausenberg or Sanz, ailing souls who unfortunately had sunk to the abysmal depths of helplessness and despair without any moral anchor, and were now in desperate need of help?

During the seven decades of his active leadership, he was renowned for his monumental *pilpul drashos*, every *Shabbos* and *Yom Tov*, every night of Chanukah, at special *seudos*, and his long, involved *shiurim* several times a week. Very few followed and understood the breadth and depth of his erudition and his *chiddushim* in Torah. But even fewer could comprehend how a man of such stature and *gadlus* could lower himself to befriend, converse with, and eventually reach the heart and soul of a morally lost

Holocaust survivor — and how he could comfort these forlorn individuals by providing them with a suit of clothing, a pair of shoes and a kosher meal.

This dichotomy had also been true of his *Zaida*, the Sanzer *Rav*. Before or after writing a complicated *teshuvah*, or before or after a lengthy heartrending *tefillas Shacharis*, the Sanzer *Rav* would discuss in great detail with the administers of the charity funds, as to how much cloth was needed for a poor bride's wedding gown, and what kind of shoes would be appropriate for her. He would be involved in every detail of the needs of the poor and how to best satisfy these needs.

In addition, the Klausenberger *Rav*'s early, cloistered life was in apparent contradiction to his later involvement in the leading of movements, communities, and projects of immense national and international proportions. Not only was he responsible for an international network of *kehillos* and Torah institutions, and projects such as *Mifal HaShas*, but also for founding Kiryat Sanz in *Eretz Yisrael*, along with the Sanz Medical Center/Laniado Hospital.

Both spiritual giant and a dedicated communal worker—was the *Rebbe* a dual personality? While he performed in one role, did he neglect the other?

No. With the Klausenberger *Rav*, there were no two distinct roles. It was not even a matter of synthesis. It was a "oneness." The common denominator, the unifying force that created this oneness, was the *Ko'ach HaTorah* — the power of Torah, which molded the Klausenberger *Rav*.

The *Hashgachah* (Divine Providence) placed the Klausenberger *Rav*—whose life was one of striving for spiritual heights—in a specific setting, in a time that demanded action, for the sake of others—*bilti l'Hashem levado*. Everything solely for *Hashem*.

⋄§ Years of His Youth

The Sanz-Klausenberg *Rav* was born on 4 Shevat, 5665 (1905), to his father, the *Rav* of Rudnik in Galicia. He, in turn, was the son of the *Rav* of Gorlitz, who was the son of the great sage and saint of Sanz, the *Divrei Chaim*.

As a young child, the *Rebbe* displayed unusual talents, but foremost was his rare diligence in Torah study and his extreme devotion in *tefillah*. He would engage in either (or both) for many hours into the night, even to the point of exhaustion. As a child, he could be found pouring out his heart before an open *Aron Kodesh* at midnight in an otherwise empty *Beis Hamidrash*.

While young Yekusiel Yehudah had the good fortune of being reared in a home that was host to many *gedolim* of Eastern Europe, he tragically was orphaned from his father at age thirteen. His three-hour *hesped* (eulogy) for his father, in which he quoted verbatim sources throughout *Shas* and Midrash, was an object of marvel amongst the *Rabbanim* throughout all of Europe.

The youth's thirst for Torah was insatiable. At age sixteen, he took to the road and spent six months in Warsaw, basking in the presence of the city's spiritual giants. While there, he heard *shiurim* in the Brisker Yeshivah. Half a century later, when the Klausenberger *Rav* met the Brisker *Rav* in *Eretz Yisrael*, he reminded the Brisker *Rav* of the contents of that *shiur* he had heard in Warsaw. He also spent time with the Belzer *Rav*, Bendiner *Rav*, Radimisheler *Rav* and Munkatcher *Rav*.

The Ostrovtzer *Rav* granted him *semichah* and asked him to stay on to help him with his writings. The Ostrovtzer's *berachah* to his new disciple was, "You should be a *maishiv halachah* for the world, and render responsa for the benefit of *Klal Yisrael*."

He also obtained *semichah* from the Radimisheler *Rav*, who commented, "If the world will be *zocheh* (worthy), we will see in Yekusiel Yehudah another *Divrei Chaim*." The Klausenberger *Rav* also received *semichah* from Rabbi Meir Arik, who honored him by requiring his *shochtim* to show their *shechitah* knives to him for inspection.

Reb Yekusiel Yehudah's fame came to the attention of Rav Chaim Tzvi Teitelbaum, *Rav* of Sighet, who took him for a son-in-law, making it known at the time that there is no *Tosafos* in all of *Shas* with which his *chassan* is not familiar. During the years after his marriage, he frequented Rudnik to assume the responsibilities of his father's *kehillah*. During his years there as well as when *Rav* in Klausenberg, he immersed himself in Torah study and devoted long hours to intense, tearful *tefillos*. The best way to lead his flock, he felt, was by example.

The Years in the Camps

Volumes have been written, and more will be written, of the personal self-sacrifice and incredible moral strength of the Klausenberger *Rav* during the War years—first in Hungary, where as a Polish national, he was a hunted man. During his years of suffering in the deportation camp, then in Auschwitz, Dachau, Mildorf and other concentration camps, and finally in the D.P. camps, he avoided violating any Torah commands. Under the most severe conditions, he abstained from non-kosher food. He kept the regular times for *davening*, and managed to review entire *meséchtos* from memory, even while he carried hundred-pound bags of cement throughout the day, day in, day out, Miraculously, he was able to keep with him a pair of *tefillin*, which he daily shared with numerous others at great risk, lest the Gestapo guards learn of this flagrant violation of camp regulations. Along with his own personal *avodah*, the *Rebbe* gave moral support to countless fellow Jews in the concentration and slave labor camps.

More remarkable were the *Rebbe's* activities in the D.P. camps after the liberation, when he was in effect alone. Other *Rabbanim* had returned to their respective towns and villages. Finding nothing there, they emigrated either to the United States or to *Eretz Yisrael* to re-establish a life for themselves and their followers. They recreated their devastated communities to preserve that which was dear to them — closing ranks, locking up, and locking out. The Klausenberger *Rav's* response to this was, "Close ranks, yes—but we dare not lock out any wounded *neshamos.*"

> His thinking on kiruv: A person is drowning....One bystander on shore says, "I'll jump in." He drowns....A second bystander says, "No, I will not jump in. I'll just stand by and watch...." The third bystander says, "We are on solid ground. Let's throw him a lifesaver."
>
> Said the Klausenberger Rav, "We are on solid ground. We are not moving from here. Let's dispatch Torah to him—a virtual lifesaver—and bring him back to us."

As long as there were survivors in the displaced persons camp, he was determined not to abandon them. Within twenty four hours of the liberation—having just learned of the brutal murder of his wife and precious eleven children—still clothed in prisoner's garb, he set about the task of resuscitating the shrunken souls housed in those dried-out bones.... During all the years in the concentration camps and liberation camps, he never shed a tear over his own misery for fear it would imply a critical view of the ways of *Hashem*.

In his new role, he could not deliver a customary three-hour *drashah* to his new "congregants" nor his standard two-hour *pilpul shiur* to his new "*talmidim.*" He was now concerned with the *aleph beis* of life and basic *emunah* for these individuals.

> ### As a People, We Are Certain...
>
> Languishing in the labor camp, I was approached by a professor, who asked me derisively: "So, what have you to say about the lot of the Jews?"
>
> "It will be good," I answered. I then explained, "I am not a prophet. Rather, my conviction is based on historic fact. Notice"—I pointed out to him—"how many nations have resolved to annihilate the Jewish people. Consider how many millions of Jews have already perished, in sanctification of G-d's Name, at the hands of mighty empires and nationalities—empires and nationalities of which there remain no living trace today. The Jewish People continue to exist, their many persecutions and travails notwithstanding. There are today sizable families, who trace their ancestry to a particular grandfather, who had perished some generations earlier *al kiddush Hashem*, even as his executioners and their commanders have fallen into total oblivion. Although I cannot tell you what will happen to me, personally, I am nevertheless certain that the Jewish People as a whole will survive and will witness the downfall of their adversaries. I can guarantee this, based on thousands of years of Jewish history, persisting to this very day." Lowering his head, the professor conceded the point to me.
>
> *(Shefa Chaim)*

He worked at establishing kosher kitchens in all of the displaced persons camps throughout Germany. He provided *tefillin* for the men; established a printing press to print *seforim* necessary for the *chinuch* of people who lost four to five years of learning and observance; founded the first *yeshivos* in Europe after the Destruction; arranged marriages between the young men and women, and provided *sheitels* for the women. His concern for these lost souls was so great that he traveled to the United States, not to settle, but to raise money for the institutions that he established in the D.P. camps, and then returned to Germany.

◆§ Arrival in the United States

When the Klausenberger *Rebbe* and a group of his followers emigrated to the United States in 1947, they settled in the

Williamsburg section of Brooklyn. With a strong sense of mission, he immediately embarked on an agenda of rebuilding—first and foremost, to establish *shuls* and yeshivos for the new arrivals.

The prevailing practice among survivors, during the late 40's, was to send teenagers and young men off to work. Even in so-called *heimishe* circles, learning was unheard-of for young men. Against great odds, the *Rebbe* established *chadorim* for boys throughout New York, as well as several girls schools. He established the first *kollel* in Williamsburg in 1952, and in 1954 he purchased a commodious six-story building to house his *kehillah's* central yeshivah, *beis hamidrash, kollel,* and old-age home. He established the first pre-school program for non-Americans, claiming that children under six, not yet in school in those years, waste an irreplaceable opportunity for absorbing valuable Torah knowledge. "If it were up to me," he said, "I would start them off while they're in their cribs."

As boundless as his love for every individual Jew was, he was a stalwart warrior against the organized forces of Reform and assimilation. In 1947, he took up the battle against the UJA and the Joint Distribution Committee for their policy of settling newly-arrived immigrants in far-flung communities, distant from centers of *Yiddishkeit.*

In one of the *Rav's* fiery speeches in Williamsburg, he credited the speedy response of the local fire and police department to an accident caused by a gas leak, with saving the life of one person. "Now," he dramatically added, "we have a situation where tens of thousands of our fellow Jews are being spiritually asphyxiated, and no one—not one single *Rav* or institution— raises his voice in protest or does anything about it."

He said what had to be said, in the place it had to be said, and to the audience for whom it was intended. In Me'ah She'arim, he was not fearful of speaking out against some of the wrongs of the *Chareidi* community. In Tel Aviv he spoke up strongly against the secular anti-religious government. In Antwerp he unhesitatingly decried the cozy relationship between the Jews and Gentiles. Nor did he have problems telling a philanthropist to increase his *tzeddakah* giving.

It is worth noting that among the earliest followers and admirers of the Klausenberger *Rebbe* in American were an appre-

Salvation At The Last Moment

I, myself, was about to be murdered on several occasions, by those evil ones ימ"ש. More than once I found myself spread out on the ground, murmuring the prayer: "In Your hand I return my spirit...may the will be that my demise be my atonement" (which, in those days, was constantly on my lips)— when suddenly I heard a command that I rise and return to the camp. Such things occurred with virtually everyone who had been there. They had been in mortal danger—but rescued at the very last moment.   (*Chumash Shiur, Toldos 5743*)

ciable number of Mesivta Torah Vodaath *bachurim*, many of them from out-of-town communities. The *Rebbe's* attraction to these boys was so profound and of such intensity, that its impact is still felt— for example, the son of one of those boys, a second-generation American, is the *Rosh Kollel* of the Sanzer Kollel in Yerushalayim. Another of those Torah Vodaath young men (originally from Council Bluffs, Iowa) became the *Rebbe's* emissary to Mexico forty years ago, dispatched to establish Torah institutions there. Although he returned to Brooklyn after several years, he is still the overseer of the institutions in Mexico, as well as the mentor and spiritual guide to hundreds of religious families in Mexico. Others of that group have remained, together with children and grand-children, devoted adherents of the Klausenberger way of life.

How does one account for this? The *menahel* of Torah Vodaath, Reb Shraga Feivel Mendlowitz זצ"ל, greatly admired the Klausenberger *Rav*, and invited the *Rav* to deliver his first major public *shiur* in America in Mesivta Torah Vodaath. Moreover, the two shared many common attitudes, including great stress on Torah study, responsibility to *Klal, Ahavas Yisrael,* and *Ahavas Eretz Yisrael.*

✎ The Rebbe as an Innovator

The *Rebbe* was a leader with unusually broad horizons. His personal tragedies did not deter him from undertaking great projects, nor did strong opposition discourage him from pursuing grand designs for the development of Torah *Yiddishkeit.*

In the mid-50's, the air was bristling with excitement over the new Jewish State; at the same time, the Torah *Yishuv* in *Eretz Yisrael* found itself overwhelmed by an uphill battle for survival. The *Rebbe* saw the situation as one of new challenges, new needs, and a new role for himself.

Amongst Holocaust survivors, there was a yearning to return to *Eretz Yisrael*, especially with the horrors they had endured on alien soil fresh in their memories. It was time to be secure at home. And then, many religious American Jews—hoping eventually to settle in *Eretz Yisrael*—wanted to get a head start.

The Klausenberger *Rav's* followers would be the first of the survivor groups to establish a full-fledged settlement in *Eretz Yisrael*. He and his people negotiated with the government for land. They turned down sites in Yerushalayim and Bnei Brak, instead buying land in Netanya. Many questioned the wisdom of establishing a religious community in a resort town, right at the beachfront, but he was not fazed.

The *Rebbe* laid the cornerstone for Kiryat Sanz in 1956. The village would, of course, contain housing and the infrastructure for a comprehensive community, including *shuls, batei midrash*, educational facilities for children of all ages including *yeshivos* expressly for Sephardic children, factories for diamond polishing and the manufacture of housing and building materials, a home for infants and orphans, an old-age home and a hospital. Slowly but surely Kiryat Sanz took root, and its influence was felt all over *Eretz Yisrael*.... Once people said that Kiryat Sanz is near Netanya; today Netanya is known to be near Kiryat Sanz.

There is no vehicular traffic through Kiryat Sanz on *Shabbos*. No secularist would invade the sanctity of *Shabbos* in Kiryat Sanz, because Kiryat Sanz people do not encroach on secularist neighborhoods. Netanya is the only major city in *Eretz Yisrael* where there is no strife between the *Dati'im* and *Chilonim*.

The men of Kiryat Sanz are gainfully employed as government employees, in private enterprise and in social welfare organizations. Many are *kollel* men involved in the publication of *seforim* or in teaching. Kiryat Sanz does not ask of Netanya; instead Kiryat Sanz graciously offers health care and other communal services to all the citizens of Netanya and environs. The beachfront of Kiryat Sanz was the first in all of *Eretz Yisrael* to have separate swimming times for men and women.

The educational system in Kiryat Sanz is traditional, in that it follows the teachings of Sanz. As unyielding as this educational system is in its non-conformance with the government's educational standards, it receives full government support and subsidy.

◆§ The Power of Torah

From the time he arrived in the United States in the mid-40's, until 1960, the Klausenberger *Rav* was a keen observer of the American Torah scene. He marvelled at the ability of *Roshei Yeshivah* to inspire young American boys to immerse themselves totally in Torah study with sincerity and diligence. He felt, however, that in view of their capabilities, they could accomplish much more. Before he was ready to make any public recommendations, however, he tested his own "learning system" in a laboratory. In the summer of 1961, he founded the Mesivta in Kiryat Sanz, gathering together young *bachurim,* ages 12 to 13, with keen minds and a desire to be engrossed in Torah. The *Rebbe* personally taught them, beginning the day at 5 a.m. He trained them to concentrate and cover much ground, and coached them in productive methods of *chazarah* (review). After several years, scores of these young boys were tested on comprehensive knowledge of 500 *blatt* of *Gemara* with *Rashi* and *Tosafos,* earning the title "*Chaver.*" Successfully passing an oral exam on 1,000 *blatt* earned one the title *"Moreinu."* The following is an excerpt from a letter the *Rebbe* wrote to one of his followers in the United States:

> *Sivan 1962*
>
> *I am sure that you have heard that I am a melamed tinokos, a teacher of children. I have taken in some twenty young boys and some bachurim in my beis hamidrash and they are under my personal supervision almost the entire day. I set a goal for them — to know 500 blatt Gemora with Rosh, Rashi, and Tosafos, by heart. Some of these boys are just Bar Mitzvah age, one is under Bar Mitzvah. I believe that because of their diligence and desire to learn, and in the merit of our Holy Land, we will succeed to sanctify the L-rd's Name and demonstrate that even in our times we can produce an elite core of talmidei chachamim and that the Holy Torah is eternal.*
>
> *You cannot imagine how overburdened I am. But teaching is the only activity that gives me much spiritual pleasure; it is not at all burdensome. It is eye-opening to observe the boys' uninterrupted learning and how they engage each other in sharp exchanges.*
>
> *I am aware that many of our followers see this activity of mine as a detriment to the Rebbistiva — my status as a Chassidic Rebbe. Teaching and being a Rebbe seems contradictory. However, my opinion is that one thousand of such Rebbes may go under, in place of one deserving Torah student. My prayer is that in merit of my holy ancestors, and in merit of our Holy Land, this will be a Kiddush Hashem, following in the footsteps of our ancestors.*
>
> *Yekusiel Yehudah Halberstam*

In 1968, before the *Rebbe* underwent heart surgery, he founded the *Shas Kollel.* This program involved the study of 70 *blatt Gemara* a month, requiring the successful completion of a written exam, offering generous stipends. In four years, each enrollee would complete all of *Shas.* In 1983, a grand *siyum* of *Shas* took place in the Binyanei Ha'uma in Jerusalem, attended by ten thousand people, including most of the prominent *Roshei Yeshivah, Rabbanim* and *Rabbe'im* of *Eretz Yisrael.*

The *Rebbe* next founded *Mifal Hashas,* which entails the study of 30 *blatt* per month and a monthly written test.

These two programs set higher standards for the quantity and quality of learning, and required obtaining successful grades on a written exam—something heretofore unknown in the yeshivah world. The *Rebbe* said, "If universities require accoun-tants, lawyers and physicians to successfully complete written exams, why not those who study in yeshivos?"

Since the inception of Mifal Hashas in 1983, 2,000 partici-pants throughout the world—including *talmidim* of sixty major *yeshivos* as well as *baalei battim*—have mastered over *seven million* additional *blatt* of *Gemora*.

Rabbi Yaakov Kamenetzky ל"צז, said, "The Klausenberger *Rebbe* is the greatest *marbitz Torah* (disseminator of Torah) in our generation; and since my lifetime spans three generations, I can say that he is the greatest in the past three generations."

Rabbi Yitzchak Ruderman ל"צז called it a counter-revolu-tion of sorts—a return to the standards he grew up with in Slobodka, where every accomplished *talmid* was familiar with all of *Shas*. Mifal Hashas, indeed, restores in our times the presti-gious *"Shas Yid"* that was prevalent in all generations, in all coun-tries, and in all Torah and yeshivah communities. Mifal Hashas thus justifies the statement of Rabbi Elazar Schach שליט"א: "The *Rebbe* made a 'revolution' in learning."

The *Rebbe* pointed with pride to a letter he received from the wife of a *kollel* man, in which she extends a heartfelt thanks to the *Rebbe*: Mifal Hashas gives her husband much needed self-esteem; a high mark on the monthly Mifal Hashas tests plus a stipend give him a sense of accomplishment.

"Learning, Learning, and More Learning"

The *Rebbe* often said, "I require only three things, to *learn*, to *review*, and to *remember*."

He never tired of pleading, admonishing, begging over and over again to learn more. In his weekly Thursday night *shiur* for *baalei battim*, he announced that anyone who does not have a set time to learn at least one *blatt Gemara* with *Tosafos* every day, should not think of asking for an audience with him.

He devoted unlimited time to planning individual programs of learning for each student. This giant in Torah would sit with a young boy, and discuss his capabilities with him. Pen in hand, the *Rebbe* would calculate the number of hours a young *bachur* can learn each day. He would list the *mesechtos*, the amount of *blatt* in each. He would spell out the amount of time required for the "first *laynen*" (initial independent study), so much time for review, and the amount of time it would take to reach specific goals. He calculated the hours available, only taking off time for sleep, eating, *davening* and biological needs—to the minute. The balance of time is for learning. The week is comprised of seven days, he insisted, with no time off from learning on *Shabbos*, *Yom Tov* or Purim. Attending the *tisch* of the *Rebbe* or collecting money for a worthy cause was out of the question; a yeshivah *bachur* is meant for learning only.

The *Rebbe* often quoted the Chazon Ish to support his system of learning, and like the Chazon Ish, the *Rebbe* pointed out that only with total commitment to undertake the completion of *Shas* and its commentaries—i.e. *Rashi*, *Tosafos*, *Rosh*, and *Maharsha*— can one attain appreciable levels of spirituality. Sanz was known for this approach to *Chassidus*. The *Rebbe* repeated in the name of the Sanzer *Rav* that the disciples of the Baal Shem Tov were all true *geonim* in Torah learning.

To the *Rebbe*, learning analytically, in depth, did not excuse covering little ground. One must first acquire knowledge and understanding of the entire *Shas* and its commentaries, he insisted, before offering innovative comments and interpretations. If one learns only the opening *blatt* of a few *mesechtos*, one runs the

Not an End, But a New Beginning

After the great devastation of our generation, many thought, at first, that *Yahadus* (Judaism) had become extinct. When I was liberated at Feldafing, where they designated a room for *davening*, a group of sincere youths attached themselves to me and, together, we cleaned it up and readied the room for use as a *Beis Midrash*. There were, however, others who were opposed to this, complaining that we were inciting another potential Hitler (G-d forbid). In addition, when we had begun to put up *chuppas*, to conduct weddings, some Jewish folks pelted us with stones. In the end, *Baruch Hashem*, we prevailed. A spirit of *teshuvah* came from above, which inspired a great many Jews who we had thought were beyond reach.... We may not have possessed any great *tzaddikim* who could revive us with a *tal shel techiah* (dew of life), it came straight from heaven in a wondrous way.

risk of saying a *chiddush* or *sevara* in contradiction to a clear statement in another section of *Shas*, or even to a *Rashi* or *Tosafos* in a later *perek* in the very same *mesechta*.

The *Rebbe's ahavas Torah* was evident in his prefacing the words *Mishnah* and *Gemara* with *"Heilige"* —holy. The same was true when he mentioned the name of a *Tanna* or Amora (Rabbi in the Talmud). Similarly, on his lips, the Vilna Gaon was the *"Heilige Gaon,"* as was the *"Heilige Chofetz Chaim."* He called the Jews of the Oriental countries *De "Heilige Shevatim* —The Holy Tribes." (In fact, he insisted that the *chinuch mosdos* he established for the Sephardim in Kiryat Sanz maintain their distinct pronunciation and *minhagim.)*

It was this *ko'ach* of *kedushas HaTorah,* power and force of Holy Torah knowledge, that enabled the *Rebbe* to withstand the trials and tribulations of the outside world, to swim in unchartered waters unknown to his predecessors or colleagues. It was this power of Torah that enabled him to grapple with every risk-ridden situation as it arose.

Union City, New Jersey

The *Rebbe* felt that young men unable to go to *Eretz Yisrael* should not be deprived of the learning program and atmosphere available in Kiryat Sanz. For this purpose he established a yeshivah community in Union City, New Jersey, outside of the bustling metropolis of New York. Here, young men would have the same opportunities as in *Eretz Yisrael*. The titles of *Chaver* and *Moreinu* would be bestowed upon those who earned them, and the *Roshei Yeshivah* and *kollel* men would live in close proximity to the Yeshivah.

This community in Union City boasts some of the country's outstanding *talmidei chachamim*, who live under austere conditions. Living expenses are far lower than in other population centers, allowing appreciable financial savings over the years.

Health Care and the Hospital

In 1960, when the *Rebbe* took up residence in *Eretz Yisrael*, he put into motion the governmental application process for the licensure of a hospital, appointing a qualified U.S. health care professional *(shomer Torah u'mitzvos)* to negotiate with the Ministry of Health. The Minister of Health, an avowed left-wing, anti-religious Socialist, refused to grant permission for the construction of the hospital, claiming that three hospitals were planned in Netanya, and the *Rebbe* should not be concerned that they would not be operated according to *halachah*. The *Rebbe* insisted on the permit to build, arguing that the three hospitals will never be built. When the Minister of Health offered the *hashgachah*/supervision of the religious activities in the government hospitals to the *Rebbe*, the *Rebbe* countered by offering the *hashgachah* of the projected Kiryat Sanz Hospital to the Minister, and tersely explained to his emissary that this is not a joking matter. They—the left-wing Zionists—monopolize building of all communal institutions, and then own and operate them according to their non-religious standards. We, the religious minority, come hat in hand, like beggars, to plead with them to allow *kashrus* in their institutions. We install, against their will, *mezuzos* on the doors of their buildings. This is wrong! We should build and own and operate these communal facilities. *Shabbos* observance and *kashrus* will be automatically guaranteed, and *mezuzos* will grace the doorposts without need to negotiate or beg.

Without our own independent economy and social welfare infrastructure, we cannot be assured of religious independence.[1] The *Rebbe*'s emissary was now more confident in his mission. The *Rebbe*'s views were presented to the Minister in a straightforward manner—no punches pulled. The permit and license were granted.

The hospital's outpatient clinic opened in 1975. The *Rebbe* was strategic planner for the orderly development of the hospital's departments and services, and he was involved in every aspect of the hospital's operation, while maintaing as before his personal, day-to-day involvement in the *yeshivos*, with *Roshei Yeshivah* and each and every *talmid*.

Some people opposed putting up the hospital because they were concerned with the risk of immodesty in dress of nurses and visitors in and around the hospital. The *Rebbe* overrode the objections, saying, "It will be easier to assure modesty in dress than run the risk of *piku'ach nefesh* without a hospital in the community."

> At a hospital board meeting, a discussion revolved around the choice of syringes for injections. One side recommended a product costing one shekel, and another side recommended a supplier selling a syringe needle for two shekel. Tzeddakah money was involved. The Rebbe asked if there was any difference between the two needles. The reply—the two-shekel needle is less painful to the patient. The Rebbe immediately ruled that the less painful needle be bought at a higher cost.

The *Rebbe*'s ruling prohibiting the hospital's employees from striking was surely a great *kiddush Hashem*. Hospital physicians, other health care workers, and several unions conducted at least seven major countrywide strikes, and many more minor strikes over the years. Not once since the founding of the hospital twenty years ago has any employee of the Sanz Medical Center participated in any of the strikes. The news media reported on the Sanz Medical Center employees' commitment to patient care because of the *Rebbe*'s *psak*.

1. Compare P.A.G.I. and R'Avrohom Mokotovsky.

Shabbos and *kashrus* would be the least of the reasons of religious Jews' involvement in hospitals. Sweeping scientific and technological advancements in medicine in the past few decades have created a host of new halachic issues to be addressed, ranging from the very beginnings of life to determining the precise moment of its end. In addition, many issues regarding personnel practices (physicians' requirements for availability), and patient care (crowding wards and corridors with emergency patients) also must be determined by halachic criteria.

⋺ The Nursing School

In the *Rebbe's* view, the "heart" of the hospital's operation is the nursing staff, which is in the hospital twenty-four hours a day; in addition, the patient looks to the nursing staff for comfort.

Even prior to the opening of the hospital, the *Rebbe* gave *shiurim* to a select group of nursing students, placing them in the category of Shifra and Puah—the nurses who received rewards directly from the Almighty for safeguarding Jewish babies.

The Sanz Medical Center/Laniado Hospital Nursing School is the only nursing school in Israel in which Torah subjects are an integral part of the curriculum. Girls from all over Israel and the Diaspora, with letters of reference from their school principals and *Rabbanim*, are eligible. In the sixteen years of its existence, every graduate of the school has passed the state exam and was licensed as a registered nurse. On four occasions, the SMC nursing students received the highest grades of any school in the country.

It seems that the Almighty holds His right hand over the nursing school to prevent wrongdoing. An illustration:

> *The halachah prohibits abortions in most circumstances. The Rebbe realized the difficulty of imposing a regulation which some expectant mothers find difficult, especially when informed of the possibility of the birth of an abnormal child. The Rebbe offered to care for any child born with a defect, if the mother would voluntarily give it up. This offer was made known throughout the medical center and nursing school.*
>
> *A student interning in the hospital was casually told by an expectant mother that the tests showed that her child would be*

malformed, and that she would favor an abortion. The nursing school student dissuaded the mother from an abortion by offering to take the child into her own custody if she carried to term, as per the Rebbe's directives. The mother agreed to carry to term. The mother gave birth to a normal child.

❧ The Rebbe's Capacity To Bear Great Pain

The *Rebbe* was known to have suffered great pain throughout his years, a matter about which he never complained. A Jew once asked the *Rebbe* for a portion of the *Olam Habbah* that would be his because of his suffering. The *Rebbe* replied, "My portion in the Hereafter for my suffering in this world is negligible, but my work on behalf of my fellow Jews after the liberation will earn me much in the Hereafter, and that I will not give away."

Another man asked the *Rebbe* for help for his daughter who was suffering severe migraine headaches. The doctors had given up hope on helping her. The *Rebbe* replied, "I, too, suffer from severe migraine headaches. I've suffered all my life, so I'll suffer some more by assuming some of your daughter's headaches." The young girl's headaches quickly disappeared.

The *Rebbe* in his later years had a cardiac condition which required by-pass surgery. Before the *Rebbe*'s physician was to perform the surgery, he asked the *Rebbe* why he agreeed to the surgery. Is it to relieve pain, or to improve the quality of life? The *Rebbe* replied, "I surely would not undergo surgery to relieve pain, to which I am already destined. I will only agree to the surgery to improve the quality of my life, to enable me to learn more, *daven* better, and be more effective in helping others."

More than the *Rebbe*'s willingness to accept his destiny of suffering pain, was a silent, fervent prayer from deep within the *Rebbe*'s heart—striving for the denial of any earthly pleasures and the welcoming of trials and tribulations, adversity and challenges.

> One of the highlights of the Rebbe's life was the laying of the cornerstone of the main Sanz Medical Center building in Netanya. Prior to this event, the Rebbe was in the United States, recuperating from cardiac surgery. He consulted with his physicians as to whether he could make the trip. They categorically forbade him.

The Rebbe, in reply to the physician, wrote: "Although I hold the opinions of my physician in very high esteem, and you know that I always follow doctor's orders, in this case I must make an exception. You cannot understand that my love for the Holy Land and its institutions—especially Kiryat Sanz and the hospital that is being built in Kiryat Sanz—is so great that it outweighs all the arguments you give me for not making this arduous trip." The Rebbe made the trip successfully, although in great pain.

To culminate the celebrations surrounding the cornerstone laying, which was attended by 25,000 people on the hospital campus, a banquet was planned, to which a select group of 250 of the country's most prominent lay citizens, religious leaders, and members of the international board of the Sanz Medical Center were invited. This dinner would also be graced by the presence of the Rebbe—indeed, a most unusual event.

On that very afternoon, before the dinner, the Rebbe instructed the travel agent to arrange for his immediate return to the United States, categorically refusing to stay for the dinner. All pleading for him to stay on, not to disappoint the dinner attendees, was of no avail. It was only on his way to the airport that he confided as to his reason for not staying: "I have already had too much honor and glory, too much kavod, more than enough."

The *Rebbe* did not suffer from the severe pains of the migraine headaches whenever he was immersed in Torah study. Especially when he gave a *shiur*, he had no headaches, without resorting to medication. The *Rebbe* said that being immersed in Torah with *kavanah* could dispel all aches and pains.

Ko'ach HaTorah—unleashing the forces and the power of Torah learning—that was his *raison d'etre*.

✥ The Rebbe's Passing

The *Rebbe*'s last will and testament prohibited any *hespeidim* at his funeral. He ordered that the tombstone identify him only by his name and his father's name, with no titles whatsoever. The *Rebbe* outlined specific schedules of study of *Gemara* and *Tosafos* for the benefit of his soul.

He concluded the *tzava'ah* (ethical will) with a passionate plea for peace amongst Torah scholars in order that they merit of the promise that, "And there shall be no stumbling blocks in their path." Beyond doubt, his efforts and achievements for *Klal Yisrael*—in fact, his very life—was a record of consummate devoting to clearing the path for others to follow in his *derech* of Torah, intense *avodah,* and selfless *chessed*.

Rabbi Yerachmiel D. Fried

A Glimpse At The Life of a Giant In Our Times: HaRav Shlomo Zalman Auerbach זצ"ל

A leading Poseik of our times, his feet walked the same earth as ours, while his head was in the heavens, and his heart was the heart of the Jewish nation

"**M**y headstone should be of conventional size, and certainly no higher than those of my parents ע"ה. You may add to the headstone the following words, 'He developed students in the Yeshivah Kol Torah and disseminated Torah to the multitudes...' Should someone wish to say words of eulogy, I strongly request that they should be concise and that they should not say words of praise about me (as even now, when I am alive, I am pained by praise)...only words that inspire love of Torah and the fear of Heaven, perfection in deed and *middos* (character traits)...."—*From the tzavaah (will) of Reb Shlomo Zalman* זצ"ל.

The Gemara, (Bava Basra 15a) cites an opinion that the final eight verses of the Torah, which recount the death of Moshe, were written by

Moshe himself with tears rather than ink. It would seem that besides the standard mode of writing, there is a type of script inscribed in tears. This brief tribute belongs to the latter category, written with pen dipped in the tears of all who knew him, the 300,000 melavim who accompanied him to his final resting place, and the countless more who loved him and revered him for all that they had heard about him.

These lines are culled from words I have heard from Reb Shlomo Zalman's distinguished sons, daughters, and sons-in-law, from his close students of half a century, and from the little I merited to observe over the past decade. Volumes would not suffice to describe a man whose feet walked upon the same earth as ours, but whose head was high in the heavens, and whose heart was the heart of the Jewish nation.

◄§ Early Years: Spiritual Richness, Material Poverty

Reb Shlomo Zalman was born on 23 Tamuz, 5670 (1910), to Hagaon Rabbi Chaim Yehuda Leib and Rebbetzin Tzivya Auerbach, scions of great rabbinical families of Yerushalayim for generations. His mother was the daughter of the esteemed Rabbi Shlomo Zalman Porush. In 1906, Reb Chaim Yehuda Leib, at age 20, established the Yeshivah Shaar Hashomayim of Kabbalah. During the day, a regular yeshivah schedule was followed, but throughout the night the students immersed themselves in the writings of the *Ari zal* and the *Kavanos HaRashash*, both exalted Kabbalistic works. Soon after, Reb Chaim Yehuda Leib established a *kollel* of seventy members and a *cheder* for children.

From the time Reb Shlomo Zalman entered the *cheder* of Eitz Chaim it became evident that he was no ordinary *talmid*. When his father taught him the first *Mishnah* in *Bava Kama*, the child noted the cases regarding cattle in the *Mishnah* and asked what would happen if the chickens in their courtyard would damage or eat another person's possessions. Reb Chaim Yehuda Leib later commented that his child had then revealed his propensity toward becoming a *poseik*, one who applies his learning to actual practice.

As Reb Shlomo Zalman grew into a young man, his peers and teachers all marveled over his unusual brilliance as well as his intense love for Torah and his unwavering *hasmadah* (intensity of study). He became very close to the revered *Rosh Yeshivah*, Hagaon Rabbi Isser Zalman Meltzer זצ״ל, who chose him as *chavrusa* (study partner). Reb Isser Zalman often spoke with lavish praise of this young, budding scholar, and his destiny as a *gaon*. He once remarked that as a 23-year old, his *talmid* possessed elements that were rare among Torah scholars of 40.

Reb Shlomo Zalman once described the *shiur* of his *Rebbe*: "Reb Isser Zalman would begin reading the *Gemara,* immediately posing simple queries. In attendance were great scholars, many of whom could recite the tractate by heart. Some were critical of the *shiur,* commenting that the answers to those queries are explicit statements of the *Gemara* in other places, or of classical commentaries on the spot. Many of them dropped the *shiur* to learn on their own. But there was more to it. By the conclusion of each of these magnificent *shiurim,* an entire thought system had been projected. From the way he structured the *sugya* (passage) together with us, I learned *how* to learn."

The Auerbach home often lacked basic necessities. As the oldest child, much of the burden of providing for the household fell upon young Shlomo Zalman's shoulders. There were times he forfeited his own portion of bread to a hungry sibling, and then engrossed himself in Torah, which stilled his nagging hunger.

✒ That Unswerving Resolution

He once commented that in light of the abject poverty of the times and the responsibilities he carried, he was halachically exempt from Torah study. "I was only able to continue to grow in learning," said Reb Shlomo Zalman, "because of my resolution to keep *sedarim*—set hours for learning, come what may—never to budge from those apportioned times, and to take care of all other matters, no matter how pressing, outside the framework of those set times."

It was then that he forged his rigorous stringency with himself and his students, his remarkable commitment to always adhere to a schedule. He kept to this stringency throughout his life, even during his later years when he won the love and appreciation of the masses because of his accessibility to one and all, responding to every type of request, petition, and halachic query. Through it all, he had maintained a room in the Shaare Chessed neighborhood, where he went daily to learn undisturbed, before his public hours. (A close *talmid* discovered the location of this hideaway, and approached the *Rosh Yeshivah* there to discuss a Torah topic with him. Not abandoning his characteristic smile, he said softly to the *talmid*, "I came to this room to escape the crowds, including yourself." And that ended the well-intensioned invasion. This *talmid*, today a highly regarded *talmid chacham*, notes that this encounter instructed him in the unyielding dedication necessary to grow toward greatness in Torah.)

When Reb Shlomo Zalman was older and too weak to walk daily to this room, he would learn at home, jealously guarding his private hours. In his final year and a half, when he had resolved to annotate the comments and *piskei halachah* (decisions) cited in his name in *Sefer Shmiras Shabbos K'Hilchaso*, written by his *talmid* Rabbi Yehoshua Neuwirth, his *ahavas Torah* drove him to overcome physical infirmities to fulfill this monumental task. The *avreich* (*Kollel* fellow) who merited to be his *chavrusa* for this undertaking relates that at times people knocked on the door during morning hours with great insistence. When the *avreich* would rise to get the door, Reb Shlomo Zalman would say, "This is the time I learn. There are others whom they can ask. And if they need me, they'll come back at 2:00."

ᶜᵉ§ Illuminating the World With His Writings

During the years around his Bar Mitzvah, he would become upset when reading halachic literature written by great contemporary scholars, challenging rulings of earlier *Acharonim*. He would on occasion attempt to justify the opinions of those authorities and send his response to these giants. Undaunted by his youth, the fire of defending what he thought to be the truth burned in his heart. Often, these rabbis publicly yielded to his sound arguments.

At age eighteen, Reb Shlomo Zalman authored a magnificent commentary on the classical work *Shev Shemeitza*. His father was impressed with the work, which shows an uncanny mastery over much of *Shas*, its commentaries, and *Shulchan Aruch*, but asked his son to put it away. Its contents were unusually perceptive for someone his age, and the father feared that the attention it would attract might cause his son to become arrogant. Out of respect for his father, he kept it unpublished, until his family printed the manuscript a few years ago.

During those years, he became very close with two of the great *poskim* of the generation, Rabbi Zvi Pesach Frank and Rabbi Zelig Reuven Bengis, both heads of Jewish courts in Jerusalem. Through their influence, he was guided to his eventual role as *poseik*, in addition to *Rosh Yeshivah*.

On *Purim Meshulash*[1] of 5690 (1930), Reb Shlomo Zalman married the woman of valor who was to ensure his continued growth and raise their family of Torah greatness: *Rebbetzin* Chaya Rivka, the daughter of Rabbi Aryeh Leib Ruchamlen, a noted teacher in Yerushalayim.

After their wedding, the couple moved in with the Ruchamlens. The *Rebbetzin* assumed the major role in raising the children when they were small, enabling Reb Shlomo Zalman to devote himself fully to his learning. On occasion, when I would pose questions to him regarding *chinuch* of small children, he would say, "I'm not sure what was done in that case with my children, because I entrusted such matters with my *Rebbetzin*, who was a wise and pious woman and the daughter of *gedolim*."

A kollel yungerman once complained to Reb Shlomo Zalman that his children caused such a ruckus at home that it was impossible for him to learn. Reb Shlomo Zalman was surprised, saying that when his children were small, they were so well behaved and quiet that his learning was never disturbed. The Rebbetzin overheard their conversation, and interrupted saying, "Excuse me, but that's not entirely accurate. Our children were as loud as any other kids. I just shielded you from the noise so you could concentrate."

Reb Shlomo Zalman decided to develop a special proficiency in the tractates *Beitzah* and *Bava Kama*, which remained his "favorites" for his entire lifetime. His study of *Beitzah* culminated in the publication in 5695 (1935) of *Me'orei Eish*, a work of rare erudition on the then-undefined subject of use of electricity on *Shabbos* and *Yom Tov*. His *Rebbe*, Reb Isser Zalman, in his approbation to the *sefer*, described the work as possessing a breadth and

---

1. When Purim (14 Adar) falls on Friday, cities such as Jerusalem, which keep Shushan Purim (15 Adar), mark different aspects of the holiday over a three-day period. Hence the name, which means "Triple Purim."

depth of knowledge befitting an accomplished sage. The *sefer* is also crowned with the approbation of a leading authority of his time, Rabbi Chaim Ozer Grodzensky of Vilna. Reb Chaim Ozer, upon learning that the author was but 25 years old, exclaimed: "*Ohr chadash al Tzion ta'ir!* (A great light will illuminate Zion)." After completing this *sefer*, Reb Shlomo Zalman left Yeshivah Eitz Chaim to join Kollel Kerem Tzion, an institution of advanced scholars where *Hilchos Eretz Yisrael*, the many complicated laws linked to the Holy Land, were studied in depth. He published articles on the subject in the Kollel's publications, and remained there until the publication of his *Maadanei Eretz*, in 5704 (1944). This comprehensive work on the laws of *Shmittah*, the Sabbatical year in *Eretz Yisrael*, was published a year before *Shmittah*, and immediately won acclaim as the authoritative work on the subject. It was followed by two similar works on *terumos* and *maasros* (tithes), which received similar praise.

When the Steipler Gaon received these works of Reb Shlomo Zalman, shortly after the Chazon Ish's passing in 1953, he said, "I thought that when the Chazon Ish died, *Toras Eretz Yisrael* vanished with him (*Batla Toras Eretz Yisrael*). Now I see that *Toras Eretz Yisrael* is still alive." In a letter to Reb Shlomo Zalman concerning *terumos*, the Steipler ends by stating that "whoever has this *sefer* cannot move without it in related matters."

Reb Shlomo Zalman frequently mentioned his intense devotion to *Eretz Yisrael*. He was under great pressure to attend weddings of grandchildren in England, but once commented that one thing he would be taking with him was that he never set foot outside of *Eretz Yisrael*.

◌ Rosh Yeshivah

Before completing a second work on *terumos*, he was offered the position of *Rosh Yeshivah* of Yeshivas Kol Torah. Reb Shlomo Zalman was in a dilemma, wanting to complete his commentary to the fifth and final chapter of *Rambam Hilchos Terumos*. He discussed his quandary with his *Rebbetzin*, who pointed out that the merit and importance of teaching students might be even greater than completing this much needed work. Considering this, he decided to enter this new stage of his life, the *Rosh Yeshivah*.

(Before his passing, he commented that he "carried" five more unpublished volumes of *Maadanei Eretz* in his mental files, but as long as he could serve as *Rosh Yeshivah*, publishing them would remain secondary among his priorities.)

Reb Shlomo Zalman was invited to deliver a pilot *shiur* at Kol Torah, which would determine his suitability for the position. Near the beginning of the lecture, Rabbi Yonah Mertzbach זצ״ל, one of the founders of the yeshivah, interrupted with a question. After a few seconds, Reb Shlomo Zalman unflinchingly said, "*Ta'isi*—I made a mistake," and went on to a different subject. When he returned home and the *Rebbetzin* asked how it went, he said, "Not so well. I admitted to a mistake hardly into the *shiur*. Although I had three answers to his question, I felt the question was closer to *emes* (truth) than my answers."

He did not know why he was accepted for the position in spite of the "bad showing" until many years later: Hagaon Rabbi Yehuda Addas, *Rosh Yeshivah* of Kol Yaakov and a close *talmid* of Reb Shlomo Zalman, relates that Rabbi Mertzbach later confided in him, "Do you know why Reb Shlomo Zalman was appointed to his position? When I asked him that question, and he answered 'I made a mistake,' it was clear to me that with that calibre of *emes*, he's our *Rosh Yeshivah*!"

Reb Shlomo Zalman once remarked that he would not be rewarded for accepting truth, because he simply found greater joy in agreeing with the truth than in defending his position, if the two seemed to conflict.

◆§ Ahavas Torah

Reb Shlomo Zalman's son, Reb Shmuel, eulogized him as loving Torah and only Torah. From when he began to learn *Gemara* until his last day, he invested all his thought and energy to probing the depths of *halachah*. A correspondent once asked why we call Talmudic academies "*yeshivos*," the writer offering the explanation that Torah is learned sitting down (*yosheiv*), hence "yeshivah." Reb Shlomo Zalman rejected that answer, because the *Avos* had yeshivos, and for close to 2,000 years, until the time of Rabban Gamliel, people stood while learning Torah. The actual reason, he wrote, is because Torah is "*ikar yishuvo shel olam*," the primary means of developing the world; all else is subservient to it.

This letter personifies his philosophy of life.

His son Reb Ezriel relates that he once entered the house and found his father with his head wrapped in a towel, learning a very difficult topic of *Gemara* (the entire commentary of the Chazon Ish on the *sugya* of *Matbe'os* at the beginning of *Perek Hazahav* in *Bava Metzia*). As brilliant as he was, he spared no effort on each new acquisition of Torah knowledge, concentrating intensely until it became part of his lifeblood.

When he married, he received a large nedunya (dowry), which he was advised to invest in a bank (owned by a non-Jew so it would be free of ribbis/usury problems). The principle would thus remain and he would not need to worry about earning a livelihood. He asked, "What would be involved in maintaining the fund?" He was told that he would be required to spend a half-hour or hour every Friday at the bank to take care of the investment. He answered, "If so, it's not for me. That would take me 'out of learning.'"

Rabbi Addas, when relating this story, added that his strongest impression of Reb Shlomo Zalman was his willingness to undergo any hardship, difficulty or embarrassment so as to learn one more *Tosafos*.

He delivered his *shiurim* with immense concentration, laced with joy. In the early years, when the *talmidim* were fewer in number, he delighted in sitting with them for hours, delving into a difficult *sugya*. And if a *talmid* would come up with a good, original *sevara* (explanation), his face flushed red with joy. His love for *talmidim* was that of a father; their children were his grandchildren.

Rabbi Addas was once discussing with him the concept of *Ahavas Hashem*, love for the Almighty. He became excited and said with sweetness and intensity: "For us, *Ahavas Hashem* means *Ahavas Torah*!" He conveyed this love to his *talmidim*.

One must never be discouraged, he would say, and never lose sight of the awesome importance of the Torah one is studying. He illustrated this with a story told to him by the *tzaddik* Rabbi Aryeh Levin about the great *mekubal*, the *Baal HaLeshem*. When his kabbalistic work *Leshem* reached the Ben Ish Chai in Baghdad, the *chacham* instructed his followers in Yerushalayim to don *Shabbos* garments and express gratitude to the *Leshem* for the wonderful *sefer* he had written. When the *Leshem* told this to Reb Aryeh, he began to cry, "If I would have known that this work is so important, I would have written another volume!" Reb Shlomo Zalman compared this to *Chazal*'s comment regarding *Aaron HaKohein*. Had he known that the Torah would record his joy upon greeting Moshe, he would have welcomed his brother with an orchestra. Reb Shlomo Zalman concluded, exclaiming, "The *Leshem* was like a *Malach Elokim*, an Angel of *Hashem*, and even he did not realize how important his *seforim* were. How much more must we constantly remind ourselves of the great significance of our Torah study!"

He knew no exemptions "because it's Friday,"—"it's Rosh Hashana," or—"it's Erev Pesach." During these times, one must find moments to learn with depth, with full concentration.

◄§ "L'orer L'Yiras Shamayim"—To Inspire Fear of Heaven

When Reb Shlomo Zalman *davened,* one saw the vision of a man standing before the King. He stood *Shemoneh Esrei* for 15 minutes on an ordinary day, without flinching, even during times of great weakness, his devotion etched upon his face.

Rabbi Chaim Brim, a well known *mussar* personality, once remarked that should one want to see how to speak to the *Ribbono Shel Olam* he should watch Reb Shlomo Zalman say *"Shehakol"* on a cup of water.... I once overheard him recite *"Asher Yatzar"* with the intensity we associate with *Ne'ilah* on Yom Kippur.

> *I was walking with Reb Shlomo Zalman to daven an early Minchah in the yeshivah in Shaare Chessed during the bein hazmanim (intersession) break. A yeshivah bachur passed by, and Reb Shlomo Zalman asked him what time Minchah was. The bachur did not know. He turned to me and exclaimed, "Lo Tov! That's not good! Chazal say, Shohin sha'ah achas kodem hatefillah—one should prepare for an hour before davening. If one doesn't know what time davening begins, how can he prepare himself beforehand?"*
>
> *Rabbi Addas once told him that a large group of bachurim began to come early to Shacharis in the yeshivah, to have tallis and tefillin on before the tzibbur began. He reacted with great joy— "That's truly wonderful! All my life I'd love to get to davening early, and say Korbanos slowly." He once remarked that a day in*

which he managed to daven all three Shemoneh Esrei tefillos with b'iurei millos—concentration upon the simple meaning of the words—"bei mir iz a groyse Yom Tov," is a great holiday for me!

After having spent a Shabbos in Kol Torah, in Bayit Vegan, he commented to his son-in-law, Rabbi Yitzchok Yeru-cham Borodiansky, "I have always had an intense desire to daven in yeshivah, but I never merited it."

Rabbi Borodiansky suggested that he daven Shabbasos at Maalos Ha-Torah, his son Reb Shmuel's yeshivah (now located in Shaare Chessed), instead of the shul he frequented.

Replied Reb Shlomo Zalman, "The yeshivah minyan does not function bein hazmanim; if I daven in the yeshivah all year and then return to the shul during bein hazmanim, I'll insult the baalei battim by demonstrating that their minyan is my second choice. That I cannot do."

During his last year, Reb Shlomo Zalman was approached for advice on behalf of a man with formidable problems. He wanted a suggestion for some added stringency to assume, as a source of merit. The *Rosh Yeshivah* answered that he could not tell others what to do; he could only share what he himself was working on presently: to concentrate on his *berachos*, "that my '*Baruch*' should be a *Baruch*, that my '*Atto*' should be an *Atto*, and that the '*Shem*' should be a *Shem*. If I can achieve this, it's more precious to me than all that *sifrei mussar* offer."

The family later discussed this confession. What could he mean that his "*Baruch*" be *Baruch*, and so on? His recitation of *berachos* was already exemplary! They concluded that the potential *kavana* (concentration) for a *berachah* is infinite, and he, with all his *gadlus* (greatness), fear of Heaven, and eight decades of accumulated practice, decided now to apply effort that his "*Baruch*" should be as close as possible to the ideal *Baruch*, his "*Attoh*" approach the ultimate *Attoh*, his "*Hashem*" truly address *Hashem*!

◄§ "And the Man Shlomo Was the Humblest of All Men"

Those who spent time with the *Rosh Yeshivah* were astonished by his simplicity and true *anivus*, his indescribable humbleness. It was manifest in his every action, the simplicity of his home and furnishings, and his relationship with others.

Reb Shlomo Zalman would often relate how Reb Isser Zalman Meltzer, in one of the mussar shmuessen (discourses on ethics) that he would deliver in Yeshivah Eitz Chaim before Maariv every Motza'ei Shabbos, mentioned the halachah that a Sefer Torah found to be pasul (invalid) must be tied with a gartel (belt) on the outside to reveal to all its disqualification. Reb Isser Zalman broke down in tears, exclaiming, "How many gartelach do I need to wrap around myself to publicize all my disqualifications!" Reb Shlomo Zalman went on to say, "Whatever Reb Isser Zalman said, he felt in his heart, and what he felt in his heart, he said," adding that he personally was profoundly moved by this public confession.

Dozens of times, when he still had his strength, he would get angry at me for attempting to open the car door for him. "What! I can't open it myself?!" This refusal reflected his fierce repulsion at accepting any type of honor.

He spoke to us as though we were his peers—nay, as if he was our peer. I would have a list of *she'eilos* prepared for each car ride. Once someone needed to speak to him on the way, leaving no time for my queries. He later thanked me kindly for the ride and apologized that "today we didn't converse in learning together." Not "I didn't answer your *she'eilos* today."

We were once driving past Shaare Tzeddek Hospital on our way to the *Rosh Yeshivah*'s home. A yeshivah student hitching a ride to the Chevron Yeshivah nearby took a step back when he saw who was in the car. I had no intention of stopping anyway, to delay the *Rosh Yeshivah*. He turned to me, very annoyed, "Why didn't you stop for him?!" I said that the boy seemed to have changed his mind.

"How could you not stop for a boy who needs a ride?" he exclaimed. "I don't understand," he continued to exclaim his wonder throughout the ride.

For many years, he rode the #12 bus from Bayit Vegan to Machaneh Yehudah, and from there took the long trek home by foot. Only when he became weak did he allow the yeshivah to call a cab, and then to accept rides home. (It was during those rides home that this writer merited to discuss most of the halachic aspects of *Yom Tov Sheini*, as well as hundreds of other questions.

Many people's lives were built from his breaks and his moments of transit.)

After becoming *Rosh Yeshivah* in Kol Torah, he would ask Rabbi Yechezkel Abramsky זצ"ל, who resided in Bayit Vegan, to deliver *shiurim* in the yeshivah. He would listen attentively, and then review the *shiur* with the *bachurim*. Once Rabbi Abramsky entered the *beis hamidrash* when the *Rosh Yeshivah* was delivering a *shiur klalli* (a lecture for the entire senior student body). He rushed to the door to greet him, and asked him to deliver a *shiur* instead. Rabbi Abramsky refused, saying he was not prepared; Reb Shlomo Zalman should continue. The latter replied that he could not give a *shiur* in Rabbi Abramsky's presence. Rabbi Abramsky answered, "*Ich bett eich*—I implore you to continue."

Slowly Reb Shlomo Zalman went back to his place, apologizing to the students: "What can I do? He requested it of me and '*Ein mesarvim legadol*—you cannot refuse a great man.'"

After Reb Shlomo Zalman got up from shivah for his Rebbetzin, Rabbi Addas remarked to him that we learned many things from the Rav during the past week. He answered, "I'm very far from being one whose actions can be learned from."

He had a profound hatred for titles of greatness being bestowed upon him, and felt they were utterly false. He asked me to remove the titles describing him in the preface to *Yom Tov Sheini K'hilchaso*: "All this is unnecessary. Besides that, it's not true." His son Reb Baruch recently published a *sefer* in which he referred to him as "*Maran*." He became visibly upset: "You're my own son and even you are doing this to me. If you don't remove it, I'll remove my letter of blessing."

He would laugh at the titles conferred upon him in some letters, other times getting angry at the correspondent, especially if he were close with him. He once rebuked a *talmid*, saying it was downright ugly to enumerate honorable titles on the envelope. "Do you need to tell the postman I'm some kind of *gaon*?" Near the end of his life he received a letter which bore the title רשכבה"ג. He became furious, and said, "The sender is a *meshuganer*," and refused to read the letter, insisting it be put into *sheimos* for burial.

Two year ago, Rabbi Addas called before Rosh Hashana to arrange to visit him before *Yom Tov*. He answered, "This year you need not come."

Rabbi Addas asked, "Why not?"

He answered, "*Chazal* say to visit a *Tofeis Yeshivah*, and I no longer head a yeshivah."

Rabbi Addas, disturbed by that comment, immediately traveled to his home and said, "The *Rav* is *Tofeis hador kulo*—the entire generation."

At that, Reb Shlomo Zalman was close to tears: "Are you also doing this to me, calling me *poseik hador*? I don't know *Mishnah k'tzurasa* (the proper meaning of a *Mishnah*), and they're calling me *poseik hador!*"[2]

◆§ Poseik

When giving a *shiur* in Kol Torah, besides the usual joy with which he delved into every topic, he would radiate with a special glow when his explanations would result in a *halachah l'maaseh*, with practical application. It is extremely rare in recent generations for one man to be a *Rosh Yeshivah* who has developed thousands of *talmidim*, and be a *poseik* on all phases of *halachah*, without exception. The writer has asked him questions in all four sections of *Shulchan Aruch*, and the "fifth" as well, and his answers always reflected not only clear knowledge and understanding, but *gadlus* (true greatness) in every nuance of *halachah*.

I heard him say countless times that he was not a *poseik* but a *Rosh Yeshivah*; he would not even allow the word "*poseik*" on his headstone. This reflected his *anivus*, his deep humility. But when he rendered a *p'sak*, it was with the full weight of his mastery of Torah, fused with the fear of Heaven not to make a mistake.[3]

We once discussed a question of *Yom Tov Sheini* at length, and he finally rendered a *kula* (leniency) because, he said, "It's a

---

2. His sons expressed wonder how the entire Jewish world recognized his singular greatness, with the exception of himself, similar to Moshe *Rabbeinu* in that only he was not aware that his face shone.

3. His greatness as a *poseik* is evident in every page of his masterful work *Minchas Shlomo*, in which his responses and treatises pave new avenues in every area of *halachah*. It is replete with his renowned straightforward and clear logic and lucidity in the most difficult areas of Torah. It immediately became a classical work, forging *halachah* for our generation, found in Torah libraries everywhere. This is in addition to his many hundreds of decisions brought forth in *Shemiras Shabbos K'hilchasa*, a *sefer* found in Torah homes everywhere, ensuring a proper adherence to the *halachos* of *Shabbos* in today's world.

question of a *d'rabbanan* (rabbinical law) and one need not fear to be lenient as one need be regarding *hilchos Shabbos.*" Several months later, when a different question of *Yom Tov Sheini* was raised, he expressed fear of being lenient. I asked him, "But the *Rosh Yeshivah* said one need not fear being lenient concerning a doubt in *Yom Tov Sheini!*"

He answered, "I only said you don't need the *same* fear as one must have regarding *Hilchos Shabbos. Aval pachad yeish*—but fear is in place!"

He had the sense of authority (*breite pleitzes*) to render decisions that were not explicitly dealt with in any of the classical works, and sometimes even seemed to contradict them at first glance. He often would not quote any specific source for his *psak,* because the source was *kol haTorah kula,* the entirety of Torah. I witnessed on numerous occasions when he utilized such a profound understanding of the reasoning of the *halachah,* that he could say it does—or does not—apply in situations with no precedent. This was similar to the greatness of *Maran* Rabbi Moshe Feinstein ל"צז, who paved new roads in unexplored territory in *halachah.* In a halachic dispute with Reb Shlomo Zalman, Reb Moshe, in *Igros Moshe,* stated that the *halachah* is like Reb Shlomo Zalman in *Eretz Yisrael.*

He lived in a fine-tuned, exacting world, where every nuance and phrase was weighed. He complained that today people like to hear "*assur,* it's forbidden." He took tremendous responsibility for any *p'sak* written in his name, and with *Yom Tov Sheini* he reviewed every comment attributed to him, made changes, additions, notes and deletions. Often his changes would be in subtleties, from "forbidden" to "one should not...." From "should not" to "improper...." From "improper" to "better to refrain...." From "obligated" to "should...." From "should" to "befitting...." or "nice...." I mentioned that the *Rosh Yeshivah* forbade a certain garment. He answered, "I never said it's 'forbidden.' I said it's 'ugly' to wear such an item."

When we would discuss problems *baalei teshuvah* face and the difficulties they go through, or of Jews being lost to assimilation, he would shake his head, clicking his tongue, his face twisted with pain.

After publishing the second edition of Yom Tov Sheini, incorporat-

ing many new decisions from the Rosh Yeshivah, I approached him with new she'eilos on the subject. I received a rebuke: "Enough of this subject, go onto something else! Do you think you can finish all of Yom Tov Sheini? Even if you, your children and your grandchildren would spend your entire lives studying nothing but Yom Tov Sheini, you still would-n't finish it. The Torah is infinite, which means that each and every halachah within it is also infinite. If the Chofetz Chaim would have added every new she'eila to the Mishnah Berurah, it would be like this [stretching his hands apart]! Nobody would learn it! Leave something over for the Jewish people to use their own seichel on, and work on some-thing new." (In spite of that rebuke, there are ten new pages of p'sakim from him, which he annotated like the rest, in anticipation of the next edition.)

Another incident: I received a book of chiddushim written by a person not celebrated for his yiras Shamayim, and asked Reb Shlomo Zalman if I was permitted to study it, and he answered in the affirma-tive. I asked him, "What about the statement of Chazal, 'If the rebbe is similar to an angel of G-d, only then learn Torah from his mouth.'"

He answered, "That halachah only deals with a case of a talmid and Rebbe, as we see from the beginning of the pasuk: 'Sifsei kohein yishmeru daas' when you're coming to learn not only what the rebbe says, but also from the sifsei kohein, from his lips — how the rebbe says it, to study his every gesture, his manner of speech, together with his Torah; then there's a prerequisite of 'ki malach Hashem Tzvakos hu, he must be like an angel of G-d.' But when learning from a sefer, you're absorbing the chiddushim and not the rebbe, so it is permitted — providing, of course, that the sefer has no apikorsus (blasphemy) and that the author is known not to be guilty of that."

This response indicates how the Rosh Yeshivah learned from his rabbeim, conveying so much to us, for whom shimush talmidei chachamim has nearly been forgotten.

⤳ Ahavas Habrios/Love For Fellow Creatures

During the shiva and sheloshim mourning following his pass-ing, a new dimension of the Rosh Yeshivah was revealed, involving thousands of personal stories of tzeddakah and chessed previously unknown. He married off untold numbers of orphans and paid for their wedding celebrations. He supported, monetarily and morally, so many young widows. He visited hundreds of sick in their homes and in the hospital. The *Chareidi* newspapers and magazines in *Eretz Yisrael* are filled with incredible accounts of his helping poor, elderly and sick people.

Upon hearing of a young woman just widowed in Lakewood, he asked for her number, spoke to her on the telephone for half an hour, and brought her back to life.

An old woman who could barely carry the daily delivery of eggs from the street to her small store, mysteriously began finding them moved for her. One morning she hid and discovered the identity of her benefactor. When did he find the time for it all and how did he manage to keep it hidden?

He was not a "*chessed* seeker." All of his acts of *chessed* were part of his *amal baTorah*, a feeling of halachic obligation, as a man whose every thought was governed by *halachah*.

He once noticed a boy of eight reciting Kaddish in shul, not knowing the proper pronunciation and niggun, and feeling uncomfortable. The boy would only come to shul sporadically. Reb Shlomo Zalman sat down with the boy, explaining the beautiful meaning of Kaddish. Another time, he explained what reciting it does for his father's soul. On a third occasion, he coached him in the proper niggun and recitation. The boy began to come regularly, and today is an outstanding talmid chacham who attributes his love for Torah to those early conversations.

The *Rosh Yeshivah's* appreciation of others for the smallest favor was legendary. Rabbi Y.R. Borodiansky visited us late Friday night at the *shalom zachor* of my son, and I informed him that his father-in-law, the *Rosh Yeshivah*, would be the *sandek* at the *bris*. He commented, "I'll tell you a secret: anything in the world you ask of him, he'll do, because you drive him home once a week. His *hakoras hatov* (gratitude) is of awesome proportions. He even cherishes taxi drivers, whom he paid to drive him, for the good they did for him, and considers them friends." (Indeed, taxi drivers were seen weeping at his funeral).

Eleven years ago, his beloved *Rebbetzin* passed away on *Shabbos*. When he was told, he continued his singing and *davening* as usual! The moment *Shabbos* was over, however, he broke down and sobbed the entire night for his tremendous loss, and his lifetime accumulation of appreciation.

At her funeral, he said he knews that it is customary to ask forgiveness of one's departed wife, but for 54 years they lived together according to the *Shulchan Aruch,* and he had nothing to ask forgiveness for, except that because of his many sins she died young.

Rabbi Ezriel Tauber once said that that startling statement helped him to understand another story. About to enter his home, Reb Shlomo Zalman buttoned his coat, brushed it, and smoothed his beard. The *avreich* with him asked if he was preparing to go to a *simchah.* When the answer was No, he asked why the *Rosh Yeshivah* was grooming himself. He answered, "*Chazal* tell us that when there's peace between husband and wife, the *Shechinah*— the Divine Presence—rests on them. I'm about to be *mekabel P'nei HaShechinah*—to receive the Divine Presence."

◄§ HaMelech Shlomo

The Rabbis teach that one who studies Torah for its own sake acquires *malchus* (majesty) (*Avos* Ch. 6). Indeed, our sages are called kings (*Gittin* 62a). The *sifrei mussar* expound on this, explaining that the true king is one in complete control of himself. This mastery was manifest in Reb Shlomo Zalman. Whoever saw the *Rosh Yeshivah* felt he was viewing a king, *HaMelech Shlomo:* A man who throughout his tumultuous life had overcome hardships through rigorous discipline and commitment, had forged nerves of steel to withstand the greatest pressures from within and without, and remained in complete control.

He suffered from a severe neurological disorder that necessitated high-risk brain surgery many years ago, and then suffered from pain that affected his facial muscles and one eye for decades. At times, he would suddenly jump from pain in the middle of a *shiur,* as if bitten by a snake, would hold his face for a moment, and continue where he left off, with his *simchah* and *ahavas Torah* undaunted.

Once, during a drive home, I told him that I had a life-and-death *she'eila* to ask him, when he had a severe attack of pain affecting his eye. I suggested forgetting the *she'eila,* and offered to rush him home. He answered, "You said it's a *she'eila* of *pikuach nefesh.* Pull over to the side for several minutes and explain the *she'eila* to me," which I did. He answered me despite the pain.

With all his sweetness when speaking to a *talmid,* he could be harsh too—especially when he detected laziness in thought or practice in the student, or sloppiness in logic.

I often observed others trying to coerce him into signing statements he preferred not to sign, or to make statements concerning matters he had opted to remain silent about. No matter how strong the pressure, he would not yield. Especially during a recent election, when the *frum* community was split, he had resolved to make no comment, in spite of monumental pressures from both sides. On two occasions, I attempted to probe him on the matter, and he rebuked me, "Are you calling me about *Yom Tov Sheini* or about elections?!"

Because of that determination, he remained the *poseik* of all factions and all types of Jews. The respect that he attained brought a third of a million Jews of all customs, backgrounds and loyalties, to the largest *levayah* since that of Rabban Yochanan Ben Zakai. It was the *malchus* that graced the simple name "Reb Shlomo Zalman," with no titles, uttered affectionately by all types of Jews; as *Chazal* say "*Gadol m'rabban shemo*" (*Eiduyos* ch. 3)—his name was the greatest title of all.

The *Rosh Yeshivah* prayed throughout his life to remain in control of his faculties until his final day. G-d granted that request, and he remained with his regal demeanor until his final moment. The last week of his life saw him render a *p'sak* in *Hilchos Shabbos* for all of *Klal Yisrael*. Wednesday of his last week, he attended the *bris* of a *talmid's* son, issuing an important *p'sak* there, as well. Afterwards, not feeling well, he returned home and completed writing some checks, balancing his accounts, sending off support for the poor, and then receiving people that night.

Thursday morning he fell while walking to *shul*, his legs giving out. He insisted on continuing on to *shul* and hearing the Torah reading. Once in *shul*, he *davened* with his usual concentration, albeit sitting down.

He was diagnosed with pneumonia, necessitating him to spend *Shabbos* in the hospital. It was already Thursday, so he asked the family to help him dress for *Shabbos*. His leg was immobile, but they managed to dress him in fresh *Shabbos* clothing, fulfilling his insistence that a stain be removed from his sweater.

Friday morning he woke up early to *daven*. His loyal *talmid* and *shammes*, Rabbi Chaim Swissa, put his *tefillin* on for him, staying with him and *davening*, reciting *Vidduy* (confessional) for an hour and a half. Then came the final blow, when his lungs began to hemorrhage. Reb Shmuel said afterwards, that when he heard that blood was entering his father's lungs, he thought: *What kind of blood is that? That's the blood he spilled all his life over his study of Torah. Now it's bringing him through the gates of Heaven. Hamelech Shlomo, our rebbe, poseik, advisor and father, has left us.*

The 300 children, grandchildren and *talmidim* present when the *Rosh Yeshivah*'s holy *neshamah* was returned to his Maker, all rent their garments, and a great wailing was heard throughout the hospital, soon to resound throughout the world.

Hamelech Shlomo was surrounded by *talmidei chachamim* and lay people, *talmidei yeshivos* and physicians, Jews of all factions, jolting the secular press with how the religious world is in complete agreement that this man was everyone's *poseik*.

The *Gemara* relates (*Berachos* 43a) that the *talmidim* of Rav were sitting on the banks of the River Dank with their clothing rent in mourning, following his burial. They were unable to resolve a question concerning *Birchas Hamazon*. Rabbi Adda Bar Ahavah stood up, turned the torn front of his garment to his back, and tore the front again, proclaiming, "Rav has passed away and we have not mastered the *halachos* of *Birchas Hamazon*."

We have only begun to feel the loss of *Moreinu v'Rabbeinu Gaon Doreinu* Reb Shlomo Zalman Auerbach זצ"ל, the loss of that towering figure of truth, love of *Klal Yisrael* and every Jew, and *ahavas Torah*. We will yet feel his loss in all areas of *halachah* and *divrei Torah*, and rend our garments again.

All we can do is to heed his request, and desire that we should, in his merit, have a new awakening of *Ahavas Torah, Yiras Shamayim, tikkun hamaasim u'middos*.

The Man Who Fled From Honor — And His Entourage of 300,000 Mourners

"Who was this man?" asked a policeman redirecting traffic in downtown Jerusalem a few weeks back. "If I knew my funeral would be like this, I'd drop dead right now."

I overheard that remark while standing on a street corner, craning my neck, trying to see something—anything—over the passing sea of heads. I know what you mean, I thought. If proving oneself worthy of other people's love and admiration is one's underlying, though unacknowledged, goal in life, then by that yardstick this particular life was a remarkable success. And if honor is what one craves, then a final ovation such as this would almost make it worthwhile to die on the spot.

But the irony is that Rabbi Shlomo Zalman Auerbach, whose funeral on February 20/20 Adar was attended by an estimated 300-400,000 people, did not in his eighty-four years achieve visible success, as success would probably be defined by most people, including the policeman. He had never amassed wealth, he was unknown to the world at large. The day after his death, the big-circulation Israeli newspapers were full of bemused speculation as to how this rabbi's death had managed to bring together religious Jews of all stripes, and how the largest funeral in the country's history had been held in honor of a man whom the journalists themselves, and most of their readership, had never heard of. He was reported to have been a great, even the foremost, halachic authority, but plenty of great halachic authorities go to their graves without anything approaching that kind of mourning. How could anybody be at once so extravagantly renowned and utterly unknown?

My own attendance at the funeral came about as the result of a personal experience dating back nine or ten years. At the time, I had been caught in the crossfire of an ongoing inner war with myself over an agonizing personal decision, a daily battle between yes and no. I decided to consult Rabbi Shlomo Zalman Auerbach. Revealing myself to a respected *Rav* on personal issues was an unappealing, embarrassing prospect, but the war was such that I called for an appointment.

The phone was answered by a woman who said that her father-in-law didn't really make appointments, but that I could show up at their home at midnight any night of the week, and that if I wanted to be first in line, perhaps I could come a little early. I knew he would meet with me without charge, but thought it appropriate to offer some sort of payment for his time anyway. She said, "Oh, no."

That evening at 11:30, having located the house with some difficulty in the old neighborhood of Shaarei Chessed, I ascended a rickety flight of wooden stairs that trembled beneath my feet, and arrived at a cramped, high-ceilinged apartment around a hundred years old. Someone who I gathered was Rav Auerbach's son led me into a living room where four or five children were sleeping; the living room doubled as the children's bedroom.

I was seventh in line. There was a row of folding chairs for those who waited and each of us sat submerged in his or her own world. At two-thirty, Rav Auerbach's son ushered me past the children into a teeny, book-lined chamber. As the rabbi rose—a little man!—to welcome me, what struck me was his utter frailty, as if he were a weightless and pale winter leaf. But then, when he smiled (I wondered, does he know me from somewhere?) his smile was of such a pure and lucid light that something in me melted from the warmth. I didn't know it at the time, but that momentary vision of his smiling face would remain with me from then on in my mind's eye. "What shall we discuss?" he inquired.

For the next forty minutes or so, he listened to my words as if the fate of the planet depended upon a correct understanding of my predicament. He considered me more important, evidently, than I considered myself. When I went out into the starry night—all the little houses silent and darkened in their pre-dawn stillness—I realized that I was feeling inexplicably buoyant, and it occurred to me that it hadn't been awkward or embarrassing, after all. The ancient-looking Yerushalmi, born and raised in this neighborhood, seemed to identify with me: I, half a century younger, who'd grown up an assimilated Jew in a distant Connecticut suburb.

A decision emerged of itself, by the way, during the next few days. I realized only later how his nonjudgmentalness towards my self-entanglement had enabled me to move on.

When I flagged down a cab to rush home for my children's return from school, the driver asked if I was coming from the funeral. I nodded. "I delivered a letter to that rabbi one time," he told me. "He was *tzenua*."

That word, meaning modest, hidden, concealed, constitutes an apt summation of Rav Auerbach's power. Recognition—the very thing that people could sense he wasn't seeking—was precisely that which the policeman could joke about giving his life to acquire. What is it that fuels the policeman's desire for recognition, just as it fuels my own? A feeling of *unimportance*. Because of that submerged feeling, we unwittingly devote our lives, no matter how worthwhile our deeds, to the cause of self-glorification, and would heartily enjoy the eulogies at our own funerals.

To Rav Auerbach there was nothing to prove. A Jew is a Jew, a human being a human being... unquestionably, eternally precious.

What was it that drew us there that day to say goodbye? Rabbi Auerbach's light. Like moths drawn to a flame, each of us had sensed in this person something beyond ego, beyond body, something even beyond self. With what uncanny perspicacity the inner eye recognizes the rare one among us who's thinking of other things than his own honor! It's he whom our hearts most respect.

Eliyahu Meir Klugman

The Ish Ha'emes:
The Man of Unimpeachable Integrity
Rabbi Shimon Schwab זכר צדיק לברכה

A faithful Rav and teacher who led his people with his deep insights, unimpeachable integrity and extraordinary warmth

Frankfurt, 1915: A six-year-old boy is sent by his mother to the store to buy groceries. With the change he buys himself some chocolate, which he eats on the way. When he arrives home, his mother asks him for the change. "Here it is," the boy answers.

"But where is the rest?" his mother asks.

"I must have lost it," the boy replies. But his mother notices a chocolate wrapper in his pocket.

"Oh," she says, with a look that he will remember for the rest of his life, "you didn't tell the *emes.*"

Note: As the subject of this appreciation loathed even the merest whiff of exaggeration, I have attempted to avoid embellishment, which is unnecessary in any case. In keeping with the statement of *Chazal* (*Yerushalmi, Eruvin* 2:5) that one does not erect monuments for righteous men, as their words are their memorial, the thoughts and *divrei Torah* contained herein are all, unless otherwise indicated, Rav Schwab's own. To facilitate reading, we have often dispensed with quotation marks.

Later that day his father comes home. He does not hit him or send him to his room. "What is this I hear that you didn't tell the *emes*? Your punishment will be that tonight, Friday night, I will not *bentsch* you. No, I won't *bentsch* you tonight." The young boy never forgot that lesson.

Radin, 1930: The young Frankfurt boy, now a Mirrer Yeshivah *bachur*, comes to visit the *Chofetz Chaim*. When the elderly sage is told that he is "a Frankfurter *bachur*," he takes his hand in his own and caresses it gently. "A yeshivah *bachur*! How fortunate! So many are drowning today. Only through Torah can one survive. How fortunate that you are learning!"

Marienbad, 1934: The Mirrer yeshivah *bachur*, by now a *Rav* in Germany, pays a visit to the saintly Gerrer *Rebbe*. The *Rebbe* tells him, "Remember, *Yungerman*! One must be very careful to safeguard the honor of Rav Hirsch, the *tzaddik* of Frankfurt, for he was a living *mussar sefer*."

Washington Heights, 1994: In the last winter of his life, the young Frankfurt lad, now *Rav* of the largest German-Jewish *kehillah* in the world and a leader of Torah Jewry, calls in a wealthy benefactor of the *kehillah*. "I don't have much time left on this world," he said, "and I will be going to *Gehinnom*. The Yeshivah's deficit is close to a million dollars and most of it is in the unpaid salaries of its *melamdim*. I am *Rav* of the *kehillah* that teaches *Torah im Derech Eretz*. Where is the *derech eretz* if we haven't paid our teachers for months? It will not be long before I will be called to give a *din vecheshbon* for my actions and I will be going to *Gehinnom* for this. I'm begging you. Please take me out of *Gehinnom*."

The man is shaken. After giving the matter some thought, he agrees to cover the entire deficit in teachers' salaries, in weekly installments to be completed before the Yeshivah's annual dinner. The last payment is made on the Friday before the dinner. The Yeshivah's dinner is on Sunday night.

The following evening, Rabbi Schwab passed away.

Who was this man who lived a life of such adherence to honesty and integrity? What is this potent combination of the ideals of Rabbi Samson Raphael Hirsch, architect of Torah Orthodoxy in the Western world, and the intense commitment to *limud haTorah* that is the legacy of the great Lithuanian yeshivos? What can we learn from his life to enable us to make this heady blend the reality of authentic Torah life in America? Specifically, what example did he set for the American *ben Torah*, whether engaged in full-time Torah study or as a working man?

I. Geography of a Life

⤴ Boyhood in Frankfurt-am-Main

Shimon Schwab was born in Frankfurt on 7 Teves, 5569 (1908), to an old German-Jewish family. In the 1850's, his great-grandfather moved from a small Bavarian village to Frankfurt, soon after Rabbi S.R. Hirsch had become rabbi, so his children could study in Rav Hirsch's *Realschule*. Like his father and grandfather, Shimon Schwab studied in the *Realschule*, which went only until the ninth grade. There he received his only formal secular education.

His parents, Leopold and Chana (Erlanger) Schwab, were *erliche*, respected *baalebattim*, who were active in the life of the Frankfurt *kehillah*. They produced five sons, each of them a man of note in his own right. Three of them were world famous—in addition to Reb Shimon, there was Reb Mordechai, renowned as a *tzaddik,* and Reb Moshe, *Mashgiach* of the Gateshead Yeshivah. (See *The Jewish Observer*, May '94, and April '81.)

What explains their success in child rearing? The Schwab brothers were fond of telling of the *Seder* night when their father asked his children which of the four sons they would like to be. Most of them answered, "the *chacham*," as could be expected; young Mordechai responded that he would like to be the "*tam*." The father then addressed his children in a stern voice: "If any of my sons becomes a *rosho*, even if only deviating from a single *din* or a *minhag*, I say to him '*li, velo lo*, I will have nothing to do with him.' I love my children more than anything in the world, but I love the *Ribbono Shel Olam* even more." His father's *yiras Shamayim*, Rabbi Schwab said decades later, chilled his bones.

He grew up in Frankfurt as a normal child, with no hint of the greatness he would attain. He often stressed that many *gedolim* were not accomplished *talmidei chachamim* at age thirteen or geniuses in their youth. Many who were *amei ha'aretz* at that age later became Torah leaders. This awareness, he felt, should be an encouragement to many lads who are nothing special at their Bar Mitzvah, yet have the potential to become great *talmidei chachamim* and Torah leaders.

After completing the *Realschule*, Shimon learned for two years under the Frankfurter *Rav* and *Rosh Yeshivah*, Rabbi Shlomo Zalman Breuer, son-in-law of Rabbi S.R. Hirsch. There he absorbed the joys of *yegias haTorah*, the delight of intense effort in trying to ascertain the correct *pshat*, and an absolute commitment to finding the *emes* in the *dvar Hashem*. This strong commitment of Reb Shlomo Breuer to unadulterated *emes* as the guiding light of his life obtained in communal matters as well as in Torah study. For the rest of his life, Rabbi Schwab always saw himself, in his words, as *"talmid talmido"* of Rabbi S.R. Hirsch—his disciple's pupil—and, indeed, he was suffused with Rav Hirsch's spirit.

In 1926, the Ponevezher *Rav*, Rabbi Yosef Shlomo Kahaneman visited Frankfurt and delivered a *shiur* in Rav Breuer's yeshivah. The young Frankfurter boy was entranced both by the *shiur* and by the *derech halimud*. He wanted more. The Ponevezher *Rav* suggested Telshe, with its emphasis on *seder* and its approach to education, as most appropriate

Shimon Schwab was among the first German *bachurim* in his time to study in a Lithuanian yeshivah, and a considerable number followed his lead. But many who had left Germany to study in the East ceased to appreciate their *mesores avos*, the hallowed traditions of *minhag Ashkenaz*, when they beheld the sublime grandeur and tasted the intoxicating sweetness of the *blatt Gemara*. Rabbi Schwab clung to every detail of his *mesora*, the continuation of close to two millennia of Torah life in Germany, channeled into the post-ghetto world by Rabbi S.R. Hirsch and his colleagues.

ᴥᔈ A Yeshivah Bachur in Lithuania

During the three years he spent in Telshe, he was awed by the regal dignity, the iron will, the sublime mind, and the singing *neshamah* (as he described it) of the Telzer Rav, Rabbi Yosef Leib

Bloch. In Telshe he learned about *malchus haTorah*, seeing the *Rosh Yeshivah* as a *nesi Elokim*. Whereas his relationship with the Telzer *Rav* was a mixture of awe and fear, for his *Rebbi*, Reb Avrohom Yitzchok Bloch, there was only the adoring enthusiasm of a seventeen-year-old yeshivah *bachur* for the *Rebbi's* sweet personality. In Telshe, he also learned a lifelong lesson: the meaning of "*shteigen*"— steady, sustained growth in Torah, *yiras Shamayim* and character development.

Rabbi Schwab spent six weeks in the summer of 1929 teaching in Montreux, Switzerland. There, he also served as the personal attendant of Rabbi Chaim Ozer Grodzenski. Those weeks of intimate daily contact with the *gadol hador* left an indelible imprint on him. Reb Chaim Ozer suggested that he go to study in the Mirrer Yeshivah in Poland, whose *mashgiach*, Rabbi Yeruchem Levovitz, would be the perfect mentor for the Frankfurter *bachur*.

So in Elul, 1929, he went to the Mir, where he developed an unusually close relationship with Reb Yeruchem. There too he was a trend setter for the many German *bachurim* who followed. Several years later, Reb Yeruchem delivered a regular *Chumash shiur* exclusively for these "*oislanders*," as they were called. Reb Yeruchem's *Daas Torah* on *Chumash* contains much from those *shiurim*. Reb Shimon stayed in the Mir for two years, and received *semichah* from the *Rosh Yeshivah*, Reb Lazer Yudel Finkel, as well as from Reb Chaim Ozer Grodzenski.

His visit to the Chofetz Chaim in 1930 is part of the public consciousness. Although he spent no more than a weekend in Radin—from Friday morning to Sunday morning—*Klal Yisrael* has learned more from those few days than from many who spent years in Radin. (See *The Jewish Observer*, Jan. 1984.)

⤳ A Rav in Germany

In 1931, Rabbi Schwab was appointed assistant to Rabbi Yonah Merzbach of Darmstadt, who later joined Rabbi Yechiel Schlesinger to found Yeshivah Kol Torah in Jerusalem. The same year, he married Recha Froelich of Gelsenkirchen, who was his devoted and cheerful companion for life, and with whom he had five children. Two years later he was appointed District Rabbi of Ichenhausen in Bavaria. Noting a lack of the spirit of the

Lithuanian yeshivah in German Jewry, he attempted to establish a yeshivah there, but the local Nazis closed it on the day it opened.

He was under constant pressure from the local Gestapo. As the situation deteriorated, he began to sleep at night with his clothes on. He later explained that one of his acquaintances who had been outspoken in his criticism of the regime was taken away in the middle of the night and was found the next morning hanging. Should the same fate await him, he wanted to meet it fully clothed, as befits a rabbi. Matters in Germany reached a point where it was only a matter of time before his arrest, and he decided to seek a rabbinical position overseas.

✑ Refugee Rabbi in Baltimore

Upon the suggestion of Rabbi Leo Jung, a leading Orthodox rabbi in New York, he was accepted as the rabbi of the German-Jewish Shearith Israel Congregation of Baltimore. He arrived in the U.S. with his family on 10 Teves, 1936.

Soon after his arrival, he was faced with his first crisis. He insisted that the by-laws of the congregation, which conferred voting rights only on *shomrei Shabbos*, be upheld. As a result, two hundred members, the overwhelming majority of the membership, who considered themselves Orthodox but were unable to resist the pressure to work on *Shabbos*, left the *shul* and established their own congregation. *Shearith Israel* was left with a skeleton of a congregation of barely two dozen members, sometimes without a *minyan* during the week, and almost no wherewithal to cover his salary. He was forced to borrow and scrape to make ends meet; there were times when he did not receive his salary for months. It was not the only time in his life when he was willing to sacrifice position and livelihood for principle. It was, in fact, one of the Hirschian tenets upon which he was weaned: "Learn how to withstand animosity and to weather unpopularity, and to carry on the struggle to uphold *Hashem's* ideals." Despite his poverty, in 1943 he auctioned off his only possession of value, a *Sefer Torah* that he had brought with him from Germany, and gave the proceeds of $2,000—a substantial sum at the time—to the *Vaad Hatzalah* for saving Jewish lives in Europe. He was active in securing affidavits to facilitate the entry of Jewish refugees into the United States, and the Schwab home in Baltimore became a way station for many poor, newly arrived refugees from the European inferno.

Baltimore of those years was hardly a spiritual oasis.

> *The kashrus situation was a mess. Rabbi Schwab told of the time, soon after he had arrived in Baltimore, when he received a request to provide a hashgachah for chickens. When he informed the owner that he would visit his plant, the man replied, "That's OK, Rabbi, we'll bring the check to you."*

The *Rebbetzin* was one of only a handful of women in the city who covered her hair. Even Yeshivah Chofetz Chaim, headed by the illustrious Rabbi Chaim Samson, had almost no *shomer Shabbos* students. One of the Schwab boys had only one *shomer Shabbos* friend. He pleaded with his mother not to give him sandwiches for lunch in school because the boys laughed at him when he washed his hands before eating.

Before the establishment of the Bais Yaakov, Rabbi Schwab would gather the few *shomer Shabbos* girls in his home for a weekly *shiur*. "*Ess passt nisht,*" he was told by a local rabbi, "for a *rav* to teach girls." Rabbi Schwab replied that the *Gemara* says that a *chassid shoteh*, a pious idiot, is one who refuses to save a woman who is drowning because she is a woman. "I don't want to be a *chassid shoteh*." Together with a few local *baalebattim*, he founded the Bais Yaakov of Baltimore, despite the derision of local rabbis who considered the undertaking a waste of time, effort, and especially resources. "Why," one Orthodox rabbi asked him, "are you bothering with these insignificant *mitzvos*?" This "insignificant *mitzvah*" is today the largest such institution outside the New York area.

◄§ The Frankfurt Kehillah in New York

In 1958, Rabbi Schwab's *Rebbi* from Frankfurt, Rabbi Joseph Breuer, when seventy-five-years old, decided that K'hal Adath Jeshurun of Washington Heights needed a vigorous presence on the rabbinate, and he invited his *talmid* to serve alongside him. It is testimony to the greatness of these two men that for the next twenty-three years they served the *kehillah* side by side with hardly an uncomfortable moment. Although many of the *kehillah* institutions were in place when he arrived, he was instrumental in founding the Mesivta and the Bais Yaakov High School, the *Beis Hamidrash* and the world-renowned Rika Breuer Teachers Seminary. It was during these years in Washington Heights that Rabbi Schwab's leadership and influence in the affairs of American Torah Jewry reached their peak.

II. The Embodiment of Malachi's Prophecy

❧ A Kingdom of Priests

The Jewish People, the *Rav* never tired of declaring, must be a *mamleches kohanim vegoy kadosh*, a nation of priests and a holy nation. A *kohein*, he explained, is one who by word and example spreads the knowledge of the Almighty. The *kohein* imperative of the Jew, which he epitomized, was the constant theme in his life.

Living in *Golus* America, a *malchus shel chessed*, only strengthened this obligation. Every form of *chillul Hashem*, he taught, lowers the awareness of the Divine presence in this world. If the perpetrator is a supposedly observant Jew—or worse, a so-called Torah scholar—then the offense is even greater. The *chillul Hashem* strengthens the hand of the non-observer, gives ammunition to the scoffers, and fosters yet more rejection of religion; and it is responsible, directly or indirectly, for the increase of frivolity, heresy and licentiousness in the world. How can one who cheated his neighbor or defrauded the government, he asked, have the audacity to stand in front of the congregation and recite *Kaddish*, a prayer for sanctifying G–d's Name in the world? There can be no whitewashing, no condoning, and no apologizing on behalf of the desecrators. It must be made clear that he who besmirches the Divine Name has defected from our ranks and joined our opponents. And the more prominent a person is, the more scrupulous and painstaking he must be in his business dealings to avoid even the slightest hint of a *chillul Hashem*. When the *Rav* was asked to assist in efforts to secure the release of a "religious" Jew who was incarcerated for fraud, he refused. "Help him be released? He's a *rodeif* of *Klal Yisrael*. Because of him, *frumme Yidden* will suffer. Let him sit!"

Traveling once with his son on the subway, the boy found

fifty cents on the floor in front of the change booth, which he intended to pocket, thinking that there was no obligation to return it. "Give it to the attendant," his father insisted, "and I will stick my beard in his window so that he sees that religious Jews do not want other people's money."

> The prophet Malachi, speaking of the End of Days, described the attributes of the kohein, and these qualities are perhaps the most accurate description of Rabbi Schwab, his life and his teachings: "Toras emes haysa befihu, ve'avla lo nimtza bi'sfasav; beShalom vemishor halach itti, verabbim heishiv me'avon. The teaching of truth was in his mouth and no injustice was found on his lips; in peace and in straightforwardness he walked with Me and he turned many away from sin."
>
> Malachi 2: 6-7

⤳ "Toras Emes..."[1]

He viewed his mission in life as being a *marbitz Torah*, giving *shiurim* to those of all ages and backgrounds in his *kehillah*—men, women and children. He had a unique approach to *aggadah* and shared with his *talmidim* and congregants countless original insights into *Chazal*. A lengthy series of *shiurim* on the *Siddur Tefillah* presenting invaluable insights were recorded for posterity. Many of his *chiddushim* on *Chumash* and *Midrash* were recently published in his magnum opus, *Maayan Bais Hashoeva* (Mesorah Publications, New York, 1994). Some of his public addresses of the last decade, and many essays of the last half century have been published in three volumes of his collected works (CIS Publishers).

He exhorted his followers to learn "with an inner glow and persistence, with ardor and singleminded passion, with noble joy and a serene spirit," and he put great effort into inspiring the youth of his *kehillah* to continue on in advanced *yeshivos*. The thousands of *bnei Torah* at his funeral and the overwhelming majority of *bnei Torah* at a *hesped* in his memory in Jerusalem— children and grandchildren of his congregants—are eloquent testimony to his success in this realm.

---

1. From the prophecy of *Malachi*, as are subsequent headings.

Besides serving for many years as the *Av Beis Din* of the just-ly respected *Beis Din* of K'hal Adath Jeshurun, and the *Beis Din* of Torah Umesorah, he was frequently called upon to decide crucial *dinei Torah* dealing with major Torah institutions.

Rabbi Schwab was not a bridge between two worlds, between East and West—bridges are not for living on. He was rather the embodiment of the *eilu v'eilu divrei Elokim chaim* ("These and those are the words of the living G–d") of two sacred traditions. He embodied in one person two diverse Torah cultures: the glorious Frankfurt tradition of Rabbi Hirsch, with its emphasis on adherence to the *emes* and insistence on putting the stamp of Torah on every area of public and private endeavor... combined with unwavering devotion to intense Torah study, which was the hallmark of the great yeshivos of Lithuania. On the one hand, he absorbed the Chofetz Chaim's caress; on the other, he observed the admonishment of the *alter* Gerrer *Rebbe* who characterized Rabbi Hirsch as *"a lebedike mussar sefer."* That combination was the reason why he was the inspiration and source of guidance to so many in the Torah community of America.

Rabbi Schwab was convinced that *Torah im Derech Eretz* offers a vision of Judaism "in a way that can be accepted... by the five-and-a-half-million uncommitted Jews in the vast spiritual waste-land that is today's America, in a language they can understand."

He exemplified the *"Torah-im-Derech-Eretz ben Torah." Torah im Derech Eretz* means "the subjugation and control of all mundane affairs by the royal sovereignty of the Torah." It is the call to take the Torah out into the world in order to sanctify the Divine Name on earth by our every action. It demands the Torah's conquest of life and not its flight from life. The *Torah-im-Derech-Eretz ben Torah* is well aware of what happens in the world that surrounds him, "for he is constantly called upon to apply the yardstick of *halachah* and the searchlight of *hashkafah* to the realities that confront him." He also knows that *Torah im Derech Eretz* cannot be separated from Rav Hirsch's *Austritt* (secession) principle, which requires absolute separation from institutionalized heresy or any view of Judaism based on anything other than Torah. Without *Austritt, Torah im Derech Eretz* is merely a cover for a convenient lifestyle, and a rejection of its essence, which is the total domination by Torah of all of life.

Torah im Derech Eretz means honesty and integrity in the business world and in the professions. It means seeing G–d in the wonders of Creation, in the magnificence of nature, in the breath-taking discoveries of science and in the grandeur of plant and animal life. It means an awareness of the fact that everything in the physical world is a manifestation of the *Shechinah*.

Rabbi Schwab himself attended neither high school nor college; knowledge of the world and the wonders of Creation were self taught. On nature walks with his children, he would tell them the names and nature of the flora and fauna. But the greatest revelation of G–d is the Torah, and without that, man will not know what to do with the awareness of His existence. Whereas nature shows the wonders of the Creator, Torah reveals, as it were, the Creator Himself.

Rabbi Chaim Ozer Grodzenski once put it all in perspective. While taking a walk in Switzerland, young Shimon Schwab pointed out the awesome Divine beauty of the Alps. "*S'iz shain,*" Reb Chaim Ozer agreed, "*ober a Yid mit a bord iz noch shenner.*" It would seem to this writer that the message was clear. One can perceive the Divine in nature as it performs G–d's will instinctively. That, however, can never match the beauty of the Jew who performs the Divine imperative in free-willed volition.

◆§ "Torah of Truth"

Early in life, his father taught him the importance of not only speaking the truth, but of living the truth. This writer recalls visiting the *Rav* as a young boy on the last day of Pesach, when the *Rav* told the following story.

> "*As a young boy around the age of Bar Mitzvah, I decided to stand for the entire tefillos on the night and day of Yom Kippur, a custom cited in the Shulchan Aruch (O.C. 619). My father, who was not one to ignore things like that, made no comment. On Motza'ei Yom Kippur, one of my younger brothers did something that was not to my liking, and I let him have it physically. My father slapped my face. 'I thought that you had perhaps attained the madreigah of observing even a custom brought as yesh omdim (some stand) in the Shulchan Aruch,' he said. 'But your behavior immediately following Yom Kippur indicates that you reached no*

such level at all, and were just showing off. For that you got the potsch.'"

His insistence on *emes* extended to things which usually go unnoticed. His stationery said...אב"ד "*Head of the Beis Din* of the Kehillah Adath Jeshurun." When Rabbi Gelley joined the rabbinate, Rabbi Schwab began to cross out the words אב"ד on the stationery, even though he was still the *Rav* of the *Kehillah,* since he no longer sat on *dinei Torah.*

His first exposure to the insistence on *emes* in public life was from his revered *Rebbi,* the Frankfurter *Rav,* Rabbi Shlomo Breuer, who followed in the footsteps of his father-in-law, Rabbi S.R. Hirsch. Reb Shlomo Breuer refused to recognize any Jewish community not absolutely governed by Torah, firmly opposed cooperation between Jewish communities and organizations based on Torah with those opposed to it. "He hated the untruth," Rabbi Schwab wrote of his *Rebbi,* "but he despised even more the easy compromise between *emes* and *sheker,* the political double talk, which in the name of unity would relegate the Torah Nation to a modest niche, to a mere 'branch' within the superstructure of a nondescript 'Jewish People.'"

✑ The Kehillah as an Instrument of Truth

The *kehillah,* Rabbi Schwab taught, is a microcosm of *Klal Yisrael* and as such

> *"is not beholden to any non-Torah authority, not associated with any board, federation, council, roof organization—local, national, or international— that is not absolutely and exclusively identified with the Law of Torah. The true kehillah will not subscribe to or encourage any Jewish orientation or philosophy which is not based on the truth of the Torah."*

This was not mere talk. The *kehillah* that he headed suffered great financial difficulty for its principled stand in this matter. Yeshivah Rabbi S.R. Hirsch is one of very few in the New York area that has refused on principle to accept funding from the Federation's Board of Jewish Education, even from special "funds" that only used the Federation as a conduit. It was unthinkable to take money from an organization created for

Jewish purposes, yet not based on allegiance to Torah as the supreme authority in Jewish life. The *Rav* was also certain that a yeshivah that derives part of its income from such sources cannot fulfill its potential in producing *talmidei chachamim*. He once told this writer that he was convinced that the yeshivos in *Eretz Yisrael* would be able to produce many more *gedolei Torah* if they were not constrained to rely on Israeli government funding for their existence. (See *Bava Metzia* 85b.)

Surely tolerance is important. Judaism has different *shitos* and philosophies. Chassidim, Litvaks, Sephardim—all must live together in peace and harmony, and can and should work togeth-er as components of one grand symphony. But all must be within the parameters of *emes*. This commitment to *emes* in organization-al life was expressed in his allegiance to Agudath Israel of America, as well as in the fact that an overwhelming proportion of his congregants are members of the Agudah.

Commitment to *emes* means that there can be no tolerance for the statement that two and two are five. If the one making such an absurd statement never learned arithmetic, we can be tolerant of him, but not of his views. One must distinguish between Reform and Conservative rabbis and leaders, who are *meisisim umeidichim* (indoctrinators of non-truth), and their adherents, who are *tinokos shenishbu* (innocent victims), to whom we must reach out.

The insistence of the absolute standard of *emes* in public life is impossible unless it is the outgrowth of unshakable honesty in one's private affairs. And it is not enough, he never tired of say-ing, to be *leshem Shamayim*. One must constantly make sure that one's *leshem Shamayim* is *leshem Shamayim*. *Kana'us* (zealousness) must be driven by the purest of motives. And it must be without anger or invective. The *kana'i* must always bear in mind that those whom he criticizes are fellow Jews, whom he must rebuke with love. Only the one who leads others astray must be hated.

◆ Revision, for the Sake of Truth

His adherence to *emes* was such that he was willing to revise long-held views, even if that meant a reassessment of publicly stated positions. His views on the relevance of *Torah im Derech Eretz* are a case in point. With the rise of Nazism in the 1930's,

Rabbi Schwab was convinced that *Torah im Derech Eretz* as expounded by Rabbi S.R. Hirsch was no longer relevant, not as an educational program and certainly not as a *Weltanschauung*. The barbarity of the Nazi beast (even before World War II), the virulent anti-Semitism in Germany, and the total failure of the ideals of enlightened humanism and Western culture to change the essential nature of gentile society led him to conclude that the only path for the Torah-observant German Jew was to return to the "Torah Only" approach, and to shun Western culture and the world at large as much as possible. Rabbi Hirsch's *Torah im Derech Eretz* ideal, he averred, was only a *hora'as sha'ah*, a temporary measure for a temporary situation. In 1934, he aired these views in a slim volume entitled *Heimkehr ins Judentum* (Homecoming into Judaism), which caused a sensation in German Orthodoxy.

But after coming to America, he concluded that the realities of the ghetto and the *shtetl* where one could spend all one's life in the local *beis hamidrash,* with its total dissociation from the rest of society, was a way of life that had also been consumed in the flames of the Holocaust. The realities of life in the United States and other Western countries, where the Jew traveled in non-Jewish circles and could not live totally apart from the society around him, were not essentially different from the siutation in the Western Europe of Rabbi Hirsch. Furthermore, a careful study of all of Rabbi Hirsch's writings led him to the inevitable conclusion that he had never meant *Torah im Derech Eretz* as a *hora'as sha'ah* at all. It was not a compromise, a *kula*, or a *hetter*. Although Rav Hirsch did not insist that it was for everyone, he certainly did not see it as time bound. Rabbi Schwab then publicly retracted his earlier insistence on "Torah Only" as the sole way of life for the Torah Jew in Western society. (Rabbi Schwab always viewed the situation in *Eretz Yisrael* as essentially unique, but that is beyond the purview of this article.) To that end he published in 1966 a booklet entitled *These and Those (Eilu v'Eilu)*, wherein he set forth the arguments and counterarguments for both positions, with the conclusion, as the title indicates, that both, in their proper time and place, are legitimate ways of life for the Torah Jew in Western society.

There is an old Ashkenazi custom to call out "Emes" in the Aleinu prayer recited during the Chazaras Hashatz of Mussaf on the Yomim Noraim. He retained this custom even in America where others had ceased to observe it. His last words to a disciple were, "Remember, you must always tell the emes. I have many failings," he continued, "but one thing I never did was chanfa (flatter) people."

⋼ "... Was in His Mouth"

He taught himself to speak and write eloquent, polished English, for that was the medium to reach the hearts and minds of American Jewry. Even the best of speakers sometimes have an off day, but of him it was said that he never spoke less than perfectly. He was always inspiring, stimulating, never humdrum. At the *Siyumei Hashas* of the *Daf Yomi*, at Agudath Israel and Torah Umesorah conventions, his carefully crafted addresses set the tone and inspired the audience. He could admonish and suggest areas in need of improvement without alienating his listeners. Why? Because he respected his audiences and never took them for granted. Because of that respect, he was always well prepared. His listeners knew that whatever he said derived from a sense of heartfelt concern. And he spoke of nothing to which he himself did not adhere.

He viewed his ability to influence others in a totally different way. He felt that it was because he was a *dachil rabbanan*, one who feared the Sages. The *Gemara* says that such a person will either become a *tzurva m'rabbanan*, a sage in his own right, or, if incapable of that, will be listened to *as if he were* a sage. He put himself in the latter category.

His son once found his father standing and talking on the telephone, at a time when he suffered terrible arthritis in his knees, which made it excruciatingly painful to stand. When asked why he was standing, he explained that he was talking to Rabbi Moshe Feinstein. "But you're not obligated to, if it's only on the phone," his son protested. "Surely, I have no chiyuv to stand," the Rav replied, "but how can I sit when talking to Reb Moshe?"

His influence was not limited to the spoken word. His articles and his *seforim* influenced many. In addition, he was a poet. At the request of Rabbi Breuer he authored a *Kinnah* (lamentation) in memory of the Six Million. This eloquent and moving elegy for the *kedoshim* is now recited on *Tishah B'Av* in congregations throughout the world.

◆§ "Injustice Was Not on His Lips"

He was scrupulous to a fault in financial matters. He hated even a suggestion of crooked dealings. "I don't want to be a *bedi'eved Yid*," he would say, "I want to be a *lechat'chila Yid*." He often wondered why people who were so stringent in regard to a *yeish omrim* (alternative opinion) in *Orach Chaim* and *Yoreh De'ah* (ritual *halachah*) simply ignore the *yeish omrim* in *Choshen Mishpat* that prohibits *gezel akum*: His tax form was exact, recording even gifts from friends. He was once called in by the IRS for an audit, as they could not believe that a man with such modest income could give so much charity. He sent an accountant, a member of the *kehillah*, to represent him. At the conclusion, the IRS agent declared that never, in all his years as an auditor, had he met anyone who was so forthcoming and meticulous in reporting income and in documenting all contributions. He followed that with a letter to Rabbi Schwab saying that the latter's scrupulous honesty "had restored my faith in humanity."

Someone once undertook to publish the writings of a certain Torah luminary of a previous generation. Knowing that the editor of the work was having difficulty raising the necessary funds to cover the publication costs, the *Rav* called him on his own initiative and offered him a loan of $10,000 to cover the initial costs. Several weeks later, he notified the editor that since the publisher of the work had been sending him books from time to time, he was afraid that those complimentary books might be construed as *ribbis* (interest). He thus decided to give the entire sum, which constituted a good portion of his life savings, as a gift, so that there would be no hint of a *she'eila*, even though halachically there was no problem whatsoever.

Kashrus, he always stressed, refers not only to food but to money as well.

> *"While those who resort to cheating, trickery, dishonesty and fraud may at times have the outward appearance of being G–d-fearing Jews, they are, in fact, irreligious. They may well be strict*

*in their observance of certain mitzvos, but in their business deal-
ings they reveal that they are kofrim (infidels) in regard to
Hashgachah Pratis, Divine Providence. Since they certainly do
not believe that G–d wants them to take what is not rightfully
theirs, they are conducting their business as though He does not
exist." Glatt yosher, as Rabbi Breuer once wrote, is no less important than glatt kosher.*

He was the ultimate *sonei betza*. He refused to accept com-
pensation for any rabbinic function, including weddings, funerals, *dinei Torah* and *kashrus* supervision. "Rabbi," he was often
asked, "what do I owe you?"

"Owe me? This is not a business. It is my responsibility to
Klal Yisrael." He refused to accept money even for *mechiras
chometz*. He did not, however, wish to hurt the income of other
rabbis, so he established a *tzeddakah* fund to which anyone who
insisted on paying for *mechiras chometz* could contribute.

*In his six decades as a Rav, he never once asked for a raise.
When, in his advanced years, the kehillah engaged Rabbi
Zechariah Gelley to serve alongside him, he requested the Board of
Trustees to reduce his own salary since he would have less respon-
sibilities. They replied that, as it was, his salary was so low that it
constituted no more than a retirement wage.*

✍ " In Peace and Straightforwardness He Walked With Me"

He was princely in his relations with others. He treated
young and old with warmth, and greeted everyone *b'seiver panim
yafos*, the hallmark of all the Schwab brothers. His smile warmed
as it shone; his sparkling eyes and his shining countenance put
his visitors at ease, no matter what their station in life.

"*Ha'emes vehashalom ehavu,*" the prophet says. Both peace
and truth are important, but one must always bear in mind that
peace is a virtue when dealing with one's personal affairs, where
one must bend and give in for the sake of peace. Judaism, however, is not one's to compromise. In matters touching upon Torah
issues, it must be *emes* first and then *shalom*. Peace, Rabbi S.R.
Hirsch often said, is the child of truth; not the reverse.

He personified the imperative of the prophet Michah to be a

hatzne'a leches im Elokecha, to walk humbly with G–d. Although requested at various times to serve on the *Moetzes Gedolei HaTorah* of Agudath Israel, he refused, saying that he was not worthy of being a member of this august body.

The *tzenius* referred to by the prophet Michah means not only humility, but more importantly, a lack of ostentation. He despised conspicuous consumption. He pleaded incessantly for *tzenius* and simplicity in *simchas*, in manner of dress and comportment, in lifestyles and vacations.

Tzenius, lack of ostentation, is no less important in spiritual matters. How does one walk with *Hashem* inconspicuously? For a person who truly walks with G–d, being in the public eye is no reason to manifest one's devoutness. *Le'olam yehei adam yerei Shamayim beseiser uvagaluy.* One must always fear G–d, in private and in public. The question is obvious: One who does not fear G–d in private does not fear G–d at all. What does it mean to fear G–d in private? *Hatzne'a leches*, the *Rav* explained, requires that one's *yiras Shamayim* be something one has no need to show off. True *yiras Shamayim* is between you and G–d, and the more *yiras Shamayim* one has, the less should others be aware of it. The *Gemara* tells us that the *Isha Hashunamis* (Shunamite woman) knew that Elisha the Prophet was a holy man because flies did not disturb him, among other private indications. Couldn't she tell that he was a *kadosh* by just looking at him and watching his behavior? The answer is that true *kedushah*, true *yiras Shamayim* is not readily apparent to the casual observer. One sees nothing extraordinary on the externals of the true *tzaddik*. He learned this, he said, from the Chofetz Chaim. If one was *zocheh*, one could see the *Shechinah* on his visage, but otherwise, he looked like a plain man dressed in the clothes of a simple laborer, with an ordinary cap pulled low over his forehead. The greater the *gadol*, the more simple the comportment. Real *kedushah* is within; as soon as it becomes manifested outwardly, it is diminished.

The *Rav* personified this in his daily life and in his davening, which was without noise or fuss. From his early youth, when no one watched or cared, the first *pesukim* of *Krias Shema* took him an inordinate amount of time to recite. Only his family knew that he began davening at home, much before he came to *shul*, and when the congregation was at *Borchu*, he was already holding by the second *beracha* of *Krias Shema*. In his later years, or when illness prevented him from *davening* with a *minyan* in *shul*, his *tefillos* at home were wrenching in their intensity—but never when anyone was watching.

For years he would buy two *esrogim* for Succos. The exquisite one, for which he spent a large sum of money, he kept at home. He took the simpler one to *shul*. The *hiddur mitzvah* was pure, with no element of public display. *Kavanah* in *mitzvos* was not limited to the more glamorous ones. One must have no less *kavanah* in one's daily *benching*, he used to say, than one has when eating the first *k'zayis* of *matzah* on Pesach.

One who walks with G–d feels that he is always in the Divine presence. Rabbi Schwab's regal bearing reflected that. He was his children's best friend, yet his son testified that until his father was eighty-three years old and in the hospital, he never saw him in bed. He spared himself little time for rest, citing Rav Hirsch on the verse, "*Vayikatz Yaakov mishnaso: Ehr hat sich ge'ekelt fun sein shluf—* He was revolted by his sleep." Yet for all his busy schedule and his dignified demeanor, he always had time for his children. His *Shabbos* and *Yom Tov* table were occasions of sheer delight.

When one walks with G–d, it is insufficient merely to start the journey with his Creator. Every step of the way must reflect that reality. The prophet Isaiah criticized the Jewish people, "*Vatehi yirasam osei mitzvas anashim melumada*—they did their *mitzvos* as if by rote." Rabbi Schwab explained that not only one's *mitzvah* performance, but even one's *yiras Shamayim* can become mechanical. Even a person's *kanaus* and path in life must be under constant scrutiny so that it not become stale.

Walking with *Hashem* means constant awareness of His presence. He always stressed that the prime necessity of the Jew was *emunah peshutah*, an uncomplicated awareness of G–d's closeness and *Hashgachah Pratis*. *Emunah* (which Rav Hirsch relates to *omein*, nurse) is the feeling of security and well-being one must have, sensing the protective and caring presence of G–d—as a nursing child feels in his mother's arms. In this manner Rabbi Schwab lived for eighty-six years, and when the time came for him to leave this world, it was in the same calm and trusting manner.

On *Rosh Chodesh* Adar I, 5755, he was hospitalized after a heart attack. On the eve of *Purim Kattan*, he suffered another severe attack. Now that his teachers were paid, he could leave the world. His family gathered around his bed and he calmly recited *Vidduy, Shema Yisrael, Baruch Shem,* and the seven-fold *Hashem Hu HaElokim*. With the seventh *Hashem Hu HaElokim*, he returned his soul to his Maker, moving on to the *Olam HaEmes* as he lived, declaring "*Hashem Hu HaElokim*," the fundamental truth of the universe.

Nisson Wolpin

A Mechanech For All Times,
A Teacher For All Ages

A Tribute to Rabbi Yehoshua Silbermintz זצ"ל

*With youthful
enthusiasm, acceptence
of guidance from Torah
authority and selfless
dedication to the Klal,
Rabbi Silbermintz
taught, led, and guided
others throughout
his life*

A ri was not functioning in the fourth grade in Yeshivah Toras
Emes. Promises and incentives, threats and punishments, all
made no dent in his refusal to respond. As a last resort, he was
demoted to grade three. On his second day in class, he raised his
hand and asked a question.

"Wonderful!" exclaimed the *Rebbe*. "Ask it again, Ari, so the
whole class can hear your *kashye*! And make sure to see me during recess. You're going to get a can of soda as a prize!"

Today, thirty years later, Ari—a popular *Rebbe* in a leading
Mesivta high school—looks back to that day as a turning point
in his education. The excitement that the *Rebbi* generated at that
moment continued to mount day after day, until Ari returned to

the fourth grade the following September as a highly motivated student.

❦ ❦ ❦

Jeffrey went to Talmud Torah (congregational afternoon school) when he was ten because his parents felt that an early start would make his *Bar Mitzvah* training less of a trauma. "What a way to spend my afternoons," he muttered. "It's gonna be a bore!"

But it wasn't. The *Moreh* was fun, and he always smiled. He taught a Hebrew song from the prayer book. And he made being Jewish a great thing, something to be proud of.

Jeffrey became Yisroel. His Talmud Torah teacher helped him get into a yeshivah high school, and years later, got him a job as a counselor in a private boys' camp in the mountains, where the teacher served as head counselor. He was there when Yisroel needed guidance in *shidduchim,* and he was there as mentor, friend, and fellow celebrant at many a future milestone in Yisroel's life. Today, Yisroel — an active figure in outreach—still remembers that man: "He is, and always will be, the single most important influence in my development as a *baal teshuva.* His guidance and good wishes remain an indestructible foundation for the *lomdus* of the *Rebbe'im* and *chavrusos* from whom I have been privileged to learn in recent years."

❦ ❦ ❦

Nochum hated to see younger East Siders while away their *Shabbos* afternoons at the local playground. So he decided to organize Pirchei groups for the kids, beginning with a gala *Melaveh Malkah.* He called up "Mr. Pirchei"—an older, experienced hand—for help. The response: "I've got another engagement that night. But I'll be there."

The kids came—a lively, ravenous group. It took just a few minutes for the noise to escalate to pandemonium and for place settings to evolve into flying missiles. Nochum and his assistants were helpless. Suddenly, a jovial fellow entered, raised his hands for silence—and got it. "We're going to all sing together—'Kail Nekamos Hashem.' You all know it. And—" a moment's suspenseful silence— "whoever sings especially *lebedik* gets a prize." He held up a bag full of trinkets and doo-dads. "Let's go!"

And they went.

The Melave Malka: a huge success.

Pirchei Agudath Israel groups became a regular *Shabbos* afternoon event on Broome Street.

❧ ❧ ❧

Avraham loved an extra challenge. So when Pirchei Agudath Israel sent a letter to his local branch that they were sponsoring a *Siyum Hashas* based on hundreds of individuals learning a minimum of one *perek Mishnayos* by heart, Avraham was the first in his group to memorize a *perek.* The next year, he committed several *Mesechtos* to memory, and by the time his *Bar Mitzvah* arrived, he memorized the entire *Shisha Sidrei Mishnah.* This earned him a trip to the national *Siyum* celebration in New York, where he was a top winner. Not too many years later, Avraham, as a *beis medrash* student in Telshe, made a *siyum* on *Shas*—the complete *Talmud.*

"No goal is unattainable if it is broken down to small steps. This I learned from my experience with the Pirchei *Mishnayos Be'al Peh,* and the great encouragement I always received from the national director."

❧ ❧ ❧

Strange neighbors: a very *Chassidishe* bungalow colony and a sleep-away camp for American yeshivah boys, next door to each other on a Catskill mountain top.

Their *Shabbos Seudah* over, the bungalow families left their homes for a stroll in the soft night air. Lively sounds wafted over the trees, beckoning the strollers to the camp dining room. The visitors entered—and were amazed at the spirited singing—a haunting "*Racheim bechasdecha...,*" followed by a joyous (almost rowdy) "*Ho-aderes ve'ho-emuna tzu vemen, tzu vemen....*"

"What is the occasion?" a *shtreimel*-bedecked visitor asked.

"*Shabbos Kodesh,*" answered a counselor.

"Every *Shabbos?*"

"Every *Shabbos.*"

"It seems like *Simchas Torah,*" said the visitor in admiration.

"Who's that clean-shaven fellow in the middle leading the *zemiros*?"

"Oh, that's the head-counselor. You should see his *Simchas Torah*! Then we really go to town!"

❈ ❈ ❈

Malka had been euphoric over her engagement to Simcha, but now she was unsure. His family was cold, unaccepting. Maybe she wasn't good enough for a young man of such *yichus* (noble lineage). Perhaps she should get out before it was too late....The telephone rang....11:15 p.m.—a wrong number? "Malkie?" The voice was familiar—of course! "I just wanted you to know how much Simcha admired the way you handled yourself at his parents' house yesterday."

The encouraging voice, joined by his wife's reassuring words on an extension line, continued. Questions were fielded, doubts were recognized and then dispelled. Finally, at 12:30 a.m., the telephone session was over. The *shadchanim*—friends (close as next-of-kin)—put everything into perspective. Malka was facing an uphill climb, but it was going to be worth it, with Simcha—and their dear, dear friends—at her side.

❈ ❈ ❈

An uncanny ability to touch so many people, both *Klal u' prat*, community and individual, in such a variety of settings, spanning several epochs in Jewish America—this was the hallmark of Rabbi Yehoshua Silbermintz (known universally as "Josh"). His unusual, broad-ranged effectiveness was undoubtedly in line with the response of Rabbi Elazar ben Arach to the question posed by Rabbi Yochanan ben Zakai: "What is the proper way that a man should choose?" Rabbi Elazar's answer was "*Lev tov*—goodness of heart." His reply encompassed the responses of all his colleagues—the good eye, the good friend, the good neighbor, and the ability to divine the future (see *Avos* II, 13).

Lev tov, according to the *S'forno*, describes the person whose actions emanate from a pure source, driven by a motive of *l'shem Shamayim*. A person so motivated inevitably attains a host of many other worthwhile attributes as well. Josh's *l'shem Shamayim* and love for his fellow Jews equipped him to succeed in a wide array of undertakings, and enabled him to reach thousands of individuals directly, tens of thousands indirectly.[1]

Indeed, through his direct one-on-one contact, through his leadership training programs, through the contests and competitions, publications and mass gatherings that he directed, through the communal work and behind-the-scenes lobbying that he conducted, his *lev tov* and his *l'shem Shamayim* had incalculable impact.

◅§ Hardly Remarkable, Yet Truly Remarkable

Reb Yehoshua Silbermintz's background is hardly remarkable. One of four sons born to Reb Yoseif Shmaryahu and Ita Rochel Silbermintz in the Williamsburg section of Brooklyn, Josh went to the local yeshivah, Torah Vodaath, as did hundreds of other boys from the neighborhood. His major talent was a lilting singing voice with perfect pitch. His major strengths were his infectious joy and an uncanny ability to know the insides of a boy's heart. Coupled with a dead-serious attitude toward all responsibilities—both *bein adam laMakom* and *bein adam lechaveiro*—he was by all accounts the consummate *mechanech* (pedagogue).

His prosaic background notwithstanding, his life was truly remarkable. Indeed, the bare facts trace a gradual escalation—from *talmid* in Mesivta Torah Vodaath (where he established a close, ongoing relationship with Rabbi Avraham Pam, א״טילש), to Yeshivah Bais Yosef (where he earned *semichah* from Rabbi Avraham Jofen, ל״צז); from Talmud Torah teacher to *Rebbe* in Yeshivah Toras Emes for forty years (his classroom was a *must* for Beth Jacob Seminary students to observe, so as to learn the nitty-gritty of classroom management and to witness the magic that love and excitement can generate); devoted husband, father and grandfather (his wife, nee Millicent Bachman, was always at his side as active partner and encouraging helpmate); from Pirchei leader in the Bushwick section of Brooklyn over fifty years ago, to

---

1. This interpretation, as well as some other insights in this article, are part of a longer tribute to Rabbi Silbermintz, written by Rabbi Shaya Cohen, National Director of Priority One, an outreach organization with headquarters on Long Island.

initiator and coordinator of local and national events—first as a volunteer, and then for a quarter of a century as the official national director of Pirchei Agudath Israel; head counselor of Camp Agudah and then Camp Munk (where his detailed record and careful assessment of each step in the camp calendar and every event in the season was duly noted and filed away, to be studied when planning the next season, and to be shared with the administrations of other camps, to give Jewish camping a professional image and—working with Rabbi Yechiel Arye Munk, צז״ל—endowing the experience with an enhanced Torah content)—in all phases, he was the paradigm *askan* (activist), totally dedicated to the needs of the *klal*, and, directing his talents accordingly, a gifted *mechanech*. The *lev tov* that pulsated within him was, as mentioned, accompanied by other aspects of his personality, in such intensity and purity that their impact was phenomenal.

Thus, he combined meticulous, detailed planning with spontaneity and joy. He could be creative and innovative, yet completely subservient to *Gedolei Yisrael*. Even when he was approaching seventy, he knew exactly what would excite little boys; and that profound sense of *achrayus* (accountability) that animated him as a teenager, stayed with him through dramatically changing conditions, to his last breath. The stories that follow are chosen to illustrate his special gifts, his *achrayus* for the *klal*, and his role as *mechanech*—their source and their application—as a tribute to Josh, and as the stuff of inspiration and instruction for the reader.

✥ Youthful Jottings: From His Own Words

In an interview with historian Dr. David Kranzler six years ago, Josh underscored the good fortune that was his by virtue of belonging to the Agudath Israel youth movement, his experiences and the lessons he learned.

As a member of the *Poilisher Shtiebel*, the senior Mr. Silbermintz was challenged by the president of the *shtiebel* as to why he allowed his sons to *daven* with the Zeirei Agudath Israel, instead of with the parent generation. *"Zei vellen oisvaksen goyim,"* he predicted. Now, that man spent every free moment in Torah study, along with others, for the *Poilisher Shtiebel* was open 24 hours a day, always filled with people learning Torah.... Years later, Josh met the president's son who confessed to keeping neither *Shabbos* nor *kashrus*: "Three days a year I do my father a favor and I go to the *Shtiebel*. That's the only time I ever *daven*." The same happened to quite a few members of that second generation. The parents were *yereim* and *shleimim* (devout Jews), but they gave their sons no place in the scheme of things.

Rabbi Moshe Wolfson, שליט״א, who is the *Mashgiach Ruchni* in Mesivta Torah Vadaath, and *Rav* of Emunas Yisroel, spoke at a national Torah assembly of Zeirei Agudath Israel several years ago, and put it all in perspective:

> As a youngster, I went to Torah Vodaath—the best yeshivah around in those days. After I graduated elementary school, there was a gathering of the boys in my class, and I realized that, of those forty boys, only four remained Shomer Shabbos. I was fortunate because I used to come to "the club," Pirchei Agudath Israel, and we had a leader by the name of Mr. Tress. He gave us a Torah hashkafah; and he imbued us with a spirit, to remain a Yid, to be marbitz Torah, to work for Torah. That helped me remain faithful to Torah.

Rabbi Wolfson's recollections are, unfortunately, an accurate reflection of the fate of far too many youngsters of that era.

◆§ *Daas Torah* and *Achrayus* to the *Klal*

Josh recounted the various forces that molded the "survivors" of that era: They were introduced to the concepts of *daas Torah* when the great *Rosh Hayeshivah* of Baranowitz, Rabbi Elchanan Wasserman, הי״ד, addressed his Zeirei group at 157 Rodney Street in Williamsburg, during his visit to America in 1939. "Ask questions and I'll try to give you answers from the Torah," he said. So they posed questions—about *chinuch,* about politics, and whatever else—and he shared his *daas Torah* with them. He had a reputation for being strong minded, yet in some ways he impressed the boys as being more broad-minded than many so-called liberals. "When I came to America," he said "everyone said there's no future for Torah in America. It's not true. I traveled throughout the United States, raising funds, and I saw that the beautiful, *Yiddishe kinder* here are in some ways superior to the children in Europe; more *temimus'dik* (sincere), for sure. But you need people to teach them. The reason American children do not learn Torah is because there's no one to draw them close and show them any interest. It is your task to be *marbitz Torah*! These children will respond to your efforts!"

"At our meetings," Josh recalled, "our Pirchei leader, Reb Elimelech 'Mike' Tress, would tell us whatever he had heard about the Knessia Gedolah (the International Congress of Agudath Israel in Marienbad, in 1938). Even though he often repeated the same information, he had us spellbound because he conveyed it with such warmth and such *hartz*. Our group functioned until we were 14."

Josh recounted that he and his friends had witnessed how Mr. Tress invariably spoke with a *Rosh Yeshivah*—any *adam gadol*—with great deference and *kavod haTorah*, and how he always accepted their views.... "We also wanted to share in that approach," he recalled.

"Similarly, Rabbi ('I am *Mr.* Mendlowitz!') Shraga Feivel Mendlowitz, *menahel* of Mesivta Torah Vodaath, had a tremendous impact on us [Josh continued]. In his *mussar shmuessen* in the *Beis Midrash*, he would constantly return to the theme that we must have an *achrayus* for other people. He founded *Aish Das* (forerunner of Bais Medrash Elyon) in Monsey as a *chinuch* institution to prepare *mechanchim* for the future. We were deeply moved by his actions. We were especially impressed with how he felt that he must bring *m'challelei Shabbos* boys closer to Torah. He invited out-of-town boys to the Mesivta, in effect running the first Shabbaton in America."

◂§ Learning to Lead

When Josh was 16 years old, Mr. Tress called a meeting of the members of the old Pirchei group (disbanded by then). He said, "You're the future of *Klal Yisrael*. You have to lead others and become involved in *klal* activities." Some of them responded to his call by volunteering in the Zeirei office, others eventually became involved in *chinuch*. (Rabbi Moshe Neuman, for example, will undoubtedly attribute the fact that he is *menahel* of the Bais

Yaakov of Queens to the spirit and sense of *achrayus* that prevailed in that Pirchei group.)

Josh became a Pirchei leader at 16, when he was approached by Gershon Kranzler to lead a group of Talmud Torah boys on Moore Street, in Bushwick. This entailed an hour's walk in each direction. On the first two *Shabbosos* he taught them the *Parshah*— *Chumash* and *Rashi*—which, considering their weak background and lack of interest, was ridiculous. The third *Shabbos*, B.G. (one of the boys) gave him such a hard time, that Josh announced that he was finished with *chinuch*. The next *Shabbos* B.G. walked to Josh's house to ask his forgiveness; he promised to be good from then on. ("He was a *vilder chaya* [wild] then," said Josh. "When I met him ten, twelve years ago in *Eretz Yisroel*, he had the same excitable personality, only now he's involved with Torah.") Mr. G. (his father) spoke Yiddish with his son, but was anti-religious. When B.G. refused to open the light on *Shabbos*, Mr. G. locked him in the bathroom (it was 95 degrees), and told him, "Sweat it out (the windows were closed) until you learn to listen to me, and put on the light on *Shabbos*." He did not give in. Many members of that group with similar backgrounds became leading figures in Torah life.

⋘ Rolling With the Punches

"When I was about 20," Josh recalled, "I was walking to Willoughby Street to lead a different Pirchei group. Even though many of the boys there attended yeshivah, they would sneak off to the movies on *Shabbos*. I singled out one boy to read the Torah, to give him a sense of importance. Instead, his father berated me for giving his son 'a job' without pay. This insult, coupled with several other disappointments, convinced me that walking to Willoughby to take care of a *minyan* and *Shalosh Seudos* was not worth the effort.

"When I told Mr. Tress of my intentions, he said to me: 'I'm involved with *Hatzolah* (rescue activites during the war). Whenever I go to Chicago, to Detroit, to raise money, they exclaim, *What wonderful things Zeirei is accomplishing for the Jews in New York—for the people in the Army!* When I come home to 616 Bedford Avenue, all my old friends attack me with complaints about what we are and are not doing. When people criticize you for your work in the public arena, you must rise above the situation, and just not listen. You know what you want to accomplish. *You* know it's worthwhile. Just do it, and forget about what people are saying.'

"I had remained with Pirchei until then because I thought I was experiencing *hatzlochah*. You lead a group of *mechallelei Shabbos* kids, you see them change, and you know that you have something to do with their becoming *shomrei Shabbos*. Now Mr. Tress helped me to learn to focus on my goals and to draw courage from my achievements. *Forget about the criticisms!*"

⋙ That Special Dedication

The youthful enthusiasm, acceptance of guidance from Torah authorities, and selfless dedication to the *klal* that surfaced in his Zeirei Agudath Israel days were all there as Josh continued to teach, lead and guide others throughout his life.

In 1942, Josh was among those who formed the Inter-Yeshivah Student Council, which was organized to convince yeshivah elementary school graduates to continue their yeshivah education on the high school level. These volunteers spoke to 8th grade classes, and spent many evenings visiting boys at home, conveying to their parents the importance of yeshivah high school. Over the years, hundreds of boys continued in their Torah education as a result of these efforts.

He used his musical gifts to serve as a *chazan* on the *Yamim Noraim*. One former *talmid* remembers coming to *shul* on Yom Kippur in Utica, New York, and recognizing the voice of the *chazan*. When he approached his former teacher from many years before, Rabbi Silbermintz looked at him and told him his name, *Bar Mitzvah Parshah,* and date of birth. The student was so touched by Rabbi Silbermintz's recall that he reestablished contact with him, which led him to become a *baal teshuvah* and ultimately a recognized *talmid chacham*.

That uncanny ability to focus on details, to touch individuals with his unconditional love, surfaced in other ways: He made a practice of sending wedding anniversary cards to friends and associates from over the years. The card always arrived a few days in advance of the intended date—to celebrate in anticipation, and to subtly remind the spouse who may have forgotten.

Whenever a *talmid* in his class in Toras Emes asked a "good *kashye*," he would note it on a postcard and mail it to his parents. In one particular case, he sent two postcards—one for the parents of the child, and one for the grandparents (in this case, a *Chassidishe Rebbe*). The grandfather telephoned Rabbi Silbermintz to express his joy and his gratitude. The child, of course, blossomed under the well-planted recognition.

In Pirchei, in the classroom, as in the camp setting, he would take note of a particular talent that a fellow had, and then give him assignments—in speaking, in writing, in leading a group—to develop that talent in service of the *klal*.

◆§ Pirchei Agudath Israel: Growth and Changes

Jewish America changed radically in the years between 1934 and 1994. Torah education developed and matured, and the needs of youth changed accordingly. Under Rabbi Silbermintz, the role of Pirchei Agudath Israel as a vehicle for complementing the yeshivah experience also evolved over the decades: from keeping boys away from the movies on *Shabbos* a half century ago, to weekly groups for fun, information, friendship and group identification a generation ago, to *Mishnayos Be'al Peh* as a central, galvanizing activity, to a panoply of educationally enriching programs today—all as part of a larger, all-embracing Torah community. Pirchei Agudath Israel still serves its original function of providing a sense of identity to an observant boy who otherwise might feel isolated (the Tucson, Arizona, branch of Pirchei consists of one boy who participates in almost all contests, gets mail addressed to him from 84 William Street, etc.), the emphasis in these past few years has been on special activities and areas of study not touched by the conventional yeshivah. One can not calculate the invaluable results of these programs in terms of lives affected, *mitzvos* performed, Torah knowledge amassed.

• Residents in nursing homes and retirement facilities are lonely, often out of touch with the important days in the Jewish year. Josh organized members of Bnos Agudath Israel (which he unofficially advised and guided over the decades) to visit these facilities regularly; he brought Pirchei kids and musical entertainment groups to perform periodically—bringing happiness and live *Yiddishkeit* to seniors, the joy of doing *mitzvos* to juniors.

• Why shouldn't children recognize, collect and revere likenesses of the holy countenances of our *Gedolei Torah*? Children filled albums with thousands of pictures as part of a "Know Your *Gedolim*" competition, and received prizes from Rabbi Silbermintz. No effort was required of the children other than to collect pictures of *Gedolim*—from old magazines, recent newspapers, cherished wedding albums, or any other format in which they were found. This contest led the participants to focus on greatness in Torah and imbued them with respect for all *Gedolim* of all generations. Many a home still has bulging scrapbooks filled by their children.

Wolf Karfiol—one-time member of a Pirchei group led by Josh, subsequently an active member of Agudath Israel, and close friend and *chavrusa* of Rabbi Silbermintz—reported[2] (in a long, touching tribute to Josh) that he perused over 150 issues of the Pirchei periodical, *Darkeinu*. In the pages were listed the winners of contests dealing with *Shmitta, Pirkei Avos, Shmiras Halashon-Sefer Chofetz Chaim, Hilchos Tefillin* (to be mastered before Bar Mitzva), *Shnayim Mikra V'echod Targum, Kibud Av V'Eim,* Understanding Your *Tefillos, Motza'ei Shabbos* learning programs for fathers and sons....Among the winners listed were many children who subsequently became leaders of Torah Jewry, both as *Rabbonim* and *baalei battim* (lay leaders). Participating in these contests taught them two invaluable lessons: the importance of Torah study, and the value of belonging to a *Klal*.

Mr. Karfiol tells of a friend whose 12-year-old son began learning *Hilchos Tefillin* in *Mishnah Berurah*. When the father took out his own set of *Mishnah Berurah* to review with his son, he found an award sticker on the inside cover for having won the set as a prize in a Pirchei contest. Rabbi Silbermintz's signature as Pirchei Director made the award official. How many thousands of others have such prizes in their homes and will on some future occasion tap into the memories of their past accomplishments achieved because of Pirchei Agudath Israel and Rabbi Silbermintz?

2. This, as well as other points in this article, are taken from Mr. Karfiol's tribute.

Someone calculated that over one million *Mishnayos* were learned under Pirchei auspices over the 31 years that it sponsored its study, and hundreds of thousands of hours were spent in Torah study by those who participated in all of the above contests. What a glorious reception these accumulated *Mishnayos* and hours must have given Rabbi Silbermintz when he ascended to the *Yeshivah Shel Maalah* on the sad *Erev Pesach,* 5754, when his *neshama* left our surroundings!

◆§ The Range of His Activities

Because of Josh's love for children and his extraordinary success in *chinuch,* one might lose sight of the fact that the driving force within him—in *chinuch,* as in other pursuits—was an *achrayus* to the *klal,* an *achrayus* that involved him in many other undertakings.

He was a major force in bringing *Hatzalah* (the volunteer emergency medical service) to Crown Heights, and then to Flatbush, when he moved there.

As an active member in the Agudist Benevolent Society, he worked with others to see that every aspect of *kavod hameis* be honored, and that the plight of the mourners be softened as much as possible. In fact, it was he who suggested that the legs of the standard padded folding chairs be sawed down to accommodate the requirement that *aveilim* sit within three *tefachim* (handbreadths) off the floor.

He personally processed hundreds of thousands of dollars of loans through the Agudist Benevolent's *Gemach* (free loan fund). While he generally involved his family in his numerous undertakings, none of them ever knew who came for what on behalf of whom in the *Gemach.*

One of his favorite aphorisms was: "Don't be a thermometer, be a thermostat. It is not enough for you to measure the climate in the room. If it is cool or lukewarm in a room, it is your task to raise the level of enthusiasm, to make it piping hot."

He saw it as his mission to fire his *talmidim* and his charges with the very same dedication to the *klal* that he was imbued with—a dedication ignited by the words and deeds of Reb Elimelech ("Mike") Tress, the inspiring calls to action of Mr.

Mendlowitz, and the lofty model projected by Reb Elchanan. As a matter of course, then, scores of his "boys" learned the lessons of Pirchei Agudath Israel well, and are today's *Roshei Yeshivah, mechanchim,* responsible *baalei battim,* and members and leaders in the Agudath Israel movement.

When Rabbi Silbermintz was honored by Agudath Israel of America in 1986 with the presentation of its prestigious Moreinu Yaakov Rosenheim Memorial Award at the annual dinner, his words of acceptance moved the entire assemblage. He said that although his life's work of *harbotzas haTorah* and the path he had taken for himself had not been an easy one, he had never regretted his choice, and if he had the opportunity to do so again, he would do it with the same dedication and *brenn.* Although he will be sorely missed, the fruits of his efforts and the impact of his inspiration are still very much alive today.

Yonason Rosenblum

A Chofetz Chessed in Our Time
Rabbi Shmuel Avraham Myski זצ"ל

*He walked in the ways
of Avraham Avinu, not
only doing acts of
chessed, but seeking it
out in creative,
imaginative ways*

R abbi Shmuel Avraham Myski may have been a household
name in Monsey, but not in Lakewood, Golders Green, or
Bnei Brak. That itself is a cause for optimism. If a Jew could have
done what he did in his forty-four years without becoming the
subject of great fanfare, without other Jews from around the
world flocking to Monsey just to see him, then maybe our generation is not as bereft of spiritual heroes as we think. If a Jew
working around the clock on every form of *chessed* project imag-
inable, projects whose scope staggers the imagination, is not yet
viewed as a curiosity, then we can only assume that there are others like him. But for now let us tell of Rabbi Shmuel Avraham
Myski.

I. Keren HaChessed

The proliferation of *gemachim* (free-loan societies) is one of the identifying characteristics of any religious Jewish community. There are literally thousands of *gemachim* around the world, but one in Monsey stands out from all the others.

In 1971, a recently married *yungerman* decided to use five hundred dollars from his wedding money to begin a *gemach.* The *gemach* opened its doors in a small Monsey basement; its "office" consisted of a brown desk, a black book, and a Parker pen. From that humble beginning, grew Keren HaChessed, which over the next twenty-two years lent more than a hundred million dollars.

By the late '80s, Keren HaChessed was lending over ten million dollars a year. The mere paperwork involved from the one-night a week of interviewing loan applicants and handling the dozens of bank accounts maintained by the *gemach,* kept a full-time staff busy all week. Rabbi Myski himself spent at least fifty hours a week on *gemach*-related work, in addition to his full-time job as a second-grade *rebbe* in Beis Dovid, his Hatzalah work and other *chessed* projects. The four phone lines in his house rang constantly. Often he was on two lines at a time, with one of his ten children on his lap helping him push the buttons.

Over the years, Keren HaChessed came to play a crucial role in the Monsey economy. Short-term loans of up to fifty thousand dollars regularly allowed yeshivos and other institutions to meet their payroll. Any time there was a communal emergency or tragedy — fire, illness, etc.—the checks were made out to Keren HaChessed, though this involved hours of added paperwork for the officers and staff of the *gemach.* A newcomer's typical tour of Monsey would inevitably include a drive past the Myski residence, where the Keren HaChessed offices occupy the ground floor, and the comment, "Here's Myski's if you need advice or any kind of help."

◆§ A Need to Give

How did a *gemach,* begun with no significant financial resources, grow to dwarf every other *gemach* in the world? The answer starts with Rabbi Myski's desire to give. He did not wait to be asked for a loan, but would tell people, "I hear you're making a *chasanah*. Perhaps you need a loan?" Before Pesach one year, he noticed that a store was not properly stocked for the peak season. Discreet inquiries revealed that the owner lacked money to purchase what he needed. A loan was forthcoming without having been requested. One man, who was mired in debt, still remembers with astonishment how "one night this Chassidic fellow knocked on my door and handed me a check for $50,000, and told me I should pay him back when things got better."

Reb Shmuel Avraham would go to weddings, pockets filled with cash. If he saw an argument developing between the host and the caterer, he would hurry over, pay the caterer, and tell him, "We'll settle this later," so that monetary disputes would not diminish the joy of the occasion. If someone was too embarrassed to come to the Keren HaChessed offices, Rabbi Myski thought nothing of waiting on an unlit street corner to deliver the money. He was himself the most frequent co-signer on loans.

It was easy for him to give because he begrudged no one any enjoyment of this world. An applicant for a loan to buy his newly-married son a house was never asked, "Why can't he rent like everyone else?" The starting assumption was that every loan application would be responded to affirmatively.

One of Monsey's most successful businessmen suffered sudden, dramatic business reversals. His only hope of saving his business from bankruptcy was the immediate infusion of over a million dollars in new capital. But before the Federal Bankruptcy Court would permit new capital to be put into the business, a way had to be found to protect the new monies against prior creditors. When Rabbi Myski was approached as to whether Keren HaChessed would serve as a guarantor for the new funds, he agreed without hesitation, even though the responsibilities involved consumed fifteen hours a week of his own time over the next year.

A half million dollars in receipts from the man's business came into the *gemach* a week, and most of it had to be wired to other accounts within hours of receipt. To make that possible, Rabbi Myski was forced to put his own reputation and long-term relationships on the line. Nearly every day, he had to ask the local banks, with whom he had built up a close relationship over the years, to stretch their rules on clearing checks. As each new hurdle in restructuring the business was overcome, Rabbi Myski's pleasure was as great as if it had been his own business.

Keren HaChessed became in time a convenient cover for Rabbi Myski's other charitable activities. Using monies he had raised separately, he would tell hard-pressed borrowers that they had miscalculated the amounts they owed, and their debts had either been paid in full or were much smaller than they had thought. He supported a number of needy families with weekly stipends, which he told them came from a "Special Fund" for people in their situation. These activities only came to light when he became ill, and his associates in the *gemach* could not locate the "Special Fund" they were continually being asked about.

Rabbi Myski was accused, with some justice, of trying to grab all the *chessed* in Monsey for himself. If he heard of a successful *chessed* project anywhere in the world, he wanted to bring it to Monsey. A home for mothers recuperating after childbirth, a food co-op for *avreichim* — these were just a few of the projects that he dreamed of or had brought to fruition. At the time of his passing, he was working on a multi-million dollar project to build 300 homes for *kolleleit* using funds from Keren HaChessed.

๙ Built on Trust

Neither the desire to give, nor the willingness to undertake risks in order to do so, are sufficient if the money to give is not there. The key to Keren HaChessed's fund-raising was the trust that people had in Rabbi Myski. People regularly lent him sixty or seventy thousand dollars on the promise that their money would always be available to them upon two day's notice. Not once has Keren HaChessed failed to make good on that promise.

The trust people placed in Rabbi Myski was a direct reflection of his own *bitachon* in *Hakadosh Baruch Hu*. There were times he began the day with two hundred thousand dollars in loans from banks or private individuals that had to be paid back. Invariably someone would approach him after his morning *minyan* and tell him that he had seventy thousand dollars that he did not need for the time being. "If I begin the day happy," he used to say, "then I know I'll have *siyata d'Shmaya*." Sometimes it took dozens of phone calls to raise the entire sum needed, but in the end it was always done.

He was, in addition, an innovative fund-raiser. One of Keren HaChessed's major sources of funds was a *Purim shpiel* put on in thirty or more homes of contributors. If a former large contributor had fallen on hard times, however, the *Purim shpiel* was also performed in his home as in years past.[1]

II. A Genius in Chessed

The *chofetz chessed* is marked by an acute sensitivity to people that enables him to give to others in ways others could not. In the same way that others struggle with a *sugya* in *Gemara*, he devotes himself to finding opportunities to give and the proper way of doing so. The sophisticated computerization of Keren HaChessed, the mastery of electronic banking required, the absolute minimum of waiting time, the layout of the offices — each room soundproofed, with music piped in, to ensure that what is said in one room will never be heard in another—all attest to the attention to every detail.

The Slonimer Rebbe, under whom Rabbi Myski studied in Jerusalem,[2] once told him that with his acute sensitivity to the feelings of others, he would have made a good psychiatrist. And, in fact, he was widely consulted by couples experiencing marital difficulties. One time a man started screaming at Rabbi Myski, but the latter took all his abuse with perfect equanimity. "Better that he should yell at me than his wife," he said.[3]

◆§ Rebbe Par Excellence

Nowhere was Rabbi Myski's sensitivity so clear as in the classroom. His warmth naturally attracted children, and he was rarely seen on the streets of Monsey without a crowd of young-

---

1. Similarly, Rabbi Myski often took over *tzedakah* projects that others had begun and could no longer afford to keep up, without telling the recipients that their original benefactor was no longer the source of their funding.

2. After studying in the Slonimer Yeshivah in Jerusalem, Rabbi Myski learned with Rabbi Binyamin Paler in Boro Park and in the *kollel* of Beis Medrash Elyon in Monsey.

3. Reb Shmuel Avrohom's *chessed* was not limited by the worthiness of the recipient. A man once threw him rudely out of his house when he came to solicit a contribution for Keren HaChessed. Two months later, the same man applied to the *gemach* for a loan and received it.

sters around him, holding his hands. He gave himself fully to his students. Despite the enormous demands on his time — the normal day began with *daf yomi* before *davening* and ended at two or three in the morning — he never permitted himself the luxury of recycling the previous year's *Parshah* sheets. Each year there were new drawings, new stories, and new ways to excite the curiosity of his young students. Each day he recorded the day's lessons on tape so that boys could call up a special "Dial-a-*Rebbe*" line at night and review that day's material.

There was a boy who had to repeat second grade. Rabbi Myski asked the boy to join him for a ride in his car. In the course of the drive, he said to the boy, "I have a very big class coming in next year, and I'm going to need a helper. Would you be willing to stay with me another year to be my special helper?" When the boy agreed, Rabbi Myski took a bicycle out of the back seat of the car as a present.

The bonds he forged with his students did not end with the school year. Each boy received at the end of the year a picture of himself together with Rabbi Myski, and many referred to him for years after as "my special *Rebbe*." He kept a pocketful of lollipops at all times to give to former students he might meet on the street and any friends that were with them.

One former student was critically ill in the intensive care unit. Rabbi Myski and a friend came to the hospital and danced and sang in front of the boy's bed. The boy's mother recalls: "All of a sudden, they started dancing and singing with intense *simchah*. It was a sight to behold, like a painting that was moving. They brought such joy into my son's life."

❧ In the Hands of a Malach

Hatzalah was another natural activity for one who never passed an accident on the highway without getting out of his car to see if he could help. The heroics of the rescue work itself were of no interest to him, though even here he was graced with special abilities. One mother described the way he treated her baby daughter who was choking on a bone: "The way he cuddled my baby with love, all the while working on her, relaxed me. I felt she was in the hands of a *malach*."

After providing the initial care, he retreated as soon as possible into the background to let the other volunteers take over. Then he would look around to see what he could do for the family of the victim. One time a young boy was in an accident just before *Shabbos*. As soon as he was no longer needed, Rabbi Myski went into the house and set up the *Shabbos blech* and candles.

When the Hatzalah ambulance had to take someone to the hospital on *Shabbos*, Rabbi Myski would sing *zemiros* the entire way. He once took a seriously ill boy to his sister's wedding in a Hatzalah ambulance, and tended the oxygen tanks throughout so the boy would not miss the *simchah*.

◆§ Giving in Secret

Reb Shmuel Avraham found ways to give without the recipient even knowing that he was receiving. Every Succos he bought many extra sets of the Four Species, and before Pesach boxes and boxes of extra *matzos*, to give to those who did not have. He always made it appear that the extras were the result of miscalculations on his part, and that the one receiving them would be doing him the greatest favor by taking them off his hands.

There were rarely less than twenty people at the Myski's *Shabbos* table. Orphans, divorcees, *ba'alei teshuvah* all basked in the warmth of the Myski home. Rabbi Myski spent hours preparing *divrei Torah* appropriate for his children of different ages and for his guests. It was not uncommon for him to translate his dramatic presentations into two or three languages for the benefit of all those present.

◆§ Chessed Begins at Home

His *chessed* did not end, as is too often the case, at home. In the middle of a conversation with the biggest contributor, Reb Shmuel Avraham would stop to take a call from his wife upstairs or mother next door, and if they needed anything, would excuse himself to take care of the matter. Rabbi Myski's father became an invalid at a young age, and as the oldest of the ten children, the responsibility fell on Rabbi Myski to marry off all his younger siblings. They naturally looked to him whenever in need. One time a sister was unable to prepare for Pesach, and she and her family joined the Myski family for Pesach. Throughout Pesach, Rabbi Myski kept repeating, "Isn't it nice that we could all be here together. Thank you so much for enhancing our *Yom Tov*." He was the special uncle to all his nieces and nephews. They never left for yeshivah or to camp without him coming over to say good-bye.

As long as his father was alive, he called him every day in Montreal to lift his spirits. He used to make a special effort to recall amusing stories for his father. One his favorites involved a middle-of-the-night emergency call for Hatzalah. In his pajamas, he rushed through the snow to the home of an elderly Jew, who feared he had suffered a heart attack. Yet when he arrived, the would-be patient's only reaction to his dedication was, "*Azoi tzu kumen?*—That's how you come to a person's house?"

The Skulener Rebbe told him not to tell anyone the severity of his condition, during his final illness, and he swore all his doctors to secrecy. His spirits were so high and he always exuded so much confidence that he would recover, that he convinced everyone else as well. To shield his mother, he would visit her with his intravenous needles hidden under his coat, and when he had to be hospitalized for days at a time, would call her each night to say that he had to be in the city in connection with Keren HaChessed. Even in his last year, when he could no longer teach, he continued to insist that he had nothing more than chronic fatigue virus — or as he sometimes termed it, CMV, *Chevlei Moshiach* Virus. When people came to visit him, he would joke, "Look how lazy I've become."

III. Chut Hameshulash—The Three-Stranded Thread

Rabbi Myski inherited his love of doing *chessed* from his mother. When left at thirty-five with the sole responsibility of supporting ten children, she did not slacken in her own *chessed* activities. Three times a year, she would make mass mailings from her house on behalf of different *chessed* projects. She would prepare food packages in the house for needy neighbors and send her children out with instructions: "This one needs eggs, this one can't eat such and such ..."

Rabbi Myski, too, was not just a doer of *chessed* but a teacher of *chessed*. A boy from a nearby yeshivah once came to visit and

Rabbi Myski asked him if the yeshivah had a *gemach* for *chassanim*. Informed that it did not, he gave the boy two hundred dollars to start one. One of Keren HaChessed's most innovative projects was the creation of *gemach* savings accounts for Orthodox children throughout the New York area. Each child received his own *gemach*-book, just like for a bank savings account. Instead of spending their money on sweets or nicknacks, children from a young age were taught the *mitzvah* of lending their money. Though more than a million dollars was raised through such accounts, only the educational purpose could have justified the time the whole project took.

In the Myski home, the children were not told, "*Tatte* is busy doing a *chessed*." Whatever he did was natural, like breathing, and needed no special notice or title. Not surprisingly, his oldest children are now actively involved in Keren HaChessed.

As is well-known, the Manchester *Rosh Yeshivah* Rabbi Yehuda Zev Segal, always recommended to those experiencing overwhelming physical or emotional suffering that they increase their commitment to *shemiras halashon* (avoiding slander and gossip). Yet when he spoke to Rabbi Myski in the last hours of his life, and just a few months before Rabbi Myski's own *petirah*, Rabbi Segal's only advice was "continue with your *chessed*." He recognized that Rabbi Myski's *chessed* was so pure, so much a part of him, that there could be no greater merit. Just as the key to *shemiras halashon* is the identification of our fellow Jews as part of ourselves, so was that the root of Rabbi Myski's *chessed* activities.

❄ ❄ ❄

"He neither sleeps nor slumbers (*Tehillim* 121)," says King David in reference to *Hashem*. The repetition is odd, and various commentators have noted that the second verb, *yishan*, can be read causitively, so that the verse means, "He neither sleeps nor allows others to sleep."

In every generation there are a select few whom *Hashem* calls to greatness and does not permit to rest. Rabbi Shmuel Avraham Myski was one of those. May the record of his deeds serve to drive a little of the slumber from our eyes, as well.

◆§ The Wellsprings of Greatness of Old

*Their majesty of Torah and dedication
in Divine service struck roots into
the rich European soil of earlier eras
of greatness*

Miriam Margoshes

The "Noda B'Yehuda":
On The Occasion Of His 200th Yahrzeit

*A giant in
Talmudic logic and
personal perfection,
his responsa continue
to light our way
in all areas of halachah*

◆§ A Towering Figure in a Generation of Giants

It was a generation of giants; in every shtetl dwelt *Geonim*; every *beis midrash* had a core of *talmidei chachamim*; and yet he stood out: Rabbi Yechezkel Landau, known by the name of his *sefer*, the *Noda B'Yehuda*. His generation depended on him as the arbiter of its doubts and dilemmas, as the *poseik hador*. He proved, in addition, to be a *poseik ledoros*—a decisor for generations to come, as well.

In the words of his student, Rabbi Eliezer Fleckeles (*in Sefer Teshuvah Me'ahava*): "He was the tallest of his generation, head and shoulders above the rest, as those who were privileged to know him realized." Physically tall and imposing, he was also of soaring stature in the spiritual sense. In this vein, Rabbi Yitzchok Hutner, זצ"ל, used to relate the following parable:

In every shtetl, the town clock was housed in a tall tower. The reason for its placement is simple: that the time could be told easily, even from a distance. But there was a deeper, underlying reason, as well. If the clock were accessible, anyone could reach up and move its hands to synchronize it with his own watch... it could be adjusted to suit one's personal time. Since the clock was not within reach, however, everyone was forced to set his watch by communal time.

So it is with a leader, Rabbi Hutner said. If he does not stand tall, on a high place, every Jew will "set" him to his own liking....

So, too, the Noda B'Yehuda. Everyone looked up to him, and no one could ever budge him from his commitment to truth.

◆§ Childhood: From Apt to Brod

Rabbi Yechezkel Halevi Landau was born in Apt, Poland, on 18 Cheshvan, 5474 (Nov. 17, 1713). He was a scion of Torah royalty, of scholars and distinguished communal leaders, and traced his descent back to Rashi. He was also descended from the famous "Rebbe Reb Heschel" of Cracow, who was celebrated for having brought Torah learning to Poland centuries before.

His father, Reb Yehuda, a leading figure in Apt, was a delegate to the *Vaad Arba Aratzos*. A man of vast Torah knowledge and nobility of character, his opinions are quoted frequently, with awe, in the *Noda B'Yehuda*. Realizing his young son's potential, Reb Yehuda provided him with special tutors and a rigorous program of Torah study, and discouraged him from childish pastimes. Reb Yechezkel named his *sefer* "*Noda B'Yehuda*" in honor of his father.

His mother, Rebbetzin Chaya, a devout and pious woman, is immortalized in the Noda B'Yehuda's *sefer* of *chiddushim* (original interpretations on Talmud), which he called *Tzion L'Nefesh Chaya* (*Tz'lach*). She was the daughter of Rabbi Eliezer of Dubno, a pious and holy man who fasted most of his life and was totally immersed in *halachah*.

When the Noda B'Yehuda was four years old, his father engaged a tutor for him: the *charif* (piercingly analytical scholar), Rabbi Yitzchok Eisik of Ludmir, who taught the young Yechezkel until his Bar Mitzvah.

In the *Tz'lach*, the Noda B'Yehuda describes how his father sent him, while yet a child, to "talk in learning" with the newly-arrived *Rav* of Apt, Rabbi Moshe Yaakov. He quotes the entire *pilpul* that took place between them on that *Erev Shabbos*, as well as his father's reaction when he heard the report. The level of accomplishment in Torah that the Noda B'Yehuda had reached at that early age is truly noteworthy. Scholars were already seeking him out for his opinion at that time. (From the introduction to *Noda B'Yehuda*)

In that era, a *beis midrash* in Brod known as the *"Broder Kloiz"* attracted an elite group of Torah scholars; over several generations, world-class *gedolim*, *poskim*, and *mekubalim* were nurtured there, such as the Rabbi Ephraim Zalman Margolios (the *Shaarei Ephraim*, whose father, grandfather, and brothers also learned there), Rabbi Gershon Kitover (brother-in-law of the Baal Shem Tov), Rabbi Meir Margolios (author of *Meir Nesivim* and *talmid* of the Baal Shem Tov), and Rabbi Meshulam Igra, among many, many others.

After his Bar Mitzvah, the Noda B'Yehuda joined that famous *Kloiz*, to immerse himself in every aspect of Torah, including *Kabbala*, which he studied with the world-famous *gaon* and *mekubal*, Rabbi Chaim Sanzur (not to be confused with the Sanzer Rav, the *Divrei Chaim*, who lived a generation later) in a special *shtiebel* near the *Kloiz* reserved for this purpose. Rabbi Chaim said of the Noda B'Yehuda: "צפה יחזקאל במעשה מרכבה"—he was well-versed in the *seforim* of the *Ari Hakodosh* and other *Kabbalah* writings, as well as works of philosophy such as the *Moreh Nevuchim*. But the Noda B'Yehuda never discussed *Kabbalah*. The hidden Torah remained hidden within him....

At eighteen he was married in Dubno, but his father-in-law soon moved the family to Brod where Reb Yechezkel re-joined the group at the "*Kloiz*," going home for *Shabbos* only. In his *sefer*, he praises his wife for accepting such a taxing lifestyle, gladly carrying the burdens of managing home and children by herself, week after week.

At twenty, the Noda B'Yehuda was part of the *Beis Din* of Brod and was soon answering halachic queries that poured in from other cities and countries. Indeed, he became "*Noda*

B'Yehuda"—famous in the Torah world.

In the words of his son, Rabbi Yakov'ka, he was "tall, well-formed, well-spoken.... His *bitachon* and contentment with his material lot gave him a joyous disposition.... He liked people, loved knowledge, was a trusted counselor, wise in business practices and quick with numbers...."

◄§ The Years in Yampola

In 5505, when the Noda B'Yehuda was thirty years old, he was appointed Rav in Yampola, a town in Vohlin (now part of Ukraine), not far from Brod. His departure from Brod was triggered by a dispute involving him and two of his colleagues, Reb Meir Margolios and Reb Avrohom Gershon Kitover. These three Torah giants had demonstrated their *mesiras nefesh* by speaking out against one of the most powerful leaders of the community, concerning issues related to the conduct of the gentleman's wife. It was a situation which they were warned not to raise—yet they were prepared to suffer the consequences of their actions. As a result, all three were asked to leave Brod. It is said that each one earned a reputation of untarnished purity and a revered position in Jewish life because they spoke out at that time without giving thought to their own security and future.

In Yampola the Noda B'Yehuda opened a yeshivah and became a *marbitz* (disseminator of) *Torah* on a grand scale. For the remainder of his life, teaching was his first priority; in his published responsa, he mentions the many and varied *shiurim* he would give regularly in *Gemara*, in *Poskim* (codes), in *Chumash* with *Rashi*, and so on. His yeshivah became famous in the region, with many of his students becoming *Rabbonim* themselves.

During his years in Yampola, the Noda B'Yehuda became an acknowledged *Gadol Hador*, as is evident in the role he played in the great *kamaiyos* controversy between Rabbi Yaakov Emden and Rabbi Yonasan Eibeschutz (*circa* 5512/1752). He toiled day and night to find an acceptable compromise and make peace between the factions. He wrote glowingly of the *Rebbe* Reb Yonasan, at the same time urging that he withdraw from circulation the amulets in question. His correspondence on this topic was published in *Luchos Ha'Edus*.

The *pilpulim* he delivered in Yampola, which joined the breadth of his knowledge with his *charifus* (acuity), were later printed in *Doresh L'Tzion*. His halachic responsa written at that time, covering the gamut of Jewish life—especially those relating to clarifying the marital status of *agunos* (women whose husbands are missing and cannot be accounted for)—are most impressive. In his *psakim* he delved extensively into sources in *Gemara*, even into the "Written Torah," to find the roots of the *halachah*, similar in method to the *Rishonim* of hundreds of years earlier.

Among his correspondents, as documented in the *sefer Noda B'Yehuda*, are such luminaries as Rabbi Yeshaya Pick (Breslau), Rabbi Chaim Sanzur (Brod), Rabbi Elazar Kalir (*Or Chodosh*), Rabbi Chaim HaKohein Rapaport (Lemberg), Rabbi Nesanel Weil (the *Korban Nesanel*), among many others of such stature. The Noda B'Yehuda writes, "I published my *sefer* so that my students may learn from it, but I have nothing to teach the *Gedolei Hador*, for they are all greater than I...."

His son, Reb Yakov'ka, once asked him why he postponed answering the queries of recognized *Gedolim* while rushing to answer those of lower-ranking *Rabbonim*. Wouldn't protocol dictate the opposite? Answered the Noda B'Yehuda, "The *Gedolim* know the answers themselves; they are just seeking my confirmation of their opinions. But a lower-ranking *Rav* may not be sure of his ground, and if I don't answer him quickly, he might commit a mistake in *halachah l'ma'aseh*."

✑§ Rav of Prague

In 5515/1755, at the age of 42, the Noda B'Yehuda succeeded Rabbi David Oppenheim as Rav in Prague. Prague was a major center of Jewish life, and it was there that the Noda B'Yehuda reached his peak of leadership and influence. Even those who were opposed to him at first, soon fell under his spell.

In Prague he again founded a yeshivah, which attracted top students from far and wide. His religious and civic obligations as *Rav* of the capital and halachic authority to the world at large, did not prevent him from giving his *shiurim* in the yeshivah. He taught and inspired a new generation of *geonim* and *poskim* like

Rabbi Eliezer Fleckeles (later *Rosh Beis Din* of Prague), Rabbi Avraham Danzig (the *Chayei Adam*), Rabbi Bezalel Regensberg, and many others. His sons and his son-in-law, Rabbi Yoseph "*Hatzaddik,*" also continued to grow in stature in Prague.

This period in Prague was a difficult one, beset by war and instability. Sieges took their toll, causing frequent financial collapses and many a moral dilemma. In addition, remnants of the followers of Shabbtai Tzvi still lingered, even while a new danger was surfacing: the early winds of *Haskalah* began to blow in Bohemia, especially in Prague. The Noda B'Yehuda fought these breaches like a lion and built up defenses against them, making Prague a stronghold of truth and constancy.

In an interesting responsum, the Noda B'Yehuda writes that he was unable to delve with sufficient depth into this particular *she'eila* because his beloved son was not feeling well, and was clinging to his presence, not letting him attend to his work. This could serve as a metaphor for his attachment to Prague: the Noda B'Yehuda loved his people like his own children; they were beset by various social and personal ills, so they clung to him, and he responded like a father and would not leave them....

In 5517 (1756), with the outbreak of the Seven Years' War (which reached America as the French-Canadian War), Prague came under siege. Frederick the Great of Prussia and his French allies were storming the gates of Prague, and the Austrian Empress Maria Theresa was trying to bolster the defenses of the city. Whoever could escape the city did so, but the Noda B'Yehuda categorically refused to flee. He stayed behind to assist his suffering flock and find them some means of sustenance. He even organized fire-fighting efforts in the Jewish quarter.

In war as in peacetime, the Noda B'Yehuda insisted on total loyalty to the Crown, which created a *kiddush Hashem* and enhanced the status of the community in the eyes of the Empress. He ordered prayers for the success of her war efforts, and when she fell sick, he issued a proclamation containing prayers and *Tehillim,* and ordering services and fasting to be offered for the Empress's recovery. He had it issued in German translation and distributed in Prague to demonstrate the devotion of the Jewish subjects to their sovereign—neutralizing the poison of the anti-

Semites who had the Queen's ear.

"My beloved son is not well...." The war wreaked havoc with the *kehillah* of Prague, and the Noda B'Yehuda undertook to reorganize it. To curb the luxurious lifestyles of the rich, and the standard they set, he drafted minutely detailed rules and regulations. This sage, to whom the entire world turned to solve its weightiest problems, did not consider it beneath him to outline what foods may be served at which *simchas*, when coffee may or may not be added, and when music would be permitted.

In contrast to the Yampola days, when his lectures were *tours de force* of *pilpul* and dazzling constructions of *drush*, in Prague the Noda B'Yehuda concentrated on *Mussar*, outlining the fundamentals of faith and observance, guiding his people through the minefields of "modern" life. The focus of his *drashos* was on the sanctity of *Shabbos* and *Yom-Tov*, as well as *tzenius*; the laws of interest, of forbidden foods, of giving charity, business law, swearing falsely; and so on. As fatherly as he was, he could also be unyielding.

His position in the case of the *Get al korcho al yedei shaliach* (a forced divorce, delivered through an agent) is a case in point. A wealth of knowledge is revealed in his discussion (published in *Noda B'Yehuda*) explaining his position. His *psak* was diametrically opposed to that of his *mechutan*, Rabbi Yitzchok Horowitz, the *Rav* of Hamburg, and almost all the *geonim* of the time. Yet he would not budge; when Rabbi Mordechai Zvi, the son of Rabbi Itzikel Hamburger, later attempted to defend his father's position in the matter, the Noda B'Yehuda cut him short, saying, "The *Gaon*, your father, is already in the next world where he himself recognizes the truth."

In 5527 (1767) there was another raging controversy; this one concerned the case of the *Get* of Cleves, wherein the divorcing husband was temporarily insane, bringing questions on the validity of his actions. It pitted Rabbi Yisroel Lipschutz—grandfather of the *mechaber* (author) of *Tiferes Yisroel*—who granted the divorce against the opinion of the sages of Frankfurt, among them Rabbi Abish'l, the *Birkas Avrohom*, who declared it invalid.

The Noda B'Yehuda concluded that the *Get* was valid after all. At first he conveyed his view in mild tones, which was his preferred way, but then with increasing sharpness. He actually swore in front of over 1000 people that the *get* was valid. As the Kotzker expressed it years later, "Heaven and earth may collapse, but one does not give an inch from the truth as one sees it." (The correspondence generated by this case appears in *Sefer Or Hayoshor*.) As a result of his stance, the Frankfurt *kehillah* resolved never to engage the Noda B'Yehuda or any of his descendants as *Rav*.

His *psak* permitting shaving on *Chol Hamoed* under certain conditions brought down another storm on the Noda B'Yehuda, but he remained steadfast in his decision.

In 5537, the Empress offered him the position of Chief Rabbi of Galicia, which he declined: "... I would have liked to return to my homeland, yet parting from here [Prague] would be like pulling the skin off a live animal"—so closely connected did he feel to his people. His fatherly feelings for an "ailing child who clung to him" came once again to the fore.

◄§ His Magnum Opus: On the Pages and Between the Lines

Over the years, while in both Yampola and Prague, the Noda B'Yehuda was so absorbed with his roles as Rav, Rosh Yeshivah, and statesman, that he had little time to publish his halachic responsa. A fire in 5533/1773, which destroyed most of his worldly possessions including many of his letters and manuscripts, alerted him to the need for publishing his works. Thus, in 1776 he set about the task of gathering his responsa, and in 1777 he published the first volume of the *sefer Noda B'Yehuda*, which includes 276 responsa covering all four sections of the *Shulchan Aruch*. It immediately became the topic of the day among scholars, young and old, as his decisions were considered, discussed and debated. Publication of this first volume provoked a stream of letters asking for clarification or challenging many of his *piskei halachos* (decisions), bringing further elucidation and promoting even greater interest in his subsequent responses, published in Volume Two.

The two volumes of his responsa are among the finest creations in their field, not only revealing the sacred truth of Torah, but the noble spirit of their author, his treasure-trove of *middos tovos*, his wisdom and his practical approach to life. His responsa demonstrate how humility and unyielding firmness can co-exist in wonderful harmony when the *kavanah* (motivation) is *l'sheim Shamayim.*

Between the lines of his responsa, the Noda B'Yehuda also reveals extensive knowledge of many subjects and trades. To a query as to whether hunting is permissible, he responded by decrying the cruel and vindictive streak of personality nurtured through pursuit of this "sport of Nimrod." He also stated that he would not address such a subject at all, had he not hoped to prevent the questioner and his family from besmirching their reputation.

Another questioner requested that his query be printed in full in the *sefer Noda B'Yehuda*. The *Rav* answered that although this was both difficult and expensive, since it involved re-setting a part of the *sefer* that was already printed, he would comply, to please the questioner.

In yet another responsum, the Noda B'Yehuda demonstrates both worldly wisdom and concern for a fellow Jew's future. A *rav* queried him about a rabbinical position that was open—should he take it or not? Answered the Noda B'Yehuda, "I advise you against it; the previous *Rav*, being childless, had few expenses and never asked for a raise, so the townspeople are not used to paying a living wage to a family man. However, if you still want the position, I will use my influence there in your favor."

His Relationship With the World of *Chassidus*

The Noda B'Yehuda was opposed to *Chassidus*, and wrote a well-known responsum against reciting the "*L'sheim Yichud*," the kabbalistic formulation said by *Chassidim* before performing a *mitzvah*. Towards the end of his life, however, he became close to the great Chassidic leader, Rabbi Yaakov Shimshon of Shpitorka, and this mitigated his opposition to some extent. His correspondents (in *Tz'lach*) included Rabbi Zvi Yehoshua Charif and his father, Rabbi Shmelke of Nicholsburg, as well as Rabbi Yosef of Yampola, a son of Rabbi Michel Zlotchover. Reb Yakov'ka writes that his father, the Noda B'Yehuda, used to speak often of the *Ba'al Hafla'ah* (a *talmid* of the Mezricher Maggid) with a deep and abiding love. (Subsequently, a great-grandson of the Noda B'Yehuda, Reb Yudel Landau of Brod, became a Kotzker *Chassid*.)

Yet the Noda B'Yehuda was revered by the great *Chassidic* personalities of his time. The Baal Shem Tov said that a good part of the world rested on the Noda B'Yehuda, and described his *shoresh neshamah* (the ethereal source of his soul) with awe. The *Baal HaTanya* said that he was unique in *hora'ah* and that he invariably arrived at the truth of a matter, even when others disagreed. Rabbi Boruch of Mezhibuzh commented similarly.

The Sanzer Rav (the *Divrei Chaim*) once said that if in his generation there were *Misnagdim* of the Noda B'Yehuda's caliber, he personally would sit under their table; so great was the Noda B'Yehuda's holiness and so pure his motives.

Once someone expressed himself strongly against the Noda B'Yehuda's responsum concerning the *"L'Sheim Yichud"* in the presence of Rabbi Avrohom Levi Chechanower. The *Rebbe* immediately put the speaker into *cheirem* until such time as he would present himself at the gravesite of the Noda B'Yehuda with a *minyan* of ten men, to ask for forgiveness.

The Noda B'Yehuda was niftar on 17 Iyar 1793 (5593), and was buried the next day in Prague. He was the acknowledged halachic authority for Torah-true Jews, *Misnagdim* and *Chassidim* alike. Sages who rarely looked into *seforim* of *Acharonim* (authorities after the 15th century) made an exception of the Noda B'Yehuda. His *seforim* of *psak* and *drashos* live on in *batei midrashim*, worldwide.

Rabbi Yehuda Aszod זצ"ל

Rav, Teacher, Battler for the Integrity of Torah and Jewry

The declaration of war against the reforming of Judaism had been issued in the early nineteenth century by the *Chasam Sofer* (Rabbi Moshe Schreiber), the revered *Rav* of Pressburg, and indeed, during his lifetime he succeeded in thwarting its spread in Austro-Hungary. But after his passing in 1839, the Reform influence experienced a strong revival, without serious challenge for close to ten years.

It was at that time that the government was prepared to refund a large sum of money to the Jews of Hungary, collected as a punitive tax for their support of the abortive revolution of 1848. The Reform leadership had convinced the Emperor Franz Joseph that the monies should be returned in the form of funding for a Reform rabbinical seminary. Similar seminaries in Paris, Breslau and Padua had all but destroyed the *rabbanus* and *kehillos* in their respective countries, and the Torah leadership of Austro-Hungary mobilized to prevent the government funds from being used in this manner.

A delegation led by the *Chasam Sofer's* son and successor as *Rav* of Pressburg, Rabbi Avrohom Shmuel Binyamin Schreiber (the *Ksav Sofer*), arranged to meet with the Emperor. After the *Ksav Sofer* presented a petition to the Emperor requesting his intervention in canceling plans for the rabbinical seminary, he was overcome by emotion and could not continue speaking.

Addressing the other members of the delegation, the Emperor asked, "Who amongst you is greatest in Torah?"

All the assembled rabbis indicated Rabbi Yehuda Aszod of Szerdahely. Franz Joseph asked Rabbi Aszod to honor him with a blessing. Reb Yehuda responded, "Honorable king, even though each one of these rabbis is greater than I am, I cannot refuse his majesty's request." Reb Yehuda then blessed the

Emperor with long life, culminated by a peaceful, natural death. Emperor Franz Joseph lived until the age of eighty-six; and while several members of his immediate family were assassinated or died an unnatural death, he died peacefully in his bed. He ruled Austro-Hungary for sixty-eight years, during one of the longest and most difficult reigns in history.

The Emperor promised to give the matter of the rabbinical seminary serious consideration, and eventually yielded to their request.

⋙ Background of a Scholar

Rabbi Yehuda Aszod — *poseik*, teacher, and defender of Torah — was born in 1794/5554 in the small Hungarian town of Aszod, northeast of Budapest. His father, Reb Yisrael, a pious upright tailor, would distribute cloth left over by his customers to the needy, despite his own financial straits. Before his *petira*, he left instructions that his coffin be made from his worktable, so that it bear witness before the Heavenly tribunal that he had never been dishonest. Yehuda, a mere child of eight, captivated the crowd with his eulogy.

After his father's death, his mother's primary concern was that her son become a great Torah scholar and she sent him to the yeshivah of Rabbi Falik Bichler in Suditz. Rabbi Bichler cherished the exceptional qualities of the young orphan, and treated him as a member of his own household.

Before long, Rabbi Bichler advised him to go to Szerdahely to study in the yeshivah of his brother, Rabbi Ahron Bichler. This yeshivah catered to exceptional students, and while there, Yehuda applied himself with great diligence. By the time he was eighteen, he had mastered five hundred *dappim* (folios) of *Gemara* and was fluent in all four sections of the *Shulchan Aruch*.

From Szerdahely, Yehuda joined the famous yeshivah of Rabbi Mordechai Benet in Nicholsburg. Rabbi Benet soon recognized the brilliance of his pupil and entrusted him with giving a *shiur* to a group of fifty *bachurim*. This aroused the envy of some students and a few of them composed an inflammatory pamphlet, slipping it between the pages of Rabbi Benet's *Gemara*.

The pamphlet enumerated three serious transgressions: that Yehuda had started his own yeshivah with fifty *bachurim*; that he was speaking ill of Rav Benet; and that he held himself in such high esteem that he was learning *Kabbalah*. When Rabbi Benet found the pamphlet, he was enraged at the slander against Yehuda, and turning to Yehuda he quoted Yaakov *Avinu's* blessing: "Yehudah, you, your brothers shall praise." Rabbi Benet added fifty more *bachurim* to Yehuda's *shiur* and expressed public approval of his learning *Kabbalah*.

Rabbi Benet was often overheard preparing his *shiurim* with: "And if my student Yehuda will ask me this, I will answer thus. And if he will ask me this, I will answer as follows."

While in Nicholsburg, Yehuda never slept on a bed, except on *Shabbos*, and invariably learned through the night while standing. Even when the *beis midrash* emptied at lunchtime, he stayed on, learning in his *tefillin*.

Yehuda lived in extreme poverty, but seemed unaffected. One year he had saved sufficient funds for a badly needed pair of new shoes, but with the approach of Succos, he bought beautiful *arba minim* instead, and happily went to *shul* on *Yom Tov* in slippers.

❧ Entering the *Rabbanus*

He married the daughter of Reb Meier Abani, and moved to Dunaszerdahely, devoting all his time to Torah study. He eventually served as *dayan* in the city for five years, and then went on to become the *Rav* of Rete (near Pressburg), where his reputation as a scholar spread.

After several years, Reb Yehuda moved to Semenitz, where he established a large yeshivah, opening his home to the many *bachurim* who did not have a place to eat. His fame grew, and halachic queries were sent to him from far and wide.

As Pesach in the year 1848 approached, the Jewish community of Semenitz was troubled by an ugly rumor. A band of thugs, under the leadership of the notorious anti-Semitic priest, Hurban, was on the rampage and would be passing through Semenitz on the first night of Pesach. Hurban and his horde were known to travel from town to town, heaping death and destruction in their path.

In anticipation, Rabbi Aszod ordered every man, woman and child to spend the first night of Pesach in the *Beis Medrash*. At midnight, Reb Yehuda instructed ten of his students to scout the outskirts of the city. Within an hour they returned, and informed the *Rav* that they could hear the din of battle. The *Rav* consoled the frightened crowd: "Don't fear, tonight you will witness a great salvation from *Hashem*."

Reb Yehuda purified himself, wrapped himself in his *tallis*, took his shofar and walked out to confront the enemy. Reaching the outskirts of the city, he encountered the mob, with Hurban at the lead, his sword drawn. Reb Yehuda calmly took the shofar, and the night sky reverberated with a loud blast. Overwhelmed with fear, the enemy camp fled. The next morning, hundreds of dead bodies were found. Hurban explained his humiliating defeat by describing the appearance before him of a man whose height reached the very heavens.

When it was rumored that Hurban would be returning, the anti-Semites of the community looked forward to the opportunity to rob and pillage Jewish homes. A baker who was a virulent anti-Semite was determined to kill Reb Yehuda. One *Shabbos* morning, as he walked to *shul* escorted by his followers, the would-be murderer suddenly appeared, his knife drawn. The people around him screamed in panic, but Reb Yehuda continued walking calmly. The baker was so overwhelmed, that instead of stabbing Reb Yehuda, he cut off his own left hand. Reb Yehuda continued on to *shul* and the assailant fled. For years after this episode, the baker spoke of the holiness of Reb Yehuda and of the bitter fate of anyone who dared harm him...Hurban never did return to Semenitz, realizing that it was this *Rav*, and no apparition from Heaven, that had saved the town.

⋖§ Call to Szerdahely

Reb Yehuda served as Rav of Semenitz for twenty-one years, and disseminated Torah to many students. When the community of Szerdahely invited him to become their *Rav*, his heart filled with longing for the city in which he had absorbed so much Torah in his youth. Unfortunately, some opposition to his appointment arose, and Reb Yehuda wanted to remove himself from consideration. The *Ksav Sofer* wrote a letter chastising the leaders of the community for allowing a small group of people to block the appointment of so great a man, urging the community leaders to receive this holy man with the proper respect due him. The controversy ceased, and Reb Yehuda was accepted as *Rav* of Szerdahely, a name that became associated with his own for generations.

Two men who had opposed his appointment traveled to Semenitz hoping to dissuade Reb Yehuda from accepting the position, by stressing the divisiveness it would cause in the community. Reb Yehuda greeted them warmly, but briefly, explaining that he had a busy schedule. After *Shacharis*, the *dayanim* of the city came to discuss matters of *halachah*. When they left, the yeshivah students were already waiting for Reb Yehuda to begin his *shiur*, which continued until the afternoon. Then came the city leaders to discuss *kehillah* problems. After they left, Reb Yehuda returned to his students until *Mincha* and *Maariv*. A large group of people was then waiting to learn Torah until late at night. After that, Reb Yehuda worked on his correspondence for several hours. Such was his daily schedule. The two malcontents were unable to find a spare moment in which to approach Reb Yehuda. They reconsidered their opposition, and became his staunchest supporters.

Szerdahely at that time had some five hundred Jewish families, three hundred of which were headed by *talmidei chachamim*. Reb Yehuda's influence was soon felt throughout the city, and the yeshivah attracted hundreds of *bachurim* from the broad countryside.

⋘ In the Path of the *Chasam Sofer*

As a loyal follower of the *Chasam Sofer*, Reb Yehuda was in the forefront of the battle against Reform and stood firm in his fight to preserve every detail of Torah Judaism.

The liberalism spawned by the French Revolution brought

the ghetto walls tumbling down, exposing its Jews to Western culture for the first time. Intoxicated by the new opportunities profferred them, many were convinced that by shedding all outward signs of their Jewishness, they would be accepted by their gentile neighbors and anti-Semitism would be eradicated. This followed the underlying ideology of the *Haskalah* (Enlightenment), founded by Moses Mendelssohn, which had as its motto: "*Sei ein Jude zur Hause und ein Mentsch in Strasse* — Be a Jew in your home, and a person (gentile) in the street."

Scores of German *kehillos* fell prey to this rallying cry, and the scourge of Enlightenment, coupled with Reform Judaism, spread from Germany to other countries of Europe. It was in large measure due to the valiant battle waged by the *Chasam Sofer* and his followers that Torah Judaism was saved from extinction in his area.

In 1845, a rabbinical conference of Reform rabbis was held in Brunswick, Germany. Many long-standing traditions, such as the recital of *Kol Nidrei* on Yom Kippur, were abolished. The Orthodox rabbis of Germany published a pamphlet condemning this conference, and included letters from Rabbi Yehuda Aszod that proclaimed it the obligation of every G-d-fearing Jew to wage battle against those who would uproot the Torah as given at Sinai.

The early *maskilim* had wanted to alter only the outward image of the Jew, so that he blend more easily into the gentile world. Our *Gedolim* had the foresight to realize that the modification of even one small custom could lead to sweeping defection from our sacred traditions. They therefore forbade even the slightest change of the most minor custom, as articulated by the *Chasam Sofer's* motto: "*Chadash assur min haTorah* — Innovation is prohibited by Torah law!" Much of Rabbi Yehuda Aszod's correspondence with Jews all over Europe — collected in *Teshuvos Mahari* — deal with the clash between tradition and modernity.

One letter from the leaders of the community of Nicholsburg dealt with the question of permitting a non-Jew to cook on *Shabbos* in a coffee house that would be established as a gathering place for Jewish youth. In his response, he expressed shock and dismay at being questioned about a *Shabbos* problem when the prohibition against joining a *moshav leitzim* — a gathering place of scoffers — applied every day of the week. He addressed the fear of the leaders of Nicholsburg that their youth would otherwise mingle with non-Jews, by stating that it was preferable that they continue to frequent those places where they had gathered previously, "and they not introduce innovation in the Jewish street." (See *Teshuvos Mahari, Orach Chaim* 34.)

The traditional Jewish synagogue was one of the first institutions to be "improved" by the Reform movement. The rabbis of Hungary thus forbade even the slightest innovation in synagogue structure based on the prohibition against "going in the ways of their statutes."

Reb Yehuda was once invited by a town to dedicate its new *shul*. Upon his arrival, he noticed the *shul's* domed roof built in the style of the local cathedrals, with the *Asseres Hadibros* (Ten Commandments) engraved on it. He wanted to leave immediately, but his hosts prevailed upon him to remain. He did stay and used the opportunity of his *Shabbos drasha* to warn the community about the dangers of modernization:

Referring to the *passuk* in *Parshas Toldos*, "*Vayisrotzetzu habanim bekirba, vatomar im kain lama zeh anochi, vatailech lidrosh es Hashem* — And the children (fetuses) struggled within her..." Reb Yehuda asked: "If *only* Yaakov struggled to emerge when Rivka passed a house of Torah learning, and *only* Eisav fought to get out when she passed a place of idol worship, why was Rivka feeling such great discomfort?" Reb Yehuda answered, "It was when she passed by a house of Torah like this one that the babies became very agitated. One thought it was a *shul*, the other thought it was a church, and both tried to get out. Rivka asked, 'If this is a church, then *lama zeh anochi*? Why does it say *Anochi* on its roof?' "

Reb Yehuda then made an impassioned plea to the congregation to resist any changes in tradition.... The dome was removed the next day.

⊷ Representing the Jewish Community

After the ill-fated Revolution of 1848, Hungary was permitted to form its own autonomous government within the Austro-Hungarian Empire, and the Minister of Education, Baron Etuash, was appointed ruler. As a gentile, he felt that Jewish interests were best served by encouraging assimilation, and he identified with the goals of the Reformers.

Many Jews had been active in the Revolution of 1848, and the Jewish community had therefore been fined a huge sum of money, as described in the outset of this article. This money was now being reimbursed in the form of a fund for educational and cultural institutions for Hungarian Jews. While both Orthodox and Reform Jews laid claim to the money, it was left to Baron Etuash to make the final decision as to the distribution of the funds. He asked the heads of Hungarian Jewry to organize a congress to represent all of the country's Jews.

The Reform rabbis had close government affiliations and succeeded in rigging the elections for representation to the congress in favor of the Reform faction. Though the congress was canceled, the Orthodox rabbis were fearful of the Reform element gaining control of this large sum of money, for the Reform movement had plans to establish a government-sponsored rabbinical seminary and school system.

An emergency meeting of Orthodox rabbis was held in Uhel, which decided to petition Emperor Franz Joseph to cancel plans for this rabbinical seminary. Seven prominent *Rabbonim* were selected to represent Hungarian Jewry, and after initial difficulty, they were finally granted an audience with Franz Joseph. Rabbi Menachem Ash later expressed the awe he felt toward his traveling companion, Rabbi Yehuda Aszod, who spent the two days en route weeping bitterly and praying that their mission be successful.

When the *Rabbonim* arrived at the palace, they were ushered into a large reception area called "*Shpiegel Zahl.*" This room was mirrored from wall to wall, and was reserved for special guests. While awaiting the arrival of the king, Reb Yehuda suddenly arose, startled, and asked the *Ksav Sofer* who the man sitting across the room was, for the *Shechinah* seemed to be hovering over him, and perhaps he would help them succeed in their mission. The *Ksav Sofer* told him that he was looking at a reflection — of none other than himself. Reb Yehuda sat down in shocked silence. He had never looked into a mirror, nor did he ever have his likeness reproduced during his lifetime.

When Franz Joseph appeared, he expressed feelings of great reverence for the holy men in his presence. As mentioned earlier, the Emperor took their petition under advisement, eventually acceding to their request.

In 5627 (1867) the Shomrei Hadath Organization was formed to unify all the religious *kehillos* of Hungary. The Reform leadership now exerted pressure on the government to convene the congress that had been canceled several years before. Jews from all over the country were invited to come and resolve the controversy once and for all. There was much fraud involved in the selection process, and the Reform delegates greatly outnumbered the Orthodox delegates.

Two weeks before the congress opened, two hundred of Hungary's most prominent *Rabbonim* met to discuss the impending crisis. The *Ksav Sofer*, continuing his father's holy work, described the great dangers threatening Hungarian Jewry and exhorted the *Rabbonim* to stand fast in their resolve.

On 22 Shevat, 5629 (1869), the schism in Hungarian Jewry became official. On that day, the congress announced its decision that the laws of the *Shulchan Aruch* were no longer binding. Rabbi Yehuda Aszod rose before the assemblage and tore his clothes in grief. This was the rallying cry, and more than fifty *Rabbonim* rose as a group and left the congress. Orthodox Jewry now constituted a distinct, separate group.

The *Chasam Sofer* was first to decree that Reform groups not be included in the corporate body of the Jewish people; but it was his loyal *talmidim* who succeeded in fulfilling his designs.

Rabbi Yehuda waged his personal battle against Reform throughout his life, never wavering in his position. He left an indelible imprint on the community he served so faithfully, and up until the destruction of European Jewry during World War II, the Jewish community of Szerdahely could boast that it never had a Neologue Temple.

During the later years of his life, Reb Yehuda suffered family tragedies with the death in their prime of his son and son-in-law, losses from which he never fully recovered. His health declined, and upon the urging of his doctors, he visited the famous baths at Baden to try to recoup his strength. After a few days, he returned, hardly improved, but satisfied that he had fulfilled the words of *Chazal*, exhorting a man to pay heed to the words of his doctors.

Hours before his *petira*, he delivered his usual *shiur*, completing the *Masechta* that he had been learning. That night, while working on his correspondence, writing a letter trying to resolve a conflict between the *Divrei Chaim* and Reb Yirmiya Lev of Uhel, his pen fell from his hand. He cried out: "*Ad kahn techum Shabbos* — until here is the Sabbath boundary." While the members of his household rushed to summon the doctors, he restrained them and said: "The time has come for me to leave this world of falsehood." Soon afterwards, the angels retrieved his holy soul and returned it to its Maker.

Rabbi Yehuda Aszod was succeeded as *Rav* of Dunaszerdahely by his son, Rabbi Aaron Shmuel Aszod. He also left a legacy of many valuable manuscripts, voluminous commentaries on all segments of the Torah. Though many of these were destroyed in the *Churban* in Europe, several are extant. His *Teshuvos Mahari,* a collection of letters and responses organized according to the four sections of the *Shulchan Aruch,* is considered one of the most significant works of its kind.

His greatest legacy, perhaps, is the rebirth of *Yiddishkeit* on American shores after the *Churban* in Europe, for it was in large measure due to the valiant struggle waged by the *Chasam Sofer* and his loyal disciples that Torah-Judaism was saved from annihilation in Europe.

In confronting the irreparable damage that Reform Judaism has inflicted upon our people, we can better appreciate the debt of gratitude we owe Rabbi Yehuda Aszod and those other giants of the spirit for their uncompromising stance against the reformers. For in reality, the battle to preserve the eternal truths of the Torah continues until this very day.

Joseph Friedenson

Heroes of the Warsaw Ghetto

*Fifty Years Since its Destruction:
5703/1943 - 5753/1993*

E very year, with the approach of Pesach, the *Yahrzeit* of the
final liquidation of the Warsaw Ghetto, my father's[1] friends
during those bitter days come to my mind. I feel I owe them a
debt, both personal and communal, to write these lines.

When people talk of the heroes of the Warsaw Ghetto, they usually refer to the handful of fighters who took up arms to battle the Nazi
occupation forces that outnumbered them and surely out-armed them
by far. I want to speak here of the spiritual heroes of the Warsaw Ghetto,
people who labored day and night to help others. They had no time to
pen memoirs, so the story of their heroism is all but forgotten.

But I saw them in action, so I feel that the task is mine—who
else will do it?—to tell their stories....

I. Rabbi Alexander Zushe Friedman, זצ"ל the Beloved Activist of Polish Jewry

Of all my father's good friends in the Warsaw Ghetto, the
one I remember best is Rabbi Alexander Zushe Friedman הי"ד.[2]
He is known to the world for his classic anthology of *Verter* (short
commentaries) on the *Chumash*: *Ma'ayana Shel Torah*. I had known
him personally since my childhood, as he was a frequent guest in

1. My father, Reb Eliezer Gershon Friedenson הי"ד , was active in the *kehilla* of Lodz, a
leader in the World Agudah Movement, one of the founders and a leader of the Beth
Jacob Movement in Poland, and edited *The Beth Jacob Journal* (for adults) and *Kindergarten*
(for children).

2. In spite of his stature as an outstanding *talmid chacham*, he insisted on being called
"Reb" or "Mr.," rather than "Rav" since he held no official rabbinical position.

This article was translated from Yiddish by Miriam Margoshes, who lives in Brooklyn, and is a
teacher in the Beth Jacob High School, as well as a free-lance writer, translator and editor.

our home in Lodz, and he always *farherred* (tested) me when he visited us.

It is no exaggeration to say that Rabbi Zushe Friedman was beloved by all in Jewish Poland. He was a *Gadol baTorah*, a *boki* (thoroughly knowledgeable) in *Shas* and *Poskim*; in his youth he was the youngest student in the Yeshivah of the Sochatzhover Rebbe, the *Avnei Nezer*. Although he never became a *Rav* or *Rosh Yeshivah* by profession, he continued to learn; all his life he was *baal mechadesh*, creative in Torah thought.

Yet his popularity in the Jewish world was not due to his unquestioned greatness in Torah; it was mainly a result of his leadership qualities and active participation in Agudath Israel in Poland. He was *the* spokesman of the Polish Agudah, second only to the Lubliner *Rav*, Rabbi Meir Shapiro, as its most effective, popular speaker. His every speaking tour, particularly in the Polish countryside, was an event. People listened to him spellbound for hours at a time, and his presentations invariably had depth and originality. He was also a talented writer and superb administrator.

For nearly 29 years, he was the organizing force behind the huge Agudath Israel movement in Poland, and the right hand of its president, Reb Itche Meir Levine (son-in-law of the *Imrei Emes*); at the same time he headed the widespread *chinuch* system of over 600 *chadorim* overseen by the Polish Agudah.

But it was in the Warsaw Ghetto that his true glory emerged. It was there that I had the *zechus* to observe him close up. As I recall, Reb Zushe was appointed to the Warsaw *Judenrat* after the Germans took over. But he was somehow able to free himself from the assignment, and instead devoted his energies to organizing aid for the large numbers of *Rebbeim, Rabbonim, Roshei Yeshivos*, and *askonim* who had fled their hometowns to seek refuge in Warsaw and were subsequently trapped in its Ghetto.

Earlier on, Rabbi Zushe had gained the confidence of many circles outside Agudath Israel as well; thus the Warsaw *Judenrat* and the American Joint Distribution Committee (whose previous director, David Guzik, was still active, clandestinely), amongst others entrusted him with hundreds of thousands of dollars to help these refugees. It was not easy to be the provider for hundreds of refugee families who had arrived in Warsaw penniless, with only the clothes on their backs, and who, of course, could find no means of sustenance for themselves in the Ghetto. It required limitless patience and sensitivity; only a person of Rabbi Zushe Friedman's stature could have done it in such a noble, *mentchliche* manner.

A frequent visitor to his quarters, I was invariably amazed at the inner resources he summoned for dealing with so many embittered souls. When I compared him with the executives of other organizations doing similar social work in the Ghetto, the contrast was striking. Other disbursers of funds became transformed into arrogant bureaucrats. More than once I saw professors standing at the doors of young functionaries (even their former students), kept waiting for days for an "appointment." But Rabbi Zushe Friedman showed not a sign of self-importance. He could easily have obtained an office in the "Jewish Self-Help" building and surrounded himself with secretaries and lackeys as the other officials did. But he would not countenance *Rabbonim* and *talmidei chachamim* coming to a public office to stand at the door with hat in hand. So from his own modest apartment he worked *bechein, bechessed uv'rachamim*—with charm, love and kindness. His door was open to all, and his heart even more so.

When he was disbursing aid to each of the hundreds of families, no recipient ever felt that he was receiving a favor. Reb Zushe would lower his eyes in embarrassment if anyone tried to thank him. One might even say that he felt guilty to be the giver and others the takers. In fact, when elderly folks or people of stature were involved, he personally delivered their stipends to them, in their homes.

I have mentioned here only a single aspect of Rabbi Zushe Friedman's activities in the Warsaw Ghetto. Actually, during the four years in the Ghetto he did much, much more. Just as he had headed the *chinuch* activities in the pre-war years, so did he do so in the Ghetto—first, officially when the Germans tolerated them, and later, underground. But that's a story for another occassion. It was the dignity that Reb Zushe personally projected and that he helped preserve for his clients that remains most vivid in my memory.

II. Rabbi Meshulam Kaminer ל״צז, Outstanding Community Leader and *Talmid Chacham*

Rabbi Meshulam Kaminer, a grandson of Reb Yudel Kaminer who was a *mechutan* of the *Chiddushei HaRim*, was about ten years older than my father. He was among the founders of the Agudath Israel in Poland during World War I, and continued to be one of its staunchest pillars until the end.

When the Agudah was founded, he was still a young man, as were most important early Agudists. He was well-learned in *Shas*, as well as in *Tanach*, philosophy and *Kabbala*. At the same time, he was a *Chassid* with every fiber of his being. In short, he possessed an all-encompassing personality. And all of it was at the service of the *Klal*. (He drew no salary for his *Klal* work, as he was independently wealthy.)

The Kaminer family had a reputation for being strong-minded people. The saying was, "Their name suits them" (*kamien* in Polish means "a stone"). But in truth, this was just a facade. They were really *baalei rachamim* and *gomlei chessed*—merciful and charitable people. According to *Chassidim*, the *Chiddushei HaRim* explicitly wished to be *meshadech* with them (his grandson, the *Sfas Emes*, married a Kaminer young lady). Their true character was finally revealed to all in the Warsaw Ghetto.

Rabbi Meshulam Kaminer used his family trait in the service of the *Klal*. When he helped to build the Agudah in Poland, the task required all his strength, stubbornness, perseverance—even audacity.... He undertook to publish the daily newspaper, *Der Yid*, and he carried this project through in spite of vocal opposition and technical difficulties. Since there was no one to write for it, he became a journalist (even though in those years, writers were denigrated in *Chassidic* and *yeshivah* circles). And when the new *chadorim* and Bais Yaakov schools needed textbooks, he—the *lamdam* who could write *chiddushei Torah*—wrote a children's storybook. He used a pseudonym for his newspaper articles, but for the children's books he signed his own name. He wanted everyone to know that to be a *cheder-rebbe* is a noble calling.

Reb Meshulam was strict in running the Warsaw *Kehillah*, too. His harshness was directed against prominent Jews who wanted to avoid paying their fair share of communal taxes, and against those who tried to use their clout in the *kehillah* to advance their own interests. He would tolerate no flattery, under-the-table deals, or endless time-wasting debates. He was a man of action.

Firmness was essential for running the Warsaw *kehillah*, where constant, bitter battles raged with the Bund, Zionists, Folk-Yiddishists, and all the others who wanted to rob the *kehillah* of its true Jewish character. Firmness was also needed to demonstrate that the religious Jews, those "easily-terrorized incompetents," could indeed run a proud and flourishing *kehillah*. Reb Meshulam was one of those who proved it, and he was instrumental in bringing about a great triumph when a Torah-true Jew, the Agudah's candidate, Reb Elya Mazur,[3] was elected *Rosh HaKohol*.

For more than twenty years, Reb Meshulam was a leading figure in the Polish Agudah and active in nearly every one of its projects. He was one of the builders of its large network of *chadorim*, and a key organizer of all the conferences and conventions of Agudath Israel. Interestingly, I have searched through all the old photo archives of *Knessios* and conferences, yet I have not been able to find a single photograph of Rabbi Meshulam Kaminer. Perhaps he simply did not have time for such "nonsense" as posing for pictures. It is also possible that as a committed *Chassid*, with the characteristic Kotzker avoidance of the public eye, he shunned photographs.

I did not know Rabbi Meshulam Kaminer before the war. I had been interested in meeting him, but my father would not take me along when he went from Lodz to Warsaw. He said that Reb Meshulam simply would not be able to understand how he could bring along a *bachur* to "kill time," listening to discussions about politics—even when directed *l'sheim Shamayim*, for constructive purposes.

---

3. Later, Reb Elya Mazur was an Agudath Israel Representative in the Israeli Knesset, along with Reb Itche Meir Levine.

But it was a very different Reb Meshulam whom father finally took me to meet in Warsaw after we had fled Lodz as refugees. He greeted us like brothers, asked for all the details of our escape, and wanted to know what we intended to do in Warsaw and how he could help us. Did we need money? Clothes? "Don't be embarrassed, Eliezer Gershon," he said to my father. "Tomorrow I might be in your shoes. Do you know the Germans? I do. From World War I days when they were our so-called friends. Don't fool yourself—this will go on for years. You won't get back to Lodz to resume your work tomorrow or the next day. You have to figure out how you're going to survive here, and if you need help, we'll help you.

"I'm going to have some spare time now," he went on, "as there's no more Agudah and no more *Kehillah*. I'm planning to devote myself to my *peirush* (commentary) on *Tehillim* that I've worked on and never had time to finish.... Nothing is more important today than *Tehillim*—we are in dire need of *Hashem's* mercy...."

As astute as he was, there was one thing he did not foresee. In the Ghetto, he did not have more time than in the "good years"—he had less! Jews fell dead in the street; they had to be laid to rest. As long as he was alive, he saw to it that the bodies were buried individually instead of in mass graves. Yeshivah *bachurim* were starving; a kitchen had to be set up for them. People were being picked up for forced labor which they could not possibly do—it would kill them; ways had to be created to exempt them. Orphaned children could not be abandoned; they had to be fed and taught. Added to the *Klal* work were the needs of personal friends who had to be helped, too. Our family, which was under his care, was only one of many such families.

With all these and many other duties, he was busy day and night, but he still did not stop working on his *peirush* on *Tehillim*. Over the years, I often wondered what had happened to that *peirush*. But recently, in the book *Ishim Shehikarti* by Dr. Hillel Seidman (who worked with Reb Meshulam in the *kehillah*), I discovered that while in the Ghetto, Reb Meshulam finished the *peirush* of two *seforim* of *Tehillim*. He gathered a roomful of *bnei Torah*, whom he had registered as employees of the *kehillah*, to prepare his notes for publication. Now, officially, they had jobs, thus sparing them from forced labor, for which they were totally unsuited.

Reb Meshulam passed away after Succos, 5702; his was the only big *levaya* (funeral) in the Warsaw Ghetto. A large crowd gathered in spite of the danger that at any moment it could become a target for the German police. It was also the only time in the Ghetto that the brilliant spokesman of Orthodox Jewry in Poland, Rabbi Alexander Zushe Friedman הי״ד, spoke in public.

III. Rabbi Shimshon Stockhammer זצ״ל and His Open Door in the Warsaw Ghetto

Rabbi Shimshon Stockhammer was one of the youngest members of the Warsaw rabbinate and one of the best-liked people in the Warsaw Ghetto.

His friendship with my father stemmed from their work in the Agudah, especially the Agudah press. Rabbi Stockhammer was the rabbinical columnist of the *Togblatt,* and his articles were very popular, even though he often wrote *mussar.* (It was said that he was—unofficially, of course—the *mashgiach* (overseer) on behalf of the *Moetzes Gedolei HaTorah* at the Orthodox *Togblatt.*) My father too was the editor of an important Orthodox journal, so the two had much in common.

Since the passing of Rabbi Dov Ber Meisels, Warsaw had had no Chief Rabbi, but all the members of the Rabbinate were experienced *Rabbanim.* Rabbi Stockhammer was young, and to my knowledge had never been a *Rav* before, even though he was an acknowledged *talmid chacham.* In addition, he was a "foreigner": He came from Galicia and was a Belzer *Chassid* in a city that contained barely a *minyan* of Belzer *Chassidim.*

His appointment to the Warsaw Rabbinate, along with such *Gaonim* as Rabbi Menachem Ziemba, Rabbi Avromele Weinberg, and Rabbi Yaakov Meir Biderman, is quite remarkable. It is an affirmation of his standing with *Rebbeim, Rabbanim, baalei battim,* and the heads of the Warsaw *Kehillah,* and he proved to be a wise choice.

✍ Putting Together the Judenrat

When the war broke out and Adam Cherniakov was ordered by the Germans to set up a Judenrat, he deliberately included on the list of appointees two Rabbanim of the younger generation: Rabbi Shimshon Stockhammer and Rabbi David Shapiro. He felt that they would be able to absorb the physical abuse and beatings they would receive at the hands of the Nazis, while older men would not.

Once named, there was no way out; Rabbi Stockhammer accepted his fate, but with a heavy heart. *Hashem* helped him through the ordeal, because unlike most of the other *Judenräte*, whose members became corrupt through inordinate pressure and a sense of power, the one in Warsaw was headed by another man of great integrity, Cherniakov. Rabbi Stockhammer used his position to actively pursue *chessed* with true *mesiras nefesh*.

Those were bitter times in which Jewish suffering grew from day to day. An influential person was surely no one to envy, constantly beleaguered by Jews in need, while his ability to help was so dreadfully limited! Other members of the *Judenrat* could not take the constant pressure and locked their doors. But not Rabbi Stockhammer. He once told me, "To simply listen to a Jew's troubles is also a *chessed*." He did, however, much more than just listen.

Judenrat members were not required to be at the office every day. The streets were often unsafe—even for a member of the *Judenrat* with a "secure" German permit—especially for a bearded man. Any low-ranking German soldier was empowered to demand the permit and tear it up, no explanation required. Nevertheless, Rabbi Stockhammer showed up at the *Judenrat* office every single day to help those who needed him.

During the early years of the Ghetto, Jewish theaters were flourishing. Rabbi Stockhammer prevailed on Cherniakov to close the theaters during the Three Weeks. Chernikov acquiesced, and as he recorded in his diaries: "The Jewish heart must honor the rhythms of its calendar."

In the Ghetto were several hundred *Rabbanim* and their families who had fled the countryside to "safe" Warsaw. Almost all of them needed help in terms of finding living quarters, food, labor exemptions and so on. To obtain such help, one had to knock on many doors, but not all doors would open. Nor were all the functionaries sympathetic to religious applicants. These people needed an intermediary, someone with influence.

Rabbi Stockhammer was the key for many of them, and he never wearied of the task. Not that it was easy; there were times when his pleas were ignored. But he rarely gave up, and, as I have said, *his* door was never closed.

One time, though, his door was closed, and to me, whom he had always greeted with friendliness! It happened that the son of a neighbor of ours wanted to become a member of the Jewish Ghetto Police. He needed a letter of recommendation from a member of the Judenrat, and my father sent me to get it for him. I was certain there would be no problem, because my father sent along a note saying that he personally knew the applicant to be a decent young man. So I was shocked when Rabbi Stockhammer turned me down abruptly, and said, "No! Go tell your father that I can't do it!"

Then, seeing that I was hurt—could he suspect that my father would mislead him?—he sat me down and explained: "I realize that you can't understand this; you probably think a Jewish policeman is an improvement over a German or Polish one. Yet I must tell you—I don't know why, but the sight of Jewish boys with sticks in their hands frightens me. Who will train them? German officers!... Who can know what they will learn from them? And finally, what will they be ordered to do? I shudder to think about it. Tell your father that it's not that I don't want to do it, but that I just can't; ask your father to forgive me...."

It was not until several years later that I understood his inability to acquiesce, when I found out what was required of our Jewish policemen, and how some could not refuse their orders.... Rabbi Stockhammer saw all this in advance.

Dr. Hillel Seidman writes in *Ishim Shehikarti* that Rabbi Stockhammer evaded the first deportation in November, 1942. Only after his whole family was deported to Treblinka was he captured and dragged off to the camps of Poniatov and Budzin.

After the liberation, people who were with him and Rabbi David Shapiro in the camps spoke of Rabbi Stockhammer with awe. He was a model of *zerizus* in *mitzvos* and of shining *middos*. Rabbi Avrohom Ziemba זצ"ל told me that even the non-*frum* respected him; that Dr. Block, the former director of the Keren HaKeyemes in Poland, who had been non-religious, began to put on *tefillin* in the camp at Budzin, where he had come under the influence of Rabbi Stockhammer.

Rabbi Stockhammer survived until a few days before the liberation. Tragically, he was killed by "friendly fire," in an American bombing raid on nearby Dachau. We may attribute his untimely death to the Nazis who brought about the tragic situation that ended his life, and thus may unhesitatingly conclude: "May *Hashem* avenge his blood!"

◆§ Mussar: Its Mentors and Their Followers

In control of their every thought and emotion no less than they were in command of the ethical texts from which they drew their insights.

written by Miriam Samsonowitz
told by Devora Dessler-Olstein

A Baal Mussar from Kelm
A Businessman in Pre-War Europe

Memoirs of my father, Reb Gedalya Dessler זצ"ל

*In appearance he was
no different from other
honest businessmen,
yet his entire
aspiration in life was
to attain sublime levels
of avodas Hashem*

◄§ Mussar Roots

Looking back from the view of half a century later, my father's personality is as towering to me now as it was when I was a child of ten. Until his death at age sixty-two, he was a guiding light to me and my brothers and sisters in every aspect of our lives. Years later, when we were faced with severe ordeals, the memory of his indomitable personality stood before our eyes and gave us the strength to persevere in our dedication to Torah and *mitzvos*.

My father, Chayim Gedalya Dessler, was born in 1873, the youngest son of Yisroel Dovid Dessler, a wealthy forest contractor in Homel, White Russia. My grandfather and his brother were immensely wealthy, but they were also strictly devoted to Torah and *mitzvos*. They contributed significantly towards maintaining the famous Talmud Torah of Kelm headed by Rav Simcha Zissel Ziv (the *Alter* of Kelm), which was founded in Kelm, Lithuania, relocated to Grubian, Russia, and then finally returned to Kelm.

My father and his older brother, Reb Reuven Dov, studied for many years in the Kelmer Talmud Torah and were profoundly influenced by the personality of the *Alter*. After their marriages, they both settled in Homel, where they managed large industrial enterprises in partnership. Their years in Kelm had left its indelible mark on them; their wealth and their business affairs always remained a secondary concern to them, while Torah study, *mussar* (ethics), and *tikkun hamiddos* (self-improvement) were the real preoccupations of their lives. My uncle and my father were extremely close. For many years they lived together in the same house and ran their businesses and *tzedakah* concerns in partnership, and my uncle's second wife was my mother's sister. They had an unusual system for dividing the profits: each would take what he needed to sustain his family, and the rest would go to *tzedakah*. People were amazed to hear this because my father had five children, whereas my uncle had only one son. Yet such was the love and harmony between them.

ᴥᔟ Relief for Refugees

My childhood memories evoke the stormy years of the Russian Revolution, the pogroms of the Black Hundreds, and the typhus epidemic that ravaged the many refugees from Lithuania and Poland who had fled to Russia. I remember some of the many efforts of my parents and relatives to help anyone they could. During the war, Rabbi Chaim Ozer Grodzenski, who was my uncle's brother-in-law, and Rabbi Elchonon Wasserman lived with us temporarily. Every room in our house was taken over by another family of relatives who had fled inland to Russia from the battlefront.

The hospitals were full of refugees who had fallen sick with typhus. Not only was it difficult to acquire medicine for them, but even food was scarce. My mother took a long roll of linen (an expensive item in those days) to the market and exchanged it for a sack of potatoes. She baked the potatoes in our oven and distributed them to the sick in the hospitals.

Rabbi Katz, from Klikel, Latvia, (father of Rabbi Dov Katz who wrote *T'nuas Hamussar*), and his family sat *shivah* at our home for his wife, who had died in the epidemic. People asked my mother, "You're a mother of five children; how can you bring people who have sick family members into your home?"

"*Hashem* will watch over us," was her firm reply.

Before the war, my father and his brother had founded a *Tiferes Bachurim* (a part-time yeshivah for young men who had to work) in Homel. With the influx of refugees, the student body swelled. I remember one woman from Poland who came to our house with her twelve-year-old son, Tzvi. "Please supervise his studies and keep an eye on him," she requested. Of course, my father did. Not only did he show special interest in him, but he frequently invited this student over to eat on *Shabbosos* and *Yomim Tovim*.*

During the war years, my father would frequently go to the train station to receive refugees — even on *Shabbos*. He would bring them home to us for a meal and sometimes to sleep. When all the beds in our house were occupied, we would take the doors off their hinges and make "beds" out of them.

Every able-bodied man of draft age was taken into the anti-Semitic Russian army — even rabbinical students — unless he was already serving a vital army need. My father and his uncle established an armament factory in Tula. At first, all the workers in their factory were yeshivah *bachurim*. When their army exemptions had been procured, my father hired elderly workers to replace them so they would be free to continue their Torah studies.

---

*After the war, this *bachur* returned with his family to Poland. Years later, in the late '20's, he stole across the border into Lithuania and came to learn in Kelm. When it came time to marry off my eldest sister Chana, many excellent Torah scholars were suggested to her. She refused them all, preferring instead to marry Tzvi Levin, who by then was an eminent scholar. They and their three children were killed by the Nazis in 1941.

◌§ My Father's Fortunes Overturn

The Communists took over Homel in 1920. My uncle Reuven Dov had gone south with my oldest brother David, who needed a specially mild climate for his lung ailment. (It turned out that his constant coughing was from a nutshell lodged in his lung, from which he died soon after.) This saved my uncle from the Communists' hands. My father wasn't as fortunate. As soon as the Communists took over, they confiscated the money, possessions, and businesses of the wealthy. Overnight, my father became destitute, since they wouldn't even give an ordinary job to a person who had been rich. Soon it became difficult even to find food for our family. The Communists confiscated a room in our house and put in a Jewish boarder.

One night, a close friend of my father approached him with a chest of jewels and gold and silver items. His business had already been confiscated, and this was all that was left of his vast holdings. He wanted my father to hold these valuables for him while he escaped the country. My father opened up some planks in the floor and hid the chest.

Our family, though, didn't have such assets to keep us going. The boarder saw that the situation at home was desperate. "Don't you have *some* item of value to sell?" he asked my father. "I'll help you sell it." My father had a small printing press hidden in the wood shack, and he gave it to the man. The next day, the police broke into our house and took my father away. The boarder was really an NKVD informer, one of many who had been planted in the homes of the formerly wealthy to check their every move. We didn't know where my father was for days.

◌§ Imprisonment

They had imprisoned him and were torturing and interrogating him. "Where is your money?" they demanded again and again. He protested that he had none.

One day, he heard the bloodcurdling screams of a woman being tortured in the next room. "That's your wife," they told him. "This will continue until you reveal all." The screams intensified. "They just shot a bullet into her leg. Soon they'll do the same to the other leg," they told him. Finally, the screams stopped. An interrogator burst into the room triumphantly. "She finally told us where the money is hidden — under the floor! But you better tell us yourself to be sure that she didn't leave out a detail, or we'll have to continue with her some more."

After days of starvation, lack of sleep, and torture, my father was caught off guard. "She told you about the chest under the floor!" he exclaimed. "It doesn't belong to us!"

"Aha! Now we got it out of you!" they gleefully spat out...The screaming woman had been just a ruse.

They came to our house that night, ripped up the floor, and took away the chest of jewels. But my father was in graver danger than before. They brought him before a court of three judges for a new crime: letting his family starve instead of giving up his bourgeois valuables. The prosecutor demanded death as the only fitting punishment for this form of "depravity." It was to my father's good fortune that one of the judges had formerly worked for my father. "I know Dessler well," he told the prosecutor. "If he didn't use the money, it wasn't because he wanted to withhold it from the government, but because he would never touch a penny that's not his." They decided instead to give him life imprisonment. For months we didn't know where he had been taken.

Finally we found out that he was imprisoned in Leningrad. An uncle paid a large sum for a food package to be taken to him in prison.

My mother decided to fight the decision of the court. Penniless, she traveled the huge distance to Moscow to appeal to Lenin himself. She rode on top of freight cars all the way. She stood in a line that was blocks long, made up of people with private requests to make of Lenin. When her turn arrived, he agreed to arrange a retrial. My mother hadn't yet returned when we received a telegram: "Dessler to be freed — Lenin." We didn't recognize my father when he returned home, for he was emaciated and his hair had turned completely white.

At home, we asked him if he had received the package of food. His answer astonished us: he had received it on *Shabbos*, and on that very day he was transferred by foot to a different prison in Leningrad that was kilometers away from the first. Since he couldn't carry his *tallis, tefillin,* and *siddur* with him because it was *Shabbos,* he had offered to give the entire food package — a veritable treasure in those turbulent times — to one of the guards if he would carry these objects for him. Keeping *Shabbos* meant more to him than the starvation he was being subjected to daily. My father's sacrifice for *Shabbos* electrified me. Years later, when I was undergoing my own set of trials in Russia, his example helped me to stay strong, time after time.

My father decided that we had to leave Russia immediately, and we settled in Kelm. Reb Reuven and his son Elya Lazer [known to us through his *Michtav M'Eliyahu* — ed. note] had already preceded us there. From their huge fortune, all that remained were 50,000 pounds sterling that they had laid away in an English bank. From this, my uncle and my father decided to start a new business endeavor, because on principle they never wanted to take a cent for their Torah scholarship.

✺§ The Education in Our House

Every aspect of my father's life was a manifestation of his devotion to Torah study and *yiras Shamayim.* The education we received was special; the values he passed on to us penetrated deeply. The fifty years of experience and knowledge that I have since accrued cannot point out one thing my father did that I could criticize.

We were in awe of him; we had only to get one look from my father to put us in line. While he was very reserved in demonstrating his feelings, we were keenly aware of how intensely he loved and cared for us.

We never heard loud voices or screaming in our house. In fact, I never heard an argument between my parents. How shocked I was when, at age fifteen, I passed by a room and heard them quietly disagreeing on a topic. I had always assumed that mothers and fathers automatically had the same view on everything.

I used to wake up in the morning to the *niggun* of his learning, and I would hear the same *niggun* when I fell asleep at night. My father would *daven* with the 6:30 a.m. *minyan* and then would learn until 12:30. My mother begged him to taste some food after *davening,* but he never would. In fact, he fasted every Monday and Thursday to the very end of his life.

There was little talk in our house that did not revolve around some aspect of Torah. My father never spoke about business or money. Food was another topic that was not worth wasting words on. There was no such thing as a child saying, "I don't like this dish!" or "This food is not tasty!" To this day it rankles in me when I hear a person talking about this. If a person felt the food lacked salt, he politely asked for the salt shaker. If he did not want to eat for whatever reason, he excused himself and left without another word, hungering until the next meal. There was no such thing as rummaging in the kitchen to find something else.

Shabbos was unquestionably the focal point of the week. Even as children we felt that the main purpose of meals on *Shabbos* was to educate us in *yiras Shamayim* and Torah. Each meal took two hours, and most of it was spent listening to my father talk. He spoke continually of *tikkun hamiddos,* and frequently he brought in the *parshah* or something he was learning. Once my brothers got into a fight. That elicited long discussions for days about how terrible *machlokes* (disagreement) is. One time I commented to a friend of mine who attended a different school that a girl in my class had received a low mark. My comment got around and brought a pile of disciplinary measures on my head. In school, I was penalized for a week by not being allowed to answer questions in class, and my classmates were not allowed to speak to me. At home, there were long talks for weeks on how detrimental it was to speak *lashon hara,* and how we must always look for the positive in people. No finger was pointed at me; it wasn't necessary. The lesson I learned was more effective than any punishment. Another time a fire broke out and burned our house down. My sister grabbed an insignificant object and ran out of the house to save it. Father spoke to us then about why, in a moment of panic, a person loses his head.

There was so much more to my father that I cannot even tell. He dressed and lived simply, and did business no differently than any other honest businessman, but his whole aspiration in life was to attain those sublime levels in *avodas Hashem* that were the outlook of all who went through the Kelmer Talmud Torah. He did an amazing amount of *chessed* too, but, like a true *mussar* personality, he was an expert at hiding it from the eyes of everyone, including his family. Many times he would leave for work in the morning and get sidetracked doing a *chessed* for a widow, a *kallah*, or a *niftar*.

⋐§ Living in Poverty

From 1922 until 1928, my uncle and father made three different attempts to start a business, but each time the effort ended in heavy losses.

After the last attempt, our financial situation was precarious. We had to move out of our large house to a small flat. Small daily expenses became an ordeal. Every month my father strained to find the money for our school tuition. Even fresh bread had become too expensive for us to afford. But of all these new developments, what pained my father the most was that he was now saddled with debts.

When, in 1926, he saw that a small town could not offer him financial opportunities, he went to Kovno. He contacted a former chemical manufacturer from Hamburg with whom his father had done business, and wrote him: "I'm Dessler's son and I've come into hard times. But if you give me the materials I want on credit, I will pay you as soon as I get remitted." The answer came back: "Since you're Yisroel Dovid Dessler's son, I'll give you anything you want." He became a manufacturer's representative, selling chemicals to different factory owners.

In Kovno he rented a small apartment with two other men. He spent all week there and occasionally came home for *Shabbos*. He subsisted on salty herring and bread, and would eat cooked meals only on *Shabbos*. "How could I afford luxuries if I owe people money?" was his answer to us when we found out years later about it. He did not buy clothes for years and did not even come home every *Shabbos* so that he could pay off his debts more quickly.

My mother also worked to pay our debts. One year she managed a small estate with a flour mill that she had inherited with her three sisters from her mother. People were amazed at how brave she was to undertake this work all alone in the middle of nowhere. Every few weeks I would walk over twenty-four kilometers to Kelm with a sum of money that would go towards paying off a bit more of the debt.

✑ Difficult Years in Kovno

In 1929 our family moved to Kovno. We lived very modestly because we still had debts to pay off.

My oldest brother had been suffering from leg tuberculosis on and off. Finally, in 1936, my mother had to leave with him for Switzerland. For three years she nursed him back to health, but these added expenses were a big drain on our finances.

The three years until 1939 were difficult ones for our family. My mother was in Switzerland, my sister Reva was in England visiting with Elya Lazar, and only my father and I were together in Kovno. Relations with Germany had become worse over the years, so my father had given up his business with the Hamburg company and had become an insurance agent for an English firm. But he carried on his way of life no differently than before. He would often go with Rabbi Gershon Gutman, a *dayan* in Kovno, to collect for all kinds of needs. *Erev Shabbos* he went with him from store to store to remind Jews to close early for *Shabbos*. Above all, I remember his Torah study, which he pursued with the same diligence as before.

We became very close during this period. I helped him out in his business often. He would frequently point out that financial stature is fleeting and unimportant. He would remind me of how my mother worked so hard for us, and of all of the things that she had done for us. He did not spare a word of praise if he felt my efforts deserved it. It was not important whether the food I prepared for him was tasty or not, only that I had worked hard to make something tasty for *Shabbos.*

In 1937, my father fell sick with cancer. The doctors in Kovno were unable to treat it, so I traveled with my father to Paris. The doctors in Paris sent us to the biggest expert on this disease, who was then in Strassbourg. After examining my father, he took me aside and told me that there was nothing to be done.

We returned to Kovno in the summer of 1937. My father had asked the doctor months before how to prepare himself so he could fast on Yom Kippur. The last Pesach, he insisted on eating a full *kezayis* of *marror*, even though by then it was very difficult for him to swallow anything. He was losing weight constantly and suffering great pain, but we never heard one groan or complaint from him. He would never tell us, "I can't eat now because it hurts." He would merely refuse with a gesture and say, "There's no need for that now." Only months later did I understand how poor his health was even then, because he hid everything from us.

My sister was still in England visiting with Elya Lazar, who had tried to find her a suitable match. My father had written him immediately upon returning to Kovno: "I want Reva to have a *ben Torah*. It doesn't matter if they don't have money."

After Pesach his condition worsened and he had to be hospitalized. But he strengthened himself and called for his close friend Rabbi Gershon Miyadnek, the *Rosh Yeshivah* in Kelm. A few days later, Rav Gershon came in with a Kelmer yeshivah *bachur* to see him. I left right away. Only weeks later did I find out what the meeting was about: he had asked this *bachur*, whom he had known during the years we lived in Kelm, if he would marry Reva. Reva was beautiful and graced with every virtue. Her outstanding quality was her selflessness; all she ever thought about was what she could do for others. So it wasn't hard for Ziesel Levin to agree. My father telegrammed Reva that he had a *chassan* for her and that she should come home. It was typical of all of us that our father's word was so highly respected that it was considered almost inviolable. Reva agreed right away and prepared to come home for her engagement.

⤙ A Businessman's Tribute

My father was getting weaker and weaker. My mother and I maintained a constant vigil by his bed. On the last day of his life, *Erev Lag B'Omer* 1938, he kept slipping into semiconsciousness. I would alarm the nurse, who would give him an injection to revive him.

During his last minutes, I was at my father's bedside together with Rabbi Miyadnek, Rabbi Gutman, and my brother-in-law. When he lost consciousness again, I cried out for the nurse to come. She shrugged her shoulders this time. "Why do you torture your father?" she rebuked me. "Don't you see that he has only four minutes to live?"

My father opened his eyes and quietly replied, "Nurse — if you know how to use them, four minutes are also important." With great effort, he turned to me and said, "Devora'la, no matter what difficulties you come across in life, always face them with the *chinuch* that we gave you in our house." I replied tearfully, "How could you think otherwise, Papa!"

He closed his eyes, and we saw his lips saying the *Viduy* (confessional prayer). And then he was still.

My sister had been delayed in Germany one day in transmit. When she arrived, the funeral possession had just begun; she had missed seeing my father alive by a few hours. The street was black with people who had come to the *levayah*.

They eulogized my father in four *shuls* in Kovno. I heard things about him that our family had never known. At some of the eulogies there was so much crowding that we could not even come in ourselves.

During the *shivah*, many prominent *rabbonim* and communal figures came to visit us. But one person I never forgot was a businessman who paid us a call and told us, "I heard many *rabbonim* eulogizing Reb Gedalya. But you haven't said all there is to say unless you have a businessman come and testify about him. He was so impeccably upright in his dealings that he preferred to lose big profits rather than to do one thing that was slightly wrong. Only a businessman who knows how tempting the world of commerce is can bear witness to how exceptional Reb Gedalya was."

Rabbi Moshe Rosenstain, זצ"ל: Mashgiach of the Yeshivah of Lomza

He brought the pursuit of Torah ethics and purity in service of Hashem to a leading Yeshivah in Poland

Every yeshivah puts its own imprint on its *talmidim*—usually the product of a combination of factors: the *Roshei Yeshivah*, the *Mashgiach*, the background of the *talmidim*, even the community where it is located. Thus the Lomza Yeshivah, founded in 1883 by Reb Lazar Shulavitz[1], was unique for many reasons, among them—in its later years—the unusual *tzidkus* and *yashrus* (saintliness and integrity) of the *Mashgiach*, Rabbi Moshe Rosenstain זצ"ל. His *seforim*, containing transcriptions of his *mussar shmuessen* (ethical discourses), of course convey his thinking in detailed exposition,[2] but the very title of his third *sefer*[3] says it in

---

1. See Chaim Shapiro's "Lomza: A Yeshivah Grew in Poland," JO March '78.
2. *Yesodei Hadaas*, vol. 1, 2
3. Published by Rabbi Shimon Morduchowitz, זצ"ל

just two words: *Ahavas Meishorim,* expressing his *love* for *Hashem* as a product of his uncompromisingly logical ("*straight*") thinking.

Whoever learned in Lomza Yeshivah will never forget the way the *Mashgiach* walked the aisle between the *shtenders* for hours on end. The Lomza Yeshivah probably had the longest *beis midrash* of all *yeshivos* in Europe, stretching scores of meters from the entrance door at the rear to the "*Mizrach* wall." The *Mashgiach* would pace that aisle back and forth, for miles—literally—every day. He once explained, "It takes many hours of thinking to come up with one pure thought." Among the products of his pure intellectual searching was his intense love for *Hakadosh Baruch Hu.*

Everyone in the Yeshivah was convinced that during his daily, unending stroll, the *Mashgiach* was totally detached from his surroundings, fully engaged in heavenly matters, yet a *talmid* once announced within his earshot: "With this *Tosafos* we can take care of Reb Akiva Eiger's *kushya,*" smacking of a dismissing tone toward Rabbi Akiva Eiger. In his next *shmuess,* the *Mashgiach* expressed shock about the *talmidim's* lack of awe for a Torah giant of the stature of Rabbi Akiva Eiger.

In the view of the *talmidim,* the *Mashgiach* personified the *Litvak par excellence.* Yet every morning, including *Shabbos* and *Yom Tov,* he prepared himself for *davening* by going to the *mikveh.* According to those who were present, he dipped himself in the waters no less than one hundred times. He would walk the great distance from the *mikva* with his hat practically over his eyes, looking only to the ground, avoiding eye contact with man or beast.

Rabbi Shimon Morduchowitz זצ״ל writes: "We *talmidim* knew that before us stood a holy man of the highest *madreiga* (level), whose mind never entertained a *machshava beteilla* (idle thought). In spite of his effort to hide his *tzidkus,* we were keenly aware of his *ge'onus* (genius) in *mussar* and *kedushah.* We were certain that he had overcome any tendency to material, earthly desires, for he was totally immersed in spirituality and G-dliness."

During the week, he slept in a dormitory room next to the *Beis Hamussar*—a room in the Yeshivah where a person could retreat to devote himself to thinking *behisbodedus* (in solitude). He would go home for *Shabbos*, but walk back to the Yeshivah to deliver a *mussar shmuess* (the third *shmuess* of the week). He fasted every day, for thirty years. In the evening, after *Maariv*, a *talmid* would bring him some food from the Yeshivah kitchen.

When his wife complained about him, he promised her one half of his *Gan Eiden* and *Olam Habba*. Upon her request, he wrote up a contract committing himself to his promise. Before she died, she asked Reb Yisrol'ke Zembrover (Rabinowitz), the oldest *talmid*—and the greatest *tzaddik*—in the Yeshivah, to place the document under her head in the *kever*![4]

◆§ Around the Clock With Reb Moshe

The city of Lomza was located on a hilltop, at the foot of which runs the Narev River. Every morning, Reb Moshe would stand at his window, watching the sun rise across the river, to appreciate the glory of the renewal of *Ma'aseh Bereishis*, G-d's act of Creation.

Unlike the common practice of *shokelen* (swaying) during *davening*, he would stand motionless during the entire *davening*. One Friday, after *Shemoneh Esrei*, he broke out weeping, whispering, "We've lost him!" Four hours later, a telegram arrived that the *Chofetz Chaim* was *niftar*.

Reb Moshe's ability to "read" faces was legendary. Once a professor of psychology asked him how one can recognize the face of a murderer. Sometimes his facial features and expressions are so delicate, you would never think that the man is capable of brutality. Reb Moshe replied, "To a murderer, killing a person is like slicing a *challeh*, like killing a fly. Yet, at some point in his life, he is struck with a spark of remorse, a moment of *teshuvah*, and then

---

4. The Germans entered Lomza on Rosh Hashanah night. Reb Yisroel was sitting at his regular place, where he had sat for so many years, learning all by himself. A German officer walked into the Yeshivah, and was so impressed by the one man sitting and singing to himself, that he politely asked Reb Yisroel to come to the door. The Zembrover did not pay the Nazi any heed, and continued learning. The German apologized and left! He was the last one to leave the Yeshivah building. He locked the doors and took along the keys, with the Yeshivah's financial assets, 1500 Zloty. He then left for Russia together with some other *talmidim*. When he was crossing the border, a guard opened fire. Witnesses claimed to have seen Reb Yisroel falling to the ground, presumably dead. After saying *Kaddish* for him for three months, he was discovered to be alive and well! While in Russia, he married, and eventually came to America, where he established a fine family of *Bnei Torah*. He published a two volume *sefer*, *Kol Bo Hechodosh*.

there is a change in his face. That is the sensitivity you discern."

One of the *bachurim*, Aaron Gildin—a happy fellow whose face was always graced with a smile—entered the *Mashgiach's* room to ask him if he would like to send a telegram to a *talmid* in honor of his *chasunah*. After he wrote the text for a message, the *Mashgiach* dismissed the boy, and then asked his son-in-law, Reb Leib Pruskin (son of Rabbi Pesach Pruskin—see JO June '78), who was present, if he had noticed anything unusual about Gildin's face. Reb Leib replied in the negative: "He seems as happy as ever."

The next day, Friday, Gildin had terrible pains. A doctor was summoned, and he could not determine the cause. On *Shabbos*, the boy requested to see the Rosh Yeshivah and the *Mashgiach*. The Rosh Yeshivah, Reb Yeshua Zelig Ruch, came at once. (Reb Yechiel Mordchai Gordon was then in America). The boys hesitated disturbing the *Mashgiach*, but Reb Leib Pruskin, recalling his father-in-law's remark the day before, called the *Mashgiach* at once.

The *Mashgiach* asked everyone to leave the room, and then talked to Gildin for several hours. The patient then turned his head to the wall, and returned his *neshamah* to heaven, leaving this life in *teshuvah*.

※ ※ ※

One day, as Reb Moshe was walking the Yeshivah aisle, he suddenly stopped and announced, "This week no one should go swimming!" (During the summer, the boys would go swimming in the river, especially on Fridays). One boy did not hear the statement, or chose to ignore it, and went swimming—and drowned.

⤴ Face Value

Rabbi Lazer Shulavitz, the founder of the Lomza Yeshivah, would tell an episode from his *Rebbi*, Reb Yisroel Salanter; its message set the tone for the Yeshivah, especially for the *Mashgiach*, who was, after all, an observer of human faces. Reb Yisroel Salanter once met a man *Erev Yom Kippur*, whose face expressed sorrow and anguish, having dreadful impact on whomever he encountered. Reb Yisroel asked him, "Reb Yankel, what happened? Did someone *challila* pass away?"

Reb Yankel replied, "Nothing happened, but tomorrow is the *Yom Hadin*, and I'm worried, frightened!"

Said Reb Yisroel Salanter, "Your heart is a *reshus hayachid*, a private domain, and in that corner you can be as terrified as you wish. But your face is a *reshus horabbim*, public domain. You have no right to alarm people like that. The rule requiring everyone to welcome others *besaiver panim yafos*—with a pleasant countenance—even applies to Yom Kippur."

Reb Moshe would underscore the above message with a *pasuk* in *Shir HaShirim*, "חכללי עינים מיין—*chaklili einayim*, shiny eyes [happy eyes, are better] *miyayin* than a glass of wine. *Ul'ven shinayim*, white teeth [a smiling face, is better] *mechalav*, than milk." Reb Moshe was indisputedly a *tzaddik* who was constantly aware of being in the presence of *Shamayim*, yet he practiced this principle, his face always wreathed with joy.

⋙ Torah and Character

The newspapers reported that a Russian scientist had succeeded in transplanting the head of one animal onto the body of another one. Asked Reb Moshe, "Suppose they succeed in grafting Bismark's head onto a horse's body. What do you suppose would happen? The horse could utilize Bismark's brilliant mind to pick out the best pasture, the greenest grass, to satisfy his animal desires.

"*Chazal* tell us, 'There is wisdom amongst the nations—believe it!' But they use it to fulfill their natural desires. If, however, they tell you, 'There is Torah amongst the nations—do not believe it.' Torah is a medium for guiding the human being to overcome his inclinations, to strive for spirituality, and to elevate his actions. This they do not have."

In 1934 a terrible pogrom took place in the town of Przytik. College students joined the mob in clubbing Jews on the head. (Jewish boys fought back with guns, killing some of the hooligans.) Said Reb Moshe in his *shmuess* that week, "They call themselves 'university students.' They attach grandiose names to their cultural attainment through higher education. In reality, those institutions of so-called learning are corrupt: they produce hooligans and murderers! That's what the *Zohar* means when it comments in regard to the *pasuk*, 'The days of Sarah were a hundred year (*shana*), twenty year (*shanah*), and seven years (*shanim*)' (*Bereishis* 23,1). Referring to the larger numbers, the Torah uses the word '*shana*'—the singular form for year, while with the small number (seven), it says '*shanim*'—plural. Thus the *Zohar* concludes: 'Whatever seems great is actually little, and whatever seems little is actually great!'

"Their bloated titles are nothing but a cover-up to conceal their deficiencies in character, while they graduate hooligans and murderers. We employ modest names like '*cheder*,' 'Talmud Torah,' 'yeshivah,' and look what we produce!"

• Everyone quotes the *Chazal* that "even a *reykan* (empty person) can be as full of *mitzvos* as a pomegranate [is full of seeds]," to give value to even the most ordinary fellow. As a *Baal Mussar*, Reb Moshe added his observation that "a person can be full of *mitzvos* and still be a *reykan*, 'empty,' if he does not have control of himself."

• It was the custom of the city's *Rav* to deliver a *mussar shmuess* to the Yeshivah during *Asseres Y'mei Teshuvah*. Reb Archik Baksht[5] delivered a *shmuess* quoting the passage from *Tehillim*, "As far as the east is from the west, so far had He removed our transgressions from us" (*Tehillim* 103, 12).

The next day, the *Mashgiach* cried in his *shmuess*, "But what can we do if the sins are lying in our laps?" After expounding on a *teshuvah* theme, he concluded with a plea, "If you want to feel the *taam* (taste) of your *Olam Habba*, open yourself up to the *hergesh* (feeling, awareness) of *kedushah* (sanctity) right here! Your *hergesh* of *Kedushas Shabbos, Yom Tov, Yom Kippur* and *Eretz Yisrael*!"

◆§ When Reb Moshe and Aaron Led the Way

In August 1920, Poland declared war against the Soviet Union. Backed by Western powers—primarily France and England—Poland was intent on stopping the spread of Communism beyond Russia's borders. A general mobilization was put into effect, and while Christian divinity seminaries were granted deferments, the anti-Semitic Polish Government refused to defer students of the Lomza Yeshivah, the only such yeshivah in all Poland.

---

5. *The Jewish Observer*, Oct. '72

The *Rosh Yeshivah*, Rabbi Yechiel Mordechai Gordon,[6] went to Warsaw to intervene. He approached the dean of the Jewish members of the Sejm (the Polish parliament), Dr. Noach Prilucki, an old *maskil*. Prilucki would only offer deferment to the yeshivah students if the yeshivah would incorporate some secular studies in the curriculum.

"A decision such as this," replied Reb Yechiel Mordechai, "I cannot take upon myself. I must seek advice."

"Even though in the meantime your boys are being drafted and sent to the battlefield?" asked Dr. Prilucki.

"Yes, even at that price," replied the *Rosh Yeshivah*.

Back in his hotel room, he fell asleep and dreamed of the *pasuk*: *"All leaven or honey you shall not burn as an offering to Hashem," Foreign elements—neither sour nor sweet—can ever be mixed before Hashem.* The message was obvious, but Reb Yechiel Mordechai would not rely on a dream to close a yeshivah. The war made communicating with the Chofetz Chaim or Reb Chaim Ozer Grodzenski of Vilna impossible, so Reb Yechiel Mordechai returned to Lomza to seek the advice of the *Mashgiach*.

After much consideration, the *Mashgiach* said, "It is clear that *Hakadosh Baruch Hu* requires *mesiras nefesh* from us for Torah. We are not obligated to display *mesiras nefesh* for secular studies, however. We cannot mix the two; *kodesh* and *chol*—the sacred and the profane—cannot dwell together."

"But boys are being drafted," protested the *Rosh Yeshivah*.

The *Mashgiach* was a firm believer in the Vilna Gaon's "*Goirel*," a lottery that indicated a decision through selection of a *pasuk*. The quotation selected—a Divine command to Moshe— read: "From twenty years old and upward, all that are able to go forth to war in Israel: you shall number them by their hosts, you and Aaron" (*Bamidbar* 1, 3).

His own name was Moshe, so with a student by the name of Aaron (Zlotowitz[7]), he set out to solve their dilemma, in accordance with the command in the *pasuk*. They established contact with the chairman of the local draft board (he refused to accept the

6. *The Jewish Observer*, Jan. '76
7. Rabbi Aaron Zlotowitz, ל"צז, later settled in America where he was active in *Rabbanus* and in Agudath Harabbonim, and raised a family with exemplary *bnei Torah*.

Polish Zloty). He agreed to free all the *bnei Torah* for American dollars. It was illegal to possess dollars, but these were his terms.

The *Mashgiach* justified this "illegal" approach, for *bnei Torah* should have been deferred as were Christian divinity students, except for Polish anti-Semitism that denied them their legal rights.

If Poland was anti-Semitic, the army was tenfold worse. Honoring *Shabbos* and *kashrus* was practically impossible. Hence, *bnei Torah* from all *yeshivos* threatened by military conscription arrived in Lomza finding a place to learn, with room and board, thus establishing residency there. With the necessary funds in American currency, they were safe. For the next twenty years—as long as Poland was independent—Lomza served as a haven for such *bnei Torah*.

✣ Early Years

Reb Moshe was born in the Lithuanian town of Uzvent in 1881. In his teens, he went to Telshe, becoming a *talmid* of Rabbi Shimon Shkop. His mother made a *shidduch* between the girl next door and the then-unknown Reb Yerucham Levovits, who later became the famous *mashgiach* of Mir[8]. At the age of 19, Reb Moshe came home for Pesach, and encountered for the first time a *Baal Mussar*, the *chassan*, Reb Yerucham. The two found a strong affinity for each other. Reb Moshe would call Reb Yerucham "my *Rebbi*," while Reb Yerucham would refer to him as "my *chaver*"— titles they used for the rest of their lives. Reb Moshe described his first encounter with Reb Yerucham: "I knew very little about *Mussar*. In that initial conversation I asked Reb Yerucham: 'How do you explain that *Bnei Yisrael*, who had witnessed so many *nissim*, nonetheless committed such terrible sins?'"

He had expected the young *chassan* to respond with a deep philosophical explanation. Instead, Reb Yerucham burst out crying, shedding many tears. In a *mussar nigun* he quoted the verses from *Tehillim*: ארבעים שנה אקוט בדור "Forty years I was angry with that generation, and said that they are an errant-hearted people, who know not My ways" (91, 10).... "That response," said Reb Moshe, "conveyed more to me than an abundance of words. It opened my eyes to a *Mussar* personality!"

---

8. *The Jewish Observer*, June '77.

"And then there was that day at the end of a summer," recalled Reb Moshe. "We were sitting in his room with an open *Gemara*, discussing a Torah topic. His mother-in-law appeared at the door of an adjacent room and glowered at me. She went away, and then returned to repeat her performance several times. Neither she nor he said a word about what was troubling her, so we continued our discussion of the *Gemara* for some time, until I went home. The next day I learned that his wife was giving birth to his first son! And—as if nothing were happening—he continued our discussion! That's a man of *mussar*! After that, whenever the opportunity arose, we walked and talked for hours on Torah and *mussar* topics.

"I had hoped that he would take me with him to Kelm, to immerse myself in *mussar*. But it was not till three years later, when I was 23 and a half, that he took me to Kelm."

Rabbi Morduchowitz recalled that when he left Poland for *Eretz Yisrael*, and he took leave of the *Mashgiach*, the latter said to him, "Surely you'll stop over in Mir. Please tell Reb Yerucham that I have a complaint against him. Why did he wait three long years to take me to Kelm?" [Seliv, Rabbi Murdochowitz's home town, was near Mir].

It was in Kelm that Reb Moshe gained the title, "*Ish HaEmmes*—the man of Truth," a strange appellation for a *tzaddik*—which *tzaddik* is not an *Ish HaEmmes*? In Lomza, however, his identification with truth was so evident, that one felt pressed to refer to him that way. His influence on the *bnei Torah* of Lomza was such that all understood that one must be *Emmes* with *Shamayim*, *Emmes* with others, *Emmes* with oneself—even *Emmes* with the *yeitzer hara*, or else one will never defeat it. And as every yeshivah contains a certain uniqueness that remains with the *talmid* for the rest of his life, for the Lomzerite, *Emmes* was second nature.

"Before the terrible times was the *Tzaddik* recalled" (*Yishayahu* 57, 1). Similarly, before the *Churban* of World War II, Heaven gathered up a number of *tzaddikim*, all within a few months: Reb Chaim Ozer Grodzenski, Reb Shimon Shkop, Reb Boruch Ber Leibowitz, זכרום לברכה, were *niftar*... and Reb Moshe Rosenstain on Erev Pesach 5701/1940, at the age of 59.

Rabbi Mordechai Schwab, זכר צדיק לברכה

Personification Of A Mussar Life

Reb Mordechai was an inspiration to all who came in contact with him. One invariably left his presence with a resolve to become a better person and a great servant of Hashem

Perhaps my *shver*, Rabbi Mordechai Schwab, זצ"ל[1], would not have approved of these lines. He certainly would not have appreciated this public accolade. Indeed, some who knew him expressed surprise that he did not request in his will that no eulogies be given at his *levayah* (funeral). At first, it does seem odd. I had occasion to observe him at a dinner at which he was being honored. Speaker after speaker noted the impact that "the *Mashgiach*" had upon his life. I observed him closely, looking for those subtle protestations one would expect from one with less than pure humility. There was none of it. His face was frozen and

---

1. The author referred to Rabbi Mordechai Schwab as "my *shver*"—Yiddish for "father-in-law"—throughout his manuscript, in deference to his relationship with him. To facilitate the reading, we have changed the text to refer to him by name.

expressionless. Nevertheless, one who knew him well could surely detect pain. He was being subjected to torture. Why then didn't he avoid this discomfort and request that no eulogies be said? In addition, the *seforim* note that excessive eulogies and exaggerations cause difficulties for the soul of the departed. He is closely scrutinized by the heavenly court to determine if he really exemplified those praises. Wouldn't this alone be sufficient reason to forgo the usual eulogies?

To one who knew and understood my *shver*, however, the answer should be apparent. He lived a life of concern for others. His own needs were secondary to the needs of others. He would willingly submit to discomfort—but in fact he experienced no discomfort—if he knew he was helping someone else. There certainly is valid reason to decline eulogies. But what of the bereaved family who takes consolation in speaking or hearing about the *niftar*? What of the long-time acquaintance who comes prepared to deliver a *hesped* and is not given the opportunity? During his life, my *shver* willingly endured anything to give satisfaction to another person. He certainly would not have wanted to cause anyone disappointment. Thus, we hope that he would not object to this article if perhaps even one reader might be inspired to emulate him.[2]

His Origins

Reb Mordechai was born *motza'ei Tishah B'Av* 5671 (August 4, 1911) in Frankfurt am Main to *Hachover* Reb Yehudah (Leopold) and Chana (Erlanger) Schwab. His father was one of the *ba'alei battim* of Rabbi Shlomo Zalman Breuer, ל״צז, and was steeped in the tradition of Rabbi Shamshon Raphael Hirsch, ל״צז[3]. Nevertheless, he was among the first to permit his sons to pursue a comprehensive Torah education in Lithuania.

---

2. Since he was opposed to stories about *gedolim* that left the reader with nothing more than admiration and awe, we limited this article to those anecdotes and stories that should be inspiring and instructive.

3. Frankfurt Jews were unique in their steadfast adherence to their tradition. When Mr. Schwab was drafted into the German Army, he refused to cut off his beard. While in the army, he exhibited remarkable *mesiras nefesh* for observance of *mitzvos*. Although he was a businessman, he had a private *rebbe* come to his house each morning at 5:00 AM to learn for an hour before *davening*. He himself delivered a *shiur* each evening for young men. My *shver's* mother was exceptional in her *tzenius*. He told that he never saw even a single hair of his mother's head.

Reb Mordechai was brought to Lithuania by his older brother, יבל"ח, Reb Shimon, שליט"א, and was subsequently joined by his younger brother, Reb Moshe, זצ"ל. As a lad of eighteen, he entered the *Beis Hamidrash* in Mir during the *mussar seder*. The sight of hundreds of young men studying *mussar* and subsequently *davening Maariv* with such fervor on an ordinary night had such an impact upon him that he was inspired to dedicate his life to Torah. After studying in Mir with great *hasmadah* (diligence) for three years, setting a pattern he followed for life,[4] he spent seven years in Kamenitz, under Rabbi Boruch Ber Lebovitz, זצ"ל, whom he considered his *Rebbe*.[5] At the outbreak of World War II, he joined the other yeshivah students who escaped to Vilna. From there, he and his wife, the former Yenta Buchalter, escaped with the Mirrer Yeshivah across Russia to Japan and eventually to Shanghai, where they remained throughout the war. During the war, he was actively involved, together with Rabbi Chaim Shmulevitz, זצ"ל, in the procurement and distribution of relief funds for the *bnei hayeshivos*.[6] At the close of World War II in 1946, he, together with the rest of the Mirrer Yeshivah, arrived at these shores.

৵৪ His Struggles

Life was very difficult for Reb Mordechai in this country. Unable to find a fitting position, he tried his hand at several jobs: he worked for a time as a bookkeeper[7], later he sold wine on commission. He had difficulty properly supporting his family with

---

4. This is a facet of his personality that is often overlooked.

5. It is told that even at this time he was recognized by his *rabbe'im* for his exemplary *middos* and *yiras Shamayim*. Rabbi Reuvain Grozovsky זצ"ל, son-in-law of Reb Boruch Ber, once remarked to Rabbi Shimon Schwab that Reb Mordechai's *yiras Shamayim* was in the realm of Reb Boruch Ber's.

6. He was chosen for this task because of his familial relationship with Mr. Robert Guggenheimer, president of the Swiss Agudah, who worked in conjunction with the Joint Distribution Committee in providing funds for the refugees in Shanghai.

7. He worked for a company that provided packages for the poor in *Eretz Yisrael*. People would pay a specific sum of money, and a voucher for that amount would be sent to a recipient in *Eretz Yisrael*. The recipient would then present this voucher at a warehouse and receive a package. Once, Reb Mordechai sold an eighteen dollar voucher to an individual and informed him several days later that the voucher had been sent to *Eretz Yisrael*. The individual protested that he had not ordered the voucher but had merely inquired as to its cost. Reb Mordechai assured him that it was no problem to cancel the voucher. Later, he reconsidered the matter and realized that the poor recipient would surely be disappointed when notified of the cancellation. He therefore decided to pay for

the income these jobs provided. Although he devoted every spare moment to Torah study[8], he longed to return to full-time involvement in Torah.

He would often say that one can become ennobled by difficulties. *Hashem* places difficulties only in the path of one with the strength and means to persevere. He spoke from experience. Unbeknown to the public, he was troubled with difficulties and anxieties throughout most of his life.

◦§ Teaching Torah, At Last

An opportunity to find a position in Torah presented itself when a *Yeshivah Ketanah* in Williamsburg needed a second grade *rebbe*.[9] After teaching there for several years, he was offered and he accepted a similar position in a *cheder* founded by Reb Rafael Eisenberg in Monsey, N.Y. Four years later, he took the position of ninth grade *rebbe* at Mesifta Beth Shraga in Monsey. By this time, he was over fifty. It was not until he was well over sixty that this position developed into that of a full-time *Mashgiach*.

> The Gemora (*Eiruvin13b*) states that "Whoever pushes time (i.e., he tries impatiently to hurry his success), will be pushed away by time (he will not succeed). Whoever yields to time, time will yield to him (he will eventually succeed)" — see Rashi. Reb Mordechai Schwab often said, "Men darf zich lozzen fihren — one must permit himself to be led." If one has sufficient trust that all that Hashem does is for the good, it is not too difficult to wait one's turn. It may take ten, twenty, fifty or even sixty years. He often quoted the saying "Sof hakavod lavo — eventually the honor materializes." He advised many people who were experiencing difficulties that if one sees the good in everything that befalls him, the situation actually develops into a good one. He knew this firsthand.

the voucher himself, even though the sum of eighteen dollars was significant in ratio to his income at the time. Several days later, Reb Mordechai was informed by Reb Rafael Eisenberg, who had included him as a partner in a business deal, that he had earned a thousand dollars from that deal.

8. While he performed routine work, he would recite those chapters of *Tehillim* that he knew by heart. He had a *mussar shtiebel* in which he learnt *mussar* during his lunch break.

9. He said that he found it advantageous teaching a younger grade since it required less time for preparation and left him more time for Torah study. Nevertheless, he devoted much time in preparing the *Chumash* he taught to ensure that his translation to *Yiddish* was exact and consistent with the interpretations of the *meforshim*.

ᴥ§ A Dual Nature

Many remember Reb Mordechai as forever smiling, always in good spirits. This is but half the picture.

> He often repeated a description of the first morning of Pesach in Volozhin, which he had heard from Rabbi Boruch Ber Lebovitz. When the Netziv, Rabbi Naftali Tzvi Yehuda Berlin, entered the Beis Hamidrash on Pesach morning, his face was radiant, aglow with inspiration from the many mitzvos he had fulfilled the previous evening. The Beis HaLevi, Reb Yosef Dov Soloveitchik, on the other hand, entered in a subdued mood. You could almost feel his apprehension and anxiety: Were the matzos baked with proper care? Were they eaten within the appropriate time span?
>
> Reb Boruch Ber did not dismiss this as a mere difference in disposition. Rather, he viewed this contrast as two conflicting viewpoints. Which of these two, Reb Boruch Ber asked, should one emulate?
>
> Reb Boruch Ber answered that toward others one should show happiness and satisfaction, like the Netziv, but inwardly one should be fearful, constantly examining and questioning his actions, as did the Beis Halevi.

Reb Mordechai lived by this maxim. Indeed, he was able to shift from one mode to another with remarkable ease. When he was with others, he radiated happiness and friendliness; he even greeted young children with a beaming smile. When he was alone, however, he would become solemn with *yiras Shamayim.*

He had a wonderful sense of humor. He was able to laugh, even heartily—at himself. If he ever spilled something on himself or missed a car ride, he would see the humor in the incident. If, at times, one of his *chumros* (halachic stringencies) seemed amusingly excessive, he would heartily join others in their laughter.

Yet inwardly he lived with the maxim *"Shivisi Hashem l'negdi samid—I always envision G–d before me."* The words of *Pirkei Avos,* "Let all your deeds be *l'sheim Shamayim*—for the sake of Heaven," were his guide. Everything he did was with contemplation: is this or is this not *ratzon Hashem*? Every *mitzvah* was performed with utmost concentration and energy, be it *Krias Shema, Tefillah, Birkas Hamazon,* or *Asher Yatzar.*

His brother, יבל"ח, Reb Shimon, שליט"א, noted that Reb Mordechai was able to conceal his *tzidkus* due to his *hatznaya leches*, but his *deveikus* and *yiras Shamayim* were clearly manifest whenever he recited the *Sheim Shamayim*.

He began every day with a lengthy session in his room, saying *Birchos Hashachar* and *Krias Shema* with utmost concentration and even physical exertion. His *zehirus* (excruciating care) in every *mitzvah* and *halachah* was overpowering.[10] It was often difficult to be in close proximity with him for an extended period of time. You measured yourself against him and became painfully aware of your shortcomings.

One of Rabbi Shimon Schwab's sons wished to spend Yom Kippur with Reb Mordechai. He discussed his plan with his father, יבל"ח, who permitted him to go, but warned him that he would be disappointed—and indeed, he was. He had expected the Yom Kippur *tefillos* to be dramatically different from those of all year. His father later explained, "To Uncle Mordechai, there is no difference between a simple *Minchah* and a Yom Kippur *tefillah*." To him, it was Yom Kippur all year.

His *tefillos* and *berachos* drew on physical as well as mental vigor. He would drink a cup of coffee before reciting *Krias Shema* at night, if he did not feel sufficiently alert to concentrate properly. When *Erev Pesach* coincided with *Shabbos*, the question was raised whether to split the morning *seuda* in two, so as to fulfill the obligation of *seudah shlishis*. He excused himself, maintaining that he hadn't the strength to recite *Birkas Hamazon* twice in such a short period of time.

He would spare no effort or expense to avoid the possibility of transgressing any *issur*, be it *bein adam laMakom* (commands relating to *Hashem*) or *bein adam lechaveiro* (interpersonal). He would attend many a *simchah* when he had neither time nor energy if he felt there was the slightest chance that someone's feelings might be hurt.

---

10. He was, however, careful that his *chumros* not impose any difficulty upon others. He would usually insist upon preparing coffee by himself on *Shabbos* because of the various *chumros* he kept pertaining to *bishul*. When others offered to prepare his coffee in accordance with his guidelines he refused, saying, "I do not wish to impose my *chumra* on someone else."

A repairman once did work in his house. When Reb Mordechai returned home and was informed that the worker had been paid in cash, he was upset that sales tax had not been paid. In addition, he was very distressed because he felt that he bore the responsibility if the worker did not report the income on his tax return; and so he tried to make amends....

His strong sense of the importance of honesty and his unique *emuna* are apparent in the following incident:

A young man had apparently lost seventy thousand dollars — practically all he owned — in a bad investment. When he came to Reb Mordechai for advice, he was asked whether the money had been honestly acquired — "ehrliche gelt." When informed that it was so, Reb Mordechai said that while he could not guarantee a profit, the money would be recovered. Ehrliche gelt does not get lost. Within a few months, the investment turned a profit.

One of the members of the Lakewood kollel *who attended a regular* vaad (mussar *group) at Reb Mordechai's house discussed a personal problem with him. Reb Mordechai promised to call the young man later that night with an answer. When he did call late that night, he dialed incorrectly and apparently awakened a woman. He was understandably very upset, all the more since he did not know which number he had reached and was unable to apologize to the woman. After several days, Reb Mordechai figured out which digit he had dialed incorrectly and made sure that his profuse apologies were conveyed to the woman. He was not satisfied until the woman verbally expressed her forgiveness.*

He was constantly alert as to a question regarding any prohibition of the Torah—not just of the *issur* itself, but of its impact on his character, as well.

During their stay in Shanghai, a group of Mirrer Yeshivah students were caught in an air raid while walking from shul on Shabbos. They all scrambled to safety in the shop of a Jewish barber — all except Reb Mordechai, who refused to enter the shop, and braced himself against the outer wall of the building instead. The Jewish proprietor came out and tried to convince him to take shel-

ter in his shop. Reb Mordechai refused: "I do not want to save myself through a Jew's chillul Shabbos."[11]

◄§ Avoiding Chillul Hashem

He was very scrupulous in avoiding *chillul Hashem*, both toward Jews and non-Jews. When leaving home, he would often check his appearance in the mirror, to avoid creating a negative impression of religious Jews.

> *There was a non-Jewish cemetery located across the road from his home*[12] *in which some army veterans were buried. At times, one would find him, even late at night, walking among the graves, picking up papers that the wind had blown onto the premises. He explained that if the cemetery was not cared for, people would say that the Jews do not respect the dead veterans.*

> *He was careful to tip for any service he had received, lest the worker think that religious Jews are stingy. When he left the hospital shortly before his* petira, *he instructed that a box of candy be sent to the nurses.*

> *Once, when spending Shabbos with one of his children, he did not realize that the posted time for Shacharis referred to Baruch She'omar, not Berachos. Thus, he entered the Beis Hamidrash late. He was distressed for fear that perhaps this constituted a chillul Hashem. Accordingly, for many years afterwards, whenever he had occasion to daven at that particular yeshivah, he made certain to arrive especially early to correct any chillul Hashem he may have caused years before.*

◄§ Finding Merit in Others

Reb Mordechai's rigorous introspection and *zehirus* made it all the more remarkable that he was able to completely put this scrutiny aside when dealing with others. His *deveikus* and *yiras Shamayim* were so deceivingly hidden by his warm, friendly and

---

11. Apparently he felt that his life was not actually endangered; otherwise, one is required to violate *Shabbos* in any life-threatening situation.
12. He would call the cemetery his *mussar sefer.*

relaxed smile. The manner in which he spoke to others was unique, as was his consideration of another's feelings and his immense satisfaction in being of assistance. His scrupulous avoidance of speaking or hearing anything negative about others and his adamant refusal to take part in any dispute demonstrated how central the feelings of others were to his *avodas Hashem*.

What gave him the ability to reach such perfection in dealing with others? How was he able to relate to people with such warmth and genuine friendliness? It seems that a single strand bound together the various aspects of his personality: Reb Mordechai toiled to uncover positive attributes in each person. At times it may have seemed naive—but he was not fooled. This was obvious to anyone who knew him well. He understood people's shortcomings and weaknesses remarkably well, but he chose to focus upon their good qualities instead.

> *Someone once complained to Reb Mordechai about a woman who entered Kever Rochel accompanied by her dog, to which he countered, "Why don't you look at it positively? Even a woman traveling with her dog has that spark of holiness that draws her to Kever Rochel."*

> *During his first Shabbos when visiting his son in Eretz Yisrael, he saw people violating the Shabbos. They were probably Arabs, he remarked, not Jews. When he saw a couple in a car, he assumed that the husband was taking his wife to the hospital to give birth. He continued in this manner during the entire Shabbos—and the next. This person must be an Arab, that one a doctor on an emergency call, and this woman must be ready to give birth. By the third Shabbos, his son was incredulous. "Pa! Do you really believe that all these women are giving birth and all these men are doctors or Arabs?"*

> *Reb Mordechai answered, "You do not understand. If a Jew sees chillul Shabbos, it affects his neshama, and his own scrupulousness for Shabbos is weakened. The only way to minimize the negative effect is to tell yourself that Shabbos has not been desecrated." He saw in the mitzvah of judging others favorably not just a courtesy to another person, but a benefit to oneself as well.*

Because he saw virtue in people, he came to love them.

Others have difficulty abstaining from *lashon hara* because they have to overcome the urge to denigrate others. Some have to force themselves to do someone a difficult favor, or to greet an unknown guest in *shul*. Such acts were natural to Reb Mordechai. He never had an urge to denigrate anyone—who would want to speak negatively of someone he loves? He found pleasure in doing a person a favor. He greeted a stranger in *shul* as if he were a friend,[13] and was generous to every collector, not only because of the *mitzvah* of *chessed*; rather, he looked upon the individual as a distinguished person in need of support and encouragement. He smiled at you, not only because it was a *mitzvah* to be kind—his smile was genuine and perfectly natural. When he greeted you, you felt that you were special to him—you *were*, and so was everyone else.

> He would give everyone, even a simple Jew, the title "Reb." Even in his personal phone book every name was entered with the title "Reb." When asked, "You greet people with a title to give them pleasure, but why write 'Reb' in a phone book that the person will never see?"
>
> He answered, "I am not writing it for him; I am writing it for myself. I need to know that the individual is a 'Reb'." He explained that kavod habriyos—honoring a fellow man, pertains not only to the manner in which one treats a person, but to the manner in which one thinks of him as well.

His demeanor when listening to a speaker was unique. He felt that he had something to learn from almost anyone. He would listen attentively, even to a bar mitzvah boy reciting his *p'shetel*, express his *yasher koach* and give a compliment for the wonderful *p'shat*. Many times he would meet someone and remind him of a *vort* he had said many years before and long since forgotten. He would relate that he had repeated the *vort* on many occasions. Even if the speaker had nothing much to say, Reb Mordechai would sit in rapt attention, and encourage the speaker, looking directly at him and nodding his head. This *chessed*, seemingly so simple and yet so appreciated by the speak-

13. He was critical of *shuls* and *yeshivos* where people did not greet strangers. He felt that it was the obligation of the *Rav* and *Rosh Yeshivah* to greet guests so that their congregants and *talmidim* emulate them.

er, is easy for someone concerned only with serving others, not with his own stature and image.

His home and heart were open to everyone. People would come from far and near at all hours, some for advice, some for reassurance and some for a *berachah*. Perhaps some came simply for the encouragement of his warm greeting. Each found in him a warm, caring and kind listener who concentrated upon their individual needs as if he had no other concern in the world. He shared in their plight, gave them encouragement, and continued to worry about them long after they had left, including their needs in his *tefillos*. Often he was busy or tired, but he would not show it. He was concerned only with the needs of others.

> *Occasionally, an acquaintance would stop by during the Shabbos meal. Reb Mordechai would go to the door and greet him, seat him at the table and make him feel at ease. The chulent on his plate got cold, the family fidgeted, and one by one left the table. He was oblivious to it all; it was of no consequence. His only concern was to treat his guest with honor and consideration. Later, with characteristic good humor, he sat down to eat his plate of cold food.*

✑ Hakoras Hatov

Reb Mordechai never forgot a favor. *Hakoras hatov* (gratitude) was an integral part of his *avodah*. He would send money to a *Rav* in *Yerushalayim* who had befriended his children there eighteen years earlier.

He even felt *hakoras hatov* to the clothing he wore. When he no longer needed an old garment, he would not simply discard it in the garbage. He would wait several days, then fold the garment neatly and put it in the garbage, saying, *"Zei hobben mir gut badint*—they served me well."

✑ Striving For Shleimus

How did Reb Mordechai Schwab become so dedicated to the well-being of others? Assuming there is a correlation between personal humility and finding merit in others—is one humbled when he perceives others as good, or does a modest person tend to find goodness in others? Either way, seeing merit in others is surely uplifting.

His exemplary *middos* must have been the result of many years of work and effort.[14] He felt that one cannot achieve *shleimus* without learning *mussar* each day, thus making it an integral part of his day. He toiled on *sheviras haratzon*—shattering his desires. He strived that his every act reflect *ratzon Shamayim*, not his own desires. He was thus able to warmly help someone who had previously wronged him as if nothing had occurred.

> *When his younger brother, Reb Moshe, זצ"ל, joined him in Yeshivah in Lithuania, he noticed that Reb Mordechai often put his hand in his pocket and handled some object. At first he resisted all Reb Moshe's queries about this habit. Eventually, he had no choice but to explain: He carried some sand in his pocket; whenever he felt any sense of pride, he would touch the sand to remind him that man is but sand.*[15]

> *After the passing of Rabbi Yaakov Kamenetsky, זצ"ל, he was approached to assume the position of Rav in Reb Yaakov's shul. At the outset, he adamantly refused, confiding to a close friend that he feared that he would be pressured to don a Rabbinical frock, which would inspire irresistible feelings of ga'ava (pride).*

Shemiras halashon was central to his *avodas Hashem*. He studied *Sefer Chofetz Chayim* at every *Shabbos* meal and encouraged others to do so, as well. He felt that all *yeshivos* and girls' schools should include *Shemiras Halashon* in their curriculum, and was instrumental in establishing its study in many schools. Shortly before his *petira*, he confided to a close acquaintance that he felt this to be the most important accomplishment of his life. (Once, when a *Chassidic Rebbe* visited Monsey, his followers requested that Reb Mordechai call on the *Rebbe*. He was not feeling physically well, but nonetheless consented on condition that they institute the study of *Hilchos Lashon Hara* in their *cheder*.) He was scrupulous about every word he uttered or heard lest there be some *lashon hara* involved.

---

14. His family has lists of the *kabbalos* (resolutions) that he accepted upon himself during the various periods in his life.

15. Told to this writer by Reb Moshe, זצ"ל.

Someone was discussing a personal matter with Reb Mordechai, involving another person's conduct. Reb Mordechai told him that while he is permitted to listen, he may not accept the story as fact. After some time, this individual had need to discuss the matter again. He was surprised to find that Reb Mordechai, who had an excellent memory, had no recollection of ever discussing the matter. Apparently, his memory would not retain lashon hara.

During his life, Reb Mordechai avoided public attention.[16] He would rather that others speak and occupy center stage. His modesty and *tzenius* would not tolerate that we speak of his *tzidkus*. Thus, these lines are written with a degree of apprehension.

There is, however, another consideration. He was an inspiration during his lifetime to all who came in contact with him. One left his presence with a resolve to better himself. Isn't it incumbent on those who knew him to share their impressions with others? If these lines are instrumental in stimulating others to emulate some of his *middos*, particularly his quality of finding merit in others, perhaps he will forgive us for writing them.

---

16. Nevertheless, when he felt there was something to be learned, he would publicly demonstrate the lesson. For example, he usually insisted upon carrying out the garbage. Often he would intentionally do so at a time when young men would pass the house to show the necessity of helping at home, regardless of how demeaning the task may seem.

◆§ Great Leaders, Revisited

Every new encounter with these Gedolim (as explored in earlier volumes in this series) reveals new facets of their greatness

The Chofetz Chaim

Sessions with the Chofetz Chaim

Disciples, visitors, and members of the family help us appreciate the singular greatness of the saint and sage of Radin

The Radiner Rosh HaYeshivah
Rabbi Menachem Mendel Yosef Zaks
Remembers His Saintly Father-in-Law[1]

◄§ Like a "Malach" — Yet in this World

TO MY DEAR TALMID:

Your wish to comprehend the greatness of my saintly father-in-law, the *Rebbe* of all *Klal Yisrael,* זכר צדיק לברכה is like seeking to understand the various angels, be it a *Malach* or a *Saraf.* The *Mesilas Yeshorim* describes such a person (Chapter 26), "One who is holy and clings constantly to G-d, his soul traveling in channels of truth, with love and awe for his Creator — such a person is as

---

1. This article is based on a letter to a *talmid* from the Radiner Rosh HaYeshivah, and from his talks taped at the Yeshivah Chofetz Chaim of Radin, in Monsey, N.Y.

one walking before G-d in the land of the living. While with us, in this world, such a person is considered a Tabernacle, a Sanctuary, an Altar...even his physical actions, such as eating and sleeping, are holy. His consuming of food is similar to the offering of a sacrifice. Such a person is literally considered as if he is united with the celestial Angels, while yet in this world."

In our generation and with our own eyes, we have had the great privilege to witness how my saintly father-in-law was a living exemplification of the first passage of the *Shulchan Aruch*, which states that a person must always picture himself as though he is standing before Hashem, for G-d's presence fills the Earth. His every movement, his every thought was to serve his Creator. When he would write a letter, be it for the Yeshivah or a personal note, he would say, *"Leshem Shamayim — For the sake of G-d."* Even when he slipped on his shoes in the morning or when he set out for the bathhouse, he would whisper, *"Leshem Shamayim!"*

With every word that he uttered, with every physical gesture, he taught us the Torah way of life.

❧ Humility and Self-Awareness

He was unusually astute; yet, in contrast, simple in his trust in G-d. Sometimes he seemed so humble that one might think that he was totally unaware of his own greatness. By contrast, I'd heard him say, "If only all of *Klal Yisrael* were here in this room! I'd tell them thus and thus!" It may be difficult to imagine such humility to be consistent with this willingness to assume authority. Examining his *seforim*, however, one can see both elements: self-effacement almost to the point of total self-negation, yet the belief in his abilities to decide on halachic matters, great and small. How? — Both were in fulfillment of G-d's command.

It is most important to note that he seldom revealed his motives, and then, only to those closest to him. Even when he gave some reason, he was usually concealing more than he was revealing. He once confided in me, "If I specify why I would like to see something done, my reason will only generate an argument with someone who sees things differently; and you know how I despise disputes!"

✦§ The Man and the Sefer: Two Wonders

The *Sefer Chofetz Chaim* on *lashon hara* was universally admired as a classic *halachah* work, drawing together far-flung notes from the entire Oral Law — truly a type of scholarship associated with earlier times.[2] As wondrous as this compendium of laws is, the Chofetz Chaim, as a living representative of its principles, was even more wondrous.

Throughout his long life, the Chofetz Chaim was active in communal affairs and in helping individuals — calling conferences, attending meetings, arbitrating bitter disputes, helping the desperately poor — forever interacting with others; yet, remarkably, he was careful not only in regard to speaking *lashon hara*, but also avoided listening to *lashon hara*. In fact, he often said to me, "All my life I succeeded in refraining from *avak lashon hara*" — (literally: "dust of slander," referring to remarks that might cause others to infer slanderous implications) — a trap that the Talmud describes as just about unavoidable.

First the public at large knew of him through his *Sefer Chofetz Chaim*. Then people came to know him as a person, and they discovered that the author and the book were one and the same, inseparable.

✦§ Working for the Klal

Laboring for Torah, strengthening religious observance, or working for any communal matters, the Chofetz Chaim frequently said, requires three conditions: First, he must view the situation with a special sense of urgency — as though nothing exists except the task at hand, that he alone is charged with doing it, and that it can only be done on that day.

Second, he should act with the utmost alacrity. Here he referred to Boaz's settling the affairs of Ruth. As Naomi said:

---

2. I once heard him remark, "I did a great favor for *klal yisrael* by preparing the *Sefer Chofetz Chaim*. Without knowing the pertinent *halachos*, people simply wouldn't be able to say a word, for they'd have to worry if they were transgressing laws of *lashon hara* (slander) or *rechilus* (tale-bearing). These are Torah prohibitions and one must be stringent with them when in doubt."

"The man [Boaz] will not rest unless he settles the matter today" (*Ruth* 3:18). Boaz only lived one day after his marriage to Ruth, which produced the grandfather of King David. The House of David and *Moshiach* would never have come into existence if not for Boaz's swift actions.

Third, dedication to the cause must be to the point of *mesiras nefesh* — at risk of life and limb. How often, in spite of old age and frail health, the Chofetz Chaim traveled to Vilna to consult with Rabbi Chaim Ozer Grodzenski on pressing issues!...until Reb Chaim Ozer begged of me to do my best to restrain him from making these trips. Reb Chaim Ozer claimed that he could not withstand the relentless pressure of the pleas of the Chofetz Chaim, whose fervor leapt like a burning, restless flame.

৵§ Ready to Die for the Cause

The day never passed that the Chofetz Chaim did not bemoan the tragic situation of Russian Jewry. After struggling to maintain his Yeshivah in post-revolutionary Russia for several years, he returned to the relative safety of Radin, yet he always regretted this move. He described the Communist regime as the only government with an ideology based on *kefirah*, denial of G-d.

The Russian government was actually in a declared war against G-d, constituting a public *Chilul Hashem* of the first order. "Instead of fleeing," he often said, "we should have revolted against the regime, and fought them tooth and nail. Of course, we were insignificant in number and strength, but when facing a spiritual threat, we are expected to throw caution to the wind, and ignore practical considerations. Then G-d also transcends the 'natural order' and performs miracles, as He did for the Chashmonaim of the Chanuka episode, delivering the many into the hands of the few, the mighty into the hands of the weak.[3] We had no right to abandon the fate of three million souls to the Bolsheviks! — When *mesiras nefesh* is demanded, an assured victory is not one of the considerations."

---

3. He often elaborated that only when Jews are confronted with a physical threat should they assess their strength to see if they are capable of military victory; if they are inferior in number — as in the time of Mordechai and Esther facing Haman — they should resort to the power of prayer and not engage in military confrontation.

This unfulfilled demand seemed to haunt him, as was evident ten years later, when the Chofetz Chaim led a delegation that also consisted of the Belzer Rebbe and the Gerrer Rebbe to Warsaw to intervene on behalf of the integrity of Torah education with Prime Minister Bartel. The Polish government had planned to take control of *chadorim* and *yeshivos*, which could have been the death knell for Torah *chinuch*. The Chofetz Chaim felt that this meeting with Bartel was a second chance for him to demonstrate *mesiras nefesh* and if he would not succeed in having the decree rescinded with his pleas, he was ready to defy the government — at the cost of his life, if need be!...Before entering the Prime Minister's chamber, the Chofetz Chaim turned to the Gerrer Rebbe, and asked him, "Are you ready to give away your life for this cause?"[4]

Replied the Rebbe: "I am ready!"

◆§ The Ways of Providence

"How great are Your deeds, O G-d; Your thoughts are exceedingly profound" (*Tehillim* 92:6). The Chofetz Chaim explained "G-d's great deeds" as referring to the wonders of creation, and "exceedingly profound thoughts" to His conduct of the world's affairs. "The latter," said the Chofetz Chaim, "is more profound than Creation itself, according to *Dovid Hamelech's* description. People complain that they do not understand G-d's ways, and they question His conduct of affairs. And I say that G-d's ways are so profound that they are always beyond the comprehension of a simple being of flesh and blood. The surprise is that we are able to grasp anything whatsoever of G-d's *chessed* with His creatures. If one truly tries, and examines events with a perceptive eye, he can detect the Hand of G-d in worldly events. The world is not *hefker*...It has not been abandoned to chance."

The Chofetz Chaim often told the following story. "Dobbe, a wagon driver, rented out a cottage to a poor widow and her

---

4. The events of the meeting and its successful outcome have been detailed elsewhere. For example, see *The Story of the Chofetz Chaim*, published by Mesorah Publications in conjunction with Torah Umesorah, 1983.

orphaned child. In the middle of a very cold winter, she was short of money to pay the rent, so Dobbe simply pushed in the cottage's thatched roof and evicted woman and child, sending them out into the snow. I wondered what punishment was awaiting this man. 'My anger will burn, and I will kill him,' the pasuk says. G-d, Father of orphans and widows, would surely not let the matter rest...I waited over thirty years, until Dobbe was bitten by a rabid dog in the middle of a winter. Dobbe went insane, howling in the night like a mad dog, dying a slow and painful death. G-d may wait, but He collects His due."

Who else connected this bizarre death with a brutal act of a third of a century before?

◆§ Ready for Moshiach

"When *Moshiach* comes," the Chofetz Chaim would ask a *Kohein*, "and the *Beis Hamikdash* is rebuilt, are you prepared to perform your assignments as a *Kohein*? Don't expect Eliyahu to teach you the order of *korbanos*! He'll only clear up your difficulties after you've studied."

The Chofetz Chaim once urged a *talmid* who was a *Kohein* to study Tractate *Kodoshim* in preparation for *Moshiach's* imminent coming, while the *talmid* wanted to study Tractate *Shabbos*. He argued, "What will you do when someone comes to you as a *Kohein*, and asks you to bring his *korban* for having unwittingly violated a *lav* (negative command)?"

"First the person will have to clarify whether or not he is guilty of this transgression. That's why we're studying Tractate *Shabbos* — to inform him correctly if he truly violated the law."

"Unnecessary," said the Chofetz Chaim. "For that you'll consult the *Mishneh Berurah*" — which he had written.

He was utterly convinced that we were on the very threshold of *Moshiach's* coming, and his enthusiasm for encouraging the study of *korbanos* continually found expression in numerous ways. Since study of *Kodoshim* (the parts of the Talmud that deal with the sacrificial order in the *Beis Hamikdash*) was a rarity even in yeshivos, he published *Torah Ohr*, a pamphlet calling for study of *Kodoshim* as well as *Eretz Yisrael*-related *mitzvos* that would be widely applicable after *Moshiach* comes. He also published all sorts of scholarly works to aid this study, ranging from *Asifos Zekeinim*, an anthology of classic commentaries that he had prepared; hitherto unpublished manuscripts, such as the *Shaagas Arye's* commentary on *Yoma* and the Vilna Gaon's glosses on *Toras Kohanim*, to which he added his own explanatory comments; *Likutei Halachos*, which cites the *Gemara's* conclusions in accordance with the Rambam's decisions, with his own most remarkable commentary, *Zevach Todah*. In addition, he founded a *kollel* of young married men, dedicated to the study of *Kodoshim*, which I had the privilege of heading during the decade before World War II.

◆§ "How Many Kohanim in Brisk?"

The Chofetz Chaim wrote: "We must therefore do our utmost to prepare ourselves with knowledge of *Kodoshim* and the *Beis Hamikdash* — this is especially incumbent on *Kohanim* and *Leviim*...but even other Jews, learned in Torah, should be expert in this area, so as to serve as consultants to *Kohanim*. Indeed, I've sent out questionnaires to rabbis asking them how many *Kohanim* live in their respective cities: how many are scholars, how many can study independently, how many 'understand learning' but are in need of teachers before they can apply their studies to actual situations" — from a proclamation issued in Spring 1927.

When these letters were dispatched, his sister's son-in-law, Rabbi Mordechai Ber, asked the Chofetz Chaim if his letter might have the undesirable side effect of provoking a *Chilul Hashem* by exposing how far removed our generation is from this involvement.

"No! No!" he protested. "We must prepare for *Moshiach!*"

Interestingly, the most detailed response came from Rabbi Yitzchok Zev Soloveitchik, the Brisker Rav, documenting the precise number of *Kohanim* in Brisk who were *gedolai Torah*, how many were acknowledged scholars...how many potential teachers there were in Brisk capable of instructing the *Kohanim*, how many of these would expect a salary, how many would teach for

nothing...how many *Kohanim* were *meyuchasim* (of definite priest-
ly parentage), how many were of assumed *yichus*...

✺ The Chofetz Chaim's Real World

So firm was the Chofetz Chaim's *emunah*, his faith in G-d,
that he was impatient when listening to proofs of G-d's existence;
they were so patently superfluous. ■ Whenever he spoke of
kedushah, such as when citing the *pasuk:* "You shall be holy
because I, G-d, am holy," he would smack his lips and say, "It is
sweeter than honey!" ■ When speaking of *tum'a,* defiled
objects, he would become nauseous. I often overheard him in
direct conversations with G-d, talking to Him in Yiddish: "You
always listen to my *tefillos*, please listen to me again this time." ■
Whenever he spoke of prophecy, one could see his intense yearning for the spiritual attainment it represented. In fact, to him one
of the worst tragedies of *p'sul mishpacha* was that it created an
insurmountable barrier to achieving prophecy. ■ He frequently
quoted the passage from *Avos:* "One hour of repentance and
good deeds in this world is worth more than all of the World-to-
Come." He would then follow with a number of *meshalim* and
parables. "In one minute well spent," he would add, "one can
become an *eved Hashem* — a servant of G-d. With all the joys the
World-to-Come brings, one cannot do anything further there to
achieve this status."

✺ Fool's Dirt, Wise Man's Gold

My saintly father-in-law was ever aware of the potential for
mitzvah fulfillment in everything he did. As he put it, "A fool
makes dirt from gold, while a wise man converts dirt into gold.
Are you aware of the golden opportunities that surround you?"

> We had just stepped down from a wagon ride, and after I
> paid the driver, I noticed that my father-in-law was displeased. "I
> tipped the man well," I assured him.
> "Fine," he replied, "but what did you have in mind?"
> I did not reply...
> "Do you know how many mitzvos you fulfilled? 'On the

same day you shall pay him'...'Give sustenance to your poor brother'...and so many more. And you paid him so casually, without thinking of the mitzvos you were fulfilling!"

◆§ God Imparts His Secrets to Those Who Fear Him

Once, when he seemed to be in a joyful frame of mind — I believe it was on Simchas Torah — I challenged him: "They say that you possess *Ruach Hakodesh* (Divine Spirit, endowing him with extra-sensory knowledge)." I then presented him with a list of occurrences of the past week that had all involved familiarity with facts that he could not possibly have known under ordinary circumstances. *"Baruch Hashem,"* he replied evasively, "G-d granted me a logical mind."

The Chofetz Chaim commented many times, "When *Moshiach* comes, I'll not push up front; I'll stand at the side. He'll be saying Torah thoughts regarding the *Beis Hamikdash* and *Korbanos,* and I'm afraid I'll be ashamed by my ignorance."

By contrast, he expressed an astonishing familiarity whenever he spoke about Eliyahu Hanavi. He frequently said, without trepidation, "When Eliyahu comes, I'll ask him thus-and-thus." He even ended his personal *tzava'ah* — his will — with, "This is only if Eliyahu Hanavi will not come. If he does, then, of course, we'll follow his counsel in everything." He did not shrink from: "Who can stand before Him... for He is like a purifying fire" (*Malachi* 3:2). There he was confident, for fear of G-d is a shield from this fury; yet he quaked in his sense of inadequacy in Torah knowledge!

Once, at a Pesach *Seder,* he rose to his feet when he filled the Cup of Elijah. I asked him why he did so, and he deftly changed the subject. *Did he see something beyond our perception?*

A Life Style of Material Austerity and Spiritual Wealth

ᴥ§ The Money-Life-Torah Equation

A frequent theme in the Chofetz Chaim's writings is his call for refraining from unnecessary expenses:

"**A person's income is allotted to him one year at a time,**" (Talmud, *Rosh Hashana*) — to which Rashi adds, "**Therefore one should refrain from spending more.**"... "**This is the curse of our times, for unfortunately, many people violate this cautionary note, do not budget their expenses...resort to dishonesty and are ultimately shamed.**" (Chofetz Chaim in *Be'ur Halachah*, 529,1)

His primary objection, however, was one that he often repeated: "Luxury items require money, which in turn can only be gained through devoting extra time to earning the money. Now, time is a segment of life, and life used for making money is life taken from Torah study. One hour of this world devoted to Torah and good deeds is worth more than all of the World-to-Come — and we exchange such a value-laden hour for decorations and frills!"

My saintly father-in-law expected his children to adhere to this same standard, spurning luxuries, living a life of material austerity, favoring spiritual wealth instead. He once blessed me on Yom Kippur Eve: "Reb Mendel, may Hashem help you that you not become wealthy!" A man standing next to me stepped back in horror: "Rebbe! What are you doing?"

He replied, reassuring the man, "May G-d grant you whatever you wish, but I chose to bless him (my son-in-law) with that which I want for myself."

ᴥ§ Decorations From the Gemara

He once visited one of his grandchildren, and noticing curtains, commented, "I see *Gemara* folios on the windows," and refused to enter the house for over a year...Taking note of carpets on another floor, he said, "When I enter that room, I feel as though I am treading on *Gemara* pages."

When a wooden floor was installed in his simple cottage, he swallowed his objections, but he insisted that they not devote undue effort to scrubbing the floors.[5] One Friday he found a member of the household cleaning the floor. She explained "*Lekovod Shabbos*." "Better to scrub the *neshamah* for *Shabbos*," he sighed.

By the same token, he praised his sister Mat'le for her earthen floors. "Isn't it cleaner to have wooden planks on the floor?" his close *talmid, HaGaon Hakadosh* Rabbi Elchonon Wasserman, protested.

"My dear Reb Chona," he answered, "if it were so, the *Avos* and the rabbis of the Talmud, who put such stress on cleanliness, would have insisted on stone floors, or whatever material was available to them." He then cited a number of references to underscore his point.

When the Rebbitzen pointed out that the home of Rabbi Chaim Ozer Grodzenski, revered head of the Vilna *Beis Din*, was furnished with draperies on the windows, the Chofetz Chaim replied, "Don't you realize that Reb Chaim Ozer is Prince of the Jewish People? 'Elevate him from amongst his brothers,' — it says, so he's forced to endure these luxuries, even though it's contrary to his wishes. But I, *Baruch Hashem*, am an ordinary person and have no need for all that."

He once confided in me, "Until 5655 (1895), I wore a sheepskin coat, but once I achieved prominence, I was afraid of the possibility of *Chilul Hashem*, so I had a *peltz* made — a cloth coat with a fur lining." Then he told me, with deep admiration and a touch of envy, how Reb Nachum Horodner had a peasant's jacket — a sheepskin *peltz'l* — which he wore on winter days, used as a cover on cold nights, rolled up under his head as a pillow, used as a basket to haul groceries when necessary...."

---

5. One of his motives, it seemed, was to keep his home open to all visitors at all times, including the poor wayfarers with mud on their boots, who might hesitate to enter if it involved the risk of tracking up his polished floors. They would enter without hesitation if the floors did not shine.

No Silver Case

He had no silver in his house — not his Chanuka menora, nor his spice box, nor his *esrog* box. The candlesticks used for *Shabbos* were brass. The only exception was an heirloom silver wine goblet, which he used for *Kiddush*. This was a wedding gift to me from *Hagaon Hakadosh* Rabbi Elchonon Wasserman, who had received it as a gift from his father-in-law, Rabbi Meir Atlas, who had received it upon *his* marriage from his own father-in-law, who had received it....

Private Restraint, Communal Glory

Benches were used in the Chofetz Chaim's home rather than chairs. "So many people can sit on one bench," he explained. "Two legs hold up the plank, and support several people. Why does each person need four legs?" Other times he elaborated, "G-d's throne is not complete until *Amalek* is defeated: כי יד על כס קה .... How can we sit so royally on grand chairs?"

The Chofetz Chaim once explained that in our *golus* situation, G-d contains His Glory; it is only fitting, then, that we exercise restraint in our private lives. In communal endeavors, which reflected *K'vod Hashem* and the Torah's glory, however, money was never a consideration. The yeshivah in Radin was housed in the town's finest building — a 50,000-ruble structure, an immense sum in those days. Similarly, the local *mikveh*, as well as all other *mikvaos* he had had a hand in building, were handsome, finely furnished structures.

Where's Your Head?

When a member of the family was excited over a new pair of rather elegant shoes, the Chofetz Chaim chided her, "Instead of putting your head into your shoes, you ought to put it into Torah."

"Involvement in material pursuits can't help but deflect a person's thinking and efforts from Torah study," he often said.

He was deeply distressed when he received 3,000 zlotys all at once, as royalties for his seforim.

"Why do I need all this money? When Reish Lakish died, his entire estate consisted of a bunch of vegetables, and he cried, 'This is the fulfillment of the curse, "They leave their wealth to others" ' (Gittin 47)!"

The Chofetz Chaim then embarked on a vigorous schedule of Klal activities, publishing a number of important pamphlets, and so on, until every last zloty was spent.

⋉§ Unfinished Meals and Broken Buttons

The Chofetz Chaim had no interest in physical pleasures. Before a meal, he would say, "Let's take care of the eating (*lomir oppattern dem essen*)." He would invariably compliment his *Rebbitzen* on her cooking, and then quietly push away the dish. I once asked him if he was keeping "the *Raavad's* fast." Said he, "And if I do?"

He once commented on the Aggada: When Moshe Rabbeinu ascended on high to receive the Torah, the Malachim asked, "What is a mortal doing here?" They were not challenging Moshe's greatness. Rather, they knew that he was destined to bring the Torah down to the people and become involved in their petty disputes. Eventually, Moshe would begin thinking like them, they argued, just as a kindergarten teacher who is occupied in the children's world of little objects and broken buttons soon becomes a captive of their level of thinking.

"We must avoid this trap," he continued. "G-d gave us His Torah in which to immerse ourselves. How foolish to let one's mind become enmeshed in material concerns and become a captive of broken buttons and insignificant objects, after which one will never be able to plumb the depths or see the light of Torah."

⋉§ His Seal is Truth

The Chofetz Chaim emphasized time and again that since Truth is G-d's seal, anything lacking in truth is repulsive to Him — the Torah does not warn us to keep our distance from anything, except: "Keep far from a falsehood" (Shemos 23:7) — and it was repulsive to the Chofetz Chaim, as well: Once a person was relating something that the Chofetz Chaim suspected was not true; his face reddened, he trembled, and began to weep.

> When an important delegation visited the Yeshivah in Radin, one of the members said, "I was here before, as you undoubtedly remember."
>
> "I'm sorry," the Chofetz Chaim replied, "but I'm getting older and I don't remember things as well as I used to."
>
> A member of the household interjected, recalling the incident when they had met, and that the Chofetz Chaim surely remembered...but the Chofetz Chaim stuck with his original apology.
>
> The family member later explained that he had meant the Yeshivah's benefit in presenting the situation as though he did recall the previous meeting. "The Yeshivah's benefit," said the Chofetz Chaim, "is not one of the circumstances permitting deviation from the truth."

⋙ Do Mouth and Heart Concur?

He once explained: "Eisav used the power of speech to entice and entrap others, but Yaakov was simple and direct — an *ish tam*. Rashi elaborates on this description: [Yaakov was] not expert in Eisav's ways, but [the utterings of] his mouth concurred with his heart. A person who doesn't mean what he says is a flatterer, a liar, and a cheat."

The Chofetz Chaim's precision in expression touched on many other areas as well: "Never describe a situation as being bad," he once remarked. "Since everything G-d does is for the good, we have no right to call something 'bad' simply because we fail to comprehend its benefit to us. Bitter, yes; that's a matter of perception. But never bad."

The Chofetz Chaim expected his family to conform to his standard of precision in expression, as an aspect of truthfulness. He once requested a family member to check over some newly printed *seforim* — he checked every single *sefer* for misprints or faulty binding before it was released for distribution.

The family member begged off: "I'm very busy now, but tonight I'll be free. I can handle a hundred for you then." That night she found exactly one hundred volumes on her table, and a waiting Chofetz Chaim...

On the other hand, we saw his greatness in *halachah* when his attention was once called to a match between an orphaned girl from Radin and a young man, made with the understanding that she was related to the Chofetz Chaim. When questioned about this, he said that yes, she was a relative. A family member later asked him about this — since she definitely was not related. "We're dealing here with the possibility of marrying off a *yesomah* (orphan), and if it all depends on her being related to us, then I'll rely on the assumption that all Jews are somehow related to one another. She's our kin."

✑ The Chofetz Chaim: In Public and In Private

The public Chofetz Chaim was identical to the private Chofetz Chaim. Whether he was on a podium facing thousands or in a room with his family, he spoke simply, directly, and without pretensions. He never assumed oratorical flourishes, nor did he deliver *drashos* (sermons) just for the sake of sermonizing — he only said what was required to instruct or inspire for the occasion.

Many times he stressed that in his *seforim*, he only wrote what was universally required, nothing beyond the basic requirements of Torah law — no extra stringencies. By contrast, we personally witnessed how his open conduct went far beyond the requirements of *halachah*.

I once asked him if a *Maggid* or a *Mashgiach* in a yeshivah may promote standards that he personally does not live up to, or attempt to inspire people to heights that he has yet to attain. "A person must be especially cautious in religious matters to avoid inaccuracies," he replied. "The ruling, *G-d despises words of false-hood*, would especially render his pleas ineffective. The only way to urge people to strive for an ideal you yourself also lack is to include yourself among those who are being addressed. G-d's gift to Jewry is that special skill He gave them — the power of speech. We must avoid misusing it or defiling it in any way, but make sure to use it effectively for Torah and *tefillah*."

This was the Chofetz Chaim — in word and in deed.

Rabbi Shimon Schwab

A Shabbos with the Chofetz Chaim זצ״ל

◄§ Only One Concern?

We live in times of terrible crises, political and spiritual. In spite of temporary lulls, *Klal Yisrael* has hardly any dependable friends in the entire world. Think of the *yishuv* in *Eretz Yisrael*, which is surrounded by hostile nations, whose lack of unity is all that prevents them from destroying the Jewish nation; think of the millions of Jews in Russia whose last spark of *Yiddishkeit* has been all but extinguished, held captive by a regime that refuses to let them out; think of all the other Jews in all the other lands, threatened by physical intimidation or spiritual annihilation. And think of the Jews in America, where one can learn Torah without disturbance, and the colossal spiritual crisis we are experiencing in this land of unfettered freedom.

Here we are — a thousand people, gathered together to address the problems facing *Klal Yisrael* and speak of the Chofetz Chaim who left this world over fifty years ago. Shivering in a spiritual freeze, groping in the darkness of our time — do we have nothing else on our minds but the Chofetz Chaim?

This brings to mind the humble Jew standing outside on a cold winter night to be *mekadesh levanah*, blessing the new moon, saying a *tefillah*: יה״ר למלאות פגימת הלבנה, May it be Your will...to fill the flaw of the moon." Does he have no other worries, nothing else to pray for? This Jew, who has no source of livelihood, is shivering on a dark night, and his only request to G-d is that He restore the moon to its original fullness! And, indeed, he need have no other worries, because when G-d does fill this flaw, it will be the time of *Moshiach* when the light of the moon will be like that of the sun...and then, all of his problems will be resolved.

We too may do well to concern ourselves with the Chofetz Chaim. Would we members of the Jewish world be worthy of it, we would again be privileged to have a Chofetz Chaim in our midst, fulfilling in our days the *tefillah*, "Restore our judges as before" — meaning one great *tzaddik* and *gaon* whom the whole world, not only segments of it, recognizes for his greatness! Under his leadership, all of our problems would indeed be resolved.

⋖§ The Insatiable Hunger

The widespread interest in the Chofetz Chaim that prevails in our community is undoubtedly an expression of the spiritual thirst that distinguishes us as a people (*Sanhedrin* 76b). A Jew can never be satiated with the spiritual creations of mankind, but remains thirsty for genuine fear of G-d and for fulfillment of His *mitzvos*. Some of us may not be aware of the nature of the thirst that plagues us, for we have a husk around our soul. But under the husk throbs a yearning that proclaims צמאה נפשי לאלקים — "My soul thirsts for G-d (*Tehillim* 42:3)." Thus a thousand Jews come together to hear about the Chofetz Chaim who passed away more than fifty years ago — because of a hunger that can never be stilled.

⋖§ Not A Legacy of "Hanhagos"

What can we learn from the Chofetz Chaim?

I once had the privilege to visit the Chofetz Chaim in Radin, and from there I went directly to Vilna where I met Rabbi Chaim Ozer Grodzenski. He asked me, "What do you say about the Chofetz Chaim?"

I was astounded at his question. "What have I to say about the Chofetz Chaim? It's not for me to comment about the *tzaddik hador* — the outstanding saint of our times!"

Reb Chaim Ozer sighed, "You too? Indeed, he is outstanding as a *tzaddik*, but he is an even greater *gaon* than he is a *tzaddik*, which you did not recognize." As an example of the Chofetz Chaim's *geonus*, Reb Chaim Ozer pointed to the *Be'ur Halachah*, printed as part of the *Mishneh Berurah*, which he said has no equal in the last hundred years.

Thus, the Chofetz Chaim was both the *tzaddik hador* and the *gaon hador*. But his *tzidkus* was of a different generation. His *han-*

hagos, his daily practices, do not constitute a message for this generation. We can marvel at them and be inspired by the greatness they represent, but they are beyond us: In his humility, he did not wear rabbinical garb. He wore a cap like a simple Jew; on *Shabbos* when he spoke to the crowd, his cap covered his eyes so you could not see them.[1] The austerity in his home was so severe that he did not have chairs in his house, only benches. This is not our legacy. This the Chofetz Chaim packed up and took along with him to *Gan Eden,* as did the other *tzaddikim* of earlier times. The message that he left for us is the product of his *geonus,* and this can be found in his *seforim* and his holy words: the *Mishneh Berurah,* the *Chofetz Chaim,* the *Shmiras HaLashon* — this is the Chofetz Chaim's legacy.

◂§ The Legacy of Learning

No home where Torah is studied is without a *Mishneh Berurah.* The pages are bent, a little torn, with notes written on the margins. By contrast, the *Chofetz Chaim* is still nicely bound, hasn't been touched since the owner received it as a Bar Mitzva gift. That is what we suffer from...

We are experiencing a great awakening in Torah study, as is evident in Daf Hayomi, involving tens of thousands of Jews through group *shiurim,* radio and telephone lectures; in the Klausenberger Rebbe's *Mifal HaShas* which is inspiring yeshivah students to strive for *bekius* — encyclopedic knowledge of the Talmud. May Hashem grant us the strength to continue this *hisorrerus,* this awakening, to act on it, and to apply it to our daily lives.

But shouldn't this include *Chofetz Chaim* and *Shmiras HaLashon?* Marking this 50th *Yahrzeit* of the Chofetz Chaim should inspire all Torah Jews to undertake the study of a fixed portion from *Sefer Chofetz Chaim* every day, and then on the following day to review the old passages and study another section.

---

1. His family explained that when he became older, the Chofetz Chaim became physically smaller, and his old cap no longer fit him. He refused the family's offers to buy him a new cap — the old one was still in fine shape. With some paper in the lining, it could still fit well. On *Shabbos,* however, the Chofetz Chaim removed the paper, and the hat tended to slide over his eyes.

Then the thirsty soul of the *Yid* would be refreshed with new knowledge, new inspiration, new guidance...The Chofetz Chaim's written words are waiting for us to consult them and learn from them.

⛤ The Chofetz Chaim: Looking Ahead

It was fifty-three years ago, when I was a young man of twenty, that I had the privilege to spend one *Shabbos* with the Chofetz Chaim. I heard him speak, and those words were, in their way, addressed to us today. I came on a Friday and left on Sunday. The Chofetz Chaim talked to me privately on my arrival in Radin. And I heard him several times on *Shabbos*.

An incident took place that weekend that gave me a glimpse into the measure of the man. Had I not been witness to it myself, I would not have believed it. It was before *Motzaei Shabbos*. The Chofetz Chaim had eaten a frugal *Seudah Shlishis*. When I came in, he was already talking — this was before *Birkas HaMazon*. The room was dark, and crowded with people. The Chofetz Chaim was speaking of the responsibility everyone present has to go out and be *mekarev rechokim*: "Go into the *shuls* and talk to the people about *mitzvos*, doing *teshuvah* — keeping *Shabbos* and *kashrus*, *tefillin* and *taharas hamishpachah*...I will also go, *bli neder, bli neder*" — which he did; he went to Grodno to speak to the people there.

(And how right he was! People are thirsting for *dvar Hashem*, even when they are unaware of it! On a recent flight, my seat companion was a very non-Jewish-looking Jew. It was in the middle of the night and he insisted on telling me that he was an atheist. After he informed me of this a third time, I realized that the man "protesteth too much," so I told him, "You are an atheist like I am an atheist. You are a *Yid* with a husk. Inside it, you have a Jewish heart. Your heart is calling out for Hashem. You are hungry and thirsty; you haven't been given any nourishment. You have to break through that husk and feed that thirst." How strong our obligation is to reach out to such Jews and quench their thirst!)

The Chofetz Chaim continued, talking about how the generations have gone down: "What love for Torah former generations had! People vied with one another to be close to anyone who was involved in Torah study. Every one of us is obligated to work at bringing people back to the ways of the *Ribbono Shel Olam!*"

Then he said, "It's time to *bentch*," and he started to *bentch*, like a simple Jew, saying one word at a time...I did not see anything special in his manner. Suddenly, when he reached רחם נא (the blessing that begins "Have mercy..."), something seemed to have happened to him. He cried out: על ישראל עמך ("...on Your nation, Israel) *oy! oy!* — על ציון משכן כבודך (...on Zion, home of Your glory) *oy! oy!* He continued in this manner until he reached the *"Harachamons"* and stopped. At this point he said, "I see what will be ten years from now. [This was 1930.] You don't see; but I do. A great conflagration will burn!" In the middle of *bentching* he suddenly had a vision of future events. "Twelve million is child's play!"

I turned to the person next to me and asked him what he meant with his comments. He replied, "He always talks about it. Twelve million is the sum total of those killed in the World War."

I never forgot this scene, and for ten years I repeated it, and waited watchfully, fearfully, for its realization — until ten years later, in 1940, when it started to come true.

This was the Chofetz Chaim.

◈§ With the Chofetz Chaim

On Friday night — it was Rosh Chodesh Nissan — the Chofetz Chaim said, "The *Chachomim*, our wise men, taught us that the *Geulah*, the redemption from Egypt, was in the month of Nissan, and the future *Geulah* will also be in Nissan. It is now Nissan, and the *Geulah* may well be this very month."

He was sitting in his own room with his cap over his eyes. There were 60 to 70 people in the room, yet he talked in a loud voice as though he were addressing an auditorium of several thousand people. In fact, I had the feeling that he was speaking to the entire world. He said, "How do you deal with the possibility of *Moshiach's* coming: maybe he's coming this very month, maybe he's not coming? *Al pi din*, objectively speaking, it's a doubt of equal possibilities. Let us assume the positive, that he will be here. You might think that everyone will be so happy. Not so. You'll run away in fear and hide in the deepest crevices. *Moshiach is coming! The Ribbono Shel Olam is revealing His Shechinah!* Out of shame, we'll hide in the bunkers...*Avraham Avinu* is passing through the streets to judge us — everybody has to run for cover!"

When he was saying this, it seemed to me as though *Yeshaya HaNavi* (Isaiah the Prophet) was saying: יטומן בעפר מפני פחד ה' מהדרת גאונו — "And they will hide in the sand for fear of G-d, from the magnificence of His glory (*Yeshayah* 2:10)."

"Are we ready?" he continued. "Who am I? Am I ready to receive *Moshiach?*

The Chofetz Chaim then spoke of something else: "The *mon* — the manna — had the taste of whatever food the person was thinking of. What happened (he asked) if someone was not think-ing at all? What taste did the *mon* have then?" Nobody answered...He continued, *"Az men tracht nit, hott es kein ta'am nisht*. If you don't think, it has no taste." He repeated this several times: *"Az men tracht nit, hott es kein ta'am nisht* — because the *mon* is *ruchniyus*, spiritual, and if you don't think, it has no taste...What can be more tasty than a piece of *Gemara?"* He kissed the tips of his fingers. "It is so sweet, but only if you think. If you don't think, you sit by the *Gemara* and it has no flavor whatsoever.

"Suppose *Moshiach* comes, and we don't think. It has no fla-vor. You won't even be aware of what is going on!"

⮜ Evaluating the Chofetz Chaim's Legacy...With His Help

When a man of such stature speaks to us, and has given us a legacy — *Mishneh Berurah, Chofetz Chaim,* and *Shmiras HaLashon* — we must value this legacy and see to carry it out, translate the concepts into practical actions.

But how do we manage it? How does one abstain from *lashon hara?* Wherever we turn, we encounter *lashon hara.* The Constitution of the United States guarantees freedom of speech and free access to information — and that constitutes *lashon hara.* All newspapers, with few exceptions, are organs of *lashon hara.* Most of our conversations involve *lashon hara.*

Indeed, the *Gemara* asks how one can avoid *lashon hara,* and advises, *Ya'asok baTorah.* As long as everybody will be conversing in Torah, then it will not be difficult to avoid slander. Further, עם הארץ ישפיל דעתו — simple folk will be humble; if a person thinks about his own shortcomings, he will rejoice that no one is talking about him. The Chofetz Chaim was of the opinion that the best antidote to *lashon hara* is studying about the *issur* (prohibition) against *lashon hara.* Once the objective facts are established, it becomes simple.

Midrash Rabbah tells of a peddler who was announcing that he was selling the elixir of life. ("Who wants life? Who wants life?") Rav Yannai asked him to come to him but the peddler explained, "My elixir is not for you." After Rav Yannai insisted, the peddler took out a *Sefer Tehillim* and read to him the passages (Chapter 34, verses 13,14) that are the elixir of life: "Who is the man who wants life...? Guard you tongue from evil." Rav Yannai said, "All my life I've been reading this passage without realizing how simple its message is until this peddler came along."[2]

What new insight did the peddler offer? A peddler does not sell on credit. He only sells on a cash-and-carry basis. And this opened Rav Yannai's eyes to an astounding truth: "If I am tempted to talk *lashon hara* — it's on the tip of my tongue and I would like to say it — and I succeed in suppressing it and don't say it, at that very moment I am buying life. That's how simple it is."

The dimensions of this life are beyond our understanding, and to this, too, the Chofetz Chaim opened my eyes during that fateful stay in Radin. The Chofetz Chaim said to me on Friday morning: " וחיי עולם נטע בתוכינו — 'You planted eternal life in our midst' — what does that mean? What do you think when you say these words in the *bracha* when you are called to the Torah?"

I did not answer him, so he continued: "I'll explain what 'Eternal Life' means: Where will you be 100 years from now? With the *Ribbono Shel Olam.* And where will you be 1,000 years from now? The same — with the *Ribbono Shel Olam.* And 5 million years from now? Again the same — with the *Ribbono Shel Olam.* This is Eternal Life!"

---

2. The title of the *Sefer Chofetz Chaim* was inspired by the passage quoted in this Midrash.

And one can buy it, as though from a peddler; and he's selling it a thousand times a day. Don't say *lashon hara*, suppress it —
and immediately, cash-and-carry, Eternal Life is yours. That's
how simple it is. This too is what the Chofetz Chaim taught me
and is teaching you.'

◆§ Silver Lining?

The Chofetz Chaim said more... What do you assume his
comment to us would be if he would see our preoccupation with
Olam Hazeh — this-worldly attainments? The glitter and glamour
of fashion, our designer wardrobes, our diamond and fur coat
accessories, our ostentatious *simchos*...? May I offer another gem
from our conversation on that Friday...

He asked me: "Were you ever in the Ural Mountains? ...I
was there and I saw how they dig for silver. They lie in the *blotteh* (mud) all day and *grob* (dig) and grab in the *blotteh*. Finally
they take something out, the object of their quest, which is also
caked in *blotteh*...What is silver if to get some you have to lie in
the *blotteh*, dig in the *blotteh*, get all dirty and become covered
with *blotteh*? Then it must be *blotteh*..."

The Chofetz Chaim's message from that Friday would be to
question most of our present-day preoccupations. For actually
our hearts are thirsting for *Emes* (truth) in a time when confusion
and falsehood and *Chilul Hashem* prevail. Since we want *Emes* for
ourselves, we must lift ourselves to a higher level, and not wal-
low in *blotteh*. Because, in the final analysis, what is it but *blotteh*
— mud?

Then the Chofetz Chaim put very strong emphasis on Torah
study. When I told him that I was learning in the Yeshivah of Mir,
he beamed and stroked my arm. "A yeshivah *bachur*. How wonderful! So many are drowning today. Only through Torah can
you survive. How fortunate that you are learning! Only Torah
study makes us Jews. Twenty *talleisim* and twenty pairs of *tefillin*
cannot make a person into a Jew, but the *brachah* that we say on
Torah every day declares that we are marked as Jews because 'He
gave us His Torah!' This and this alone distinguishes us as Jews."

That same Friday afternoon, the Chofetz Chaim asked me, "Are you a *Kohein?*"

"No," I replied.

He went on, "Maybe you are a *Levi?*"

"No."

"What a pity! *Moshiach* is coming and the *Beis Hamikdash* will be rebuilt. There will be a tremendous yearning to enter the *Beis Hamikdash*. The *kedushah* exerts such an irresistible attraction. If you're not a *Kohein* you can't enter the *Beis Hamikdash*. And you're not even a *Levi* — who can gain entry into some places. You're left completely outside...Perhaps you've heard — I'm a *Kohein*. — Tell me, why aren't you a *Kohein?*"

I was puzzled by the question. "Because my father isn't a *Kohein*," I answered.

"And why isn't he a *Kohein?*" he asked further.

The explanation would be the same, of course, but I decided not to answer. He obviously had something in mind.

"I'll tell you why," he went on. "Because 3,000 years ago, at the incident of the Golden Calf, your ancestors didn't run when Moshe Rabbeinu called out, '*Mi LaHashem Eilai* — Whoever is with G-d should come to me!' My father, and all the other *Leviim*, ran to Moshe. Your father did not. So we are the *Kohanim* and the *Leviim*. Now take it to heart. When you hear the call, *Mi LaHashem Eilai*, come running!"

This is the message of the Chofetz Chaim. We are living in a time when any thinking person can hear a Great Shofar blasting from all sides, calling out: *Mi LaHashem Eilai!* — and it is incumbent on us to come running.

Let us all be in the forefront of those responding to this call.

Two Winters in Radin

I had come to the yeshivah in Mir for Ellul 5690 (1930) with several American *chaveirim*. After particularly moving *Yomim Noraim* and a joyful Simchas Torah, I wanted to visit the Chofetz Chaim in Radin before beginning the new *zman* (semester). When I asked the Rosh Yeshivah, Reb Leizer Yudel (Rabbi Eliezer Yehuda Finkel), for permission, he replied: "Yesterday we celebrated Simchas Torah. Today you should begin learning."

"I would like to see the Chofetz Chaim first."

"You certainly should, but you can visit him Pesach, or next year... "

"But he's already in his mid '90s..." I said, leaving the rest to his understanding.

Reb Leizer Yudel looked at me with an expression that seemed to say: "*Nor an Amerikaner kenn azoi reden* — only an American can talk like that." Then he said, "*Der Chofetz Chaim vett zein aibik* — the Chofetz Chaim is eternal," and left it at that.

Nonetheless, I felt compelled to go to Radin for a day. I met the Chofetz Chaim, and decided to remain in the yeshivah there.

⊷§ "I Must Go to Vilna!"

I made it a practice to *daven* with the Chofetz Chaim's *minyan* every day. Early that winter — it was 12 Kislev — someone reported to the Chofetz Chaim that *taharas hamishpachah* was not as widespread as should be expected in Vilna. He was deeply disturbed, and announced, "I must go to Vilna and correct this situation." His family told him that it would be impossible for him to go to Vilna; he could scarcely walk across the room without assistance. "I am going to Vilna to speak to Reb Chaim Ozer. I need my coat." There was no holding him back.

A bus was chartered that very day, and loaded with the Chofetz Chaim's entourage and several *bachurim* including myself. The Chofetz Chaim was wrapped in a blanket and carried aboard the bus, yet he shivered the entire two-hour bus ride. The bus stopped at 66 Kavolna, Reb Chaim Ozer's residence, where the Chofetz Chaim disembarked — he was literally carried into the house where Reb Chaim Ozer was meeting with several *morei hara'a* (halachic authorities).

The Chofetz Chaim's entrance made quite a stir, as would be expected. He got right to the point: A public gathering should be called to strengthen *taharas hamishpachah*. A reminder is always in place, for *zechira* (remembering the *mitzvos*) promotes *shemirah* (keeping them). The principal speaker would be the Chofetz Chaim.

In a matter of hours, Vilna was plastered with placards calling all women to Der Alter Stodt Shul on the Vilna Gaon's Hof (Court) for a public assembly that night (Monday), and a similar meeting for men on the following night. Needless to say, the 600-year-old *shul* was crowded with women that evening. The Chofetz Chaim entered — on a chair — followed by a small group of men, myself included. Once on the *bimah*, he spoke warmly but very softly. When he finished, the Ivye Rav (later Lomza Rav), Rabbi Moshe Shatzkes, repeated the Chofetz Chaim's message in his booming voice, and explained it in more detail. The evening concluded with a *brachah* from the Chofetz Chaim, to which the women responded with a resounding *Amein!*

Tuesday night the same program was repeated for men, and on Wednesday we returned to Radin. That Friday, when the Chofetz Chaim went to the *mikveh* to prepare for *Shabbos*, he met the Rosh Yeshivah, Rabbi Moshe Landynski, who later commented that the Chofetz Chaim's face had a special glow that day. Reb Moshe told the Chofetz Chaim that he marveled at his energy to undertake the trip. "I didn't *go* to Vilna," he replied. "*S'hott zich getonn* — it just happened."

❧ Inside View

I had several occasions for personal exchanges with the Chofetz Chaim. It was necessary to speak loudly to him because he was hard of hearing in his old age — a condition that he seemed to relish because it spared him the pain of listening to forbidden talk — he was confident that no one would shout *lashon hara* in his presence. I found it easier to speak through an intermediary, such as Reb Hirsh Broyde, his assistant, than to shout at him.

On one occasion, in the summer of 1931, Reb Mendel Zaks asked me to translate an English-language letter for him. It was from an organization called Ner Israel, and opened with the salutation: "Dear Reverend Sir." It asked for the Chofetz Chaim's backing for an agrarian movement that would "solve" the Jews' economic hardships by sponsoring their move from the crowded cities to farms. The Chofetz Chaim refused to sign, remarking, "When *Moshiach* blows his *shofar*, I'm afraid the people on the farms won't come running."

ᵉᔆ "Who Knows?"

Late one winter evening — it was about 10:30 — I had a problem that I wanted to discuss with the Chofetz Chaim; so I passed his house on my way home from the *beis medrash*. The light was on, and I entered to ask his *brachah*.

...I later commented to Reb Hirsh that he seemed to be in an exceptionally good mood. Reb Hirsh explained that the Chofetz Chaim had learned that day that the Joint Distribution Committee gained permission from the Russian government to ship matzos to the Jews there. "Who knows?" said the Chofetz Chaim. "They may even permit *Yiddishe Kinder* to learn Torah. *Halevai!*"

ᵉᔆ Life is Like a...

I personally heard the Chofetz Chaim repeat three *masholim* explaining the urgency of using every minute of life productively:

■ Life is like a postcard — we usually begin writing in a large, leisurely scrawl, but as the message begins to fill the page, there's so much more to say and so little space left...so we crowd in another line and squeeze in another word. Similarly, we take it easy in our youth, leisurely wasting time — not realizing how much will be left to do, with so little time to do it.

■ Tuesday was market day, when every minute of daylight had to be used to do business. Pity the poor fellow who spent the day in line at the bank to prepare himself with an assortment of change, and then came to the marketplace at the day's end only to find all the stalls closed!

■ (When the Chofetz Chaim told the following parable to Rabbi Elchonon Wasserman, he laughed aloud — a rare occurrence!) A *yeshuv'nik* (country fellow) was preparing to board a train for the first time in his life, for a business appointment in the big city. He was wearing his overalls, and asked his fellow passengers where he could change to his "*Shabbos* clothes." A prankster advised him, "Just be patient. After you board the train, there'll be a special time when the train gets dark, and everybody will have a chance to change. You'll see." So he boarded "as is."

Later, the train entered a tunnel and it was pitch dark in the car. "Now," said the joker. As soon as the *yeshuv'nik* removed his clothes, the train was out of the tunnel, and there he stood — *ah nahkitten* — naked, in broad daylight!

Life is a fast-moving journey. We would be well advised to put on our *Shabbos* clothing — to be equipped with all our spiritual needs, and not wait for some distant transition point — lest we be caught "*ah nahkitten*" to our everlasting shame.

The Chofetz Chaim:
Close to Every Man, Closer to G-d

◄§ No Room for Despair

I came to Europe with the intention of learning in Baranovitch. When I arrived there, the Rosh Yeshivah, Reb Elchonon Wasserman, was overseas on a mission, so I decided to go to Radin for the duration of his absence. I stayed on for two years.

I was among the ten to twenty people who *davened Shacharis* with the Chofetz Chaim every morning. (More people joined us for *Shabbos tefillos,* and at *Shalosh Seudos* some forty or fifty people would come.) As such, I often heard him comment on events and the general situation of *Klal Yisrael.*

Two things impressed me. The Chofetz Chaim was keenly aware of the terrible poverty that prevailed in the era. This, coupled with the lack of prospects of *shidduchim* for the yeshivah students, created a depressed feeling in the community. He often addressed this situation. The other aspect: The Chofetz Chaim would speak to the *Ribbono Shel Olam* as though He were a visible presence in the room, כביכול. Both of these traits were always in evidence when we were with him.

Every so often he would pound on the table, and speak. For instance: "You [G-d] Yourself said, 'And on that day I will send Eliyahu Hanavi...' Where is he?... What complaints can You have against them? What do You want from them? 'Poverty corrupts' and You see how desperately poor they are!"

Yet the Chofetz Chaim would comment, "Poverty — what a treasure house of discipline and self-improvement!"

❀ ❀ ❀

He would call in the yeshivah boys before the holiday inter-session and remind them: "You know that every Jew must ulti-mately answer to: 'Did you set aside time for Torah study?' This applies to you as well. The test of your ability to answer is how you spend your vacation. Make sure to reserve time for learning."

He wanted the boys to sign pledge sheets committing them-selves to a number of undertakings: to study during vacation, or to refrain from *lashon hara*, or to memorize the list of all the *mitzvos* ("We have to know all the *mitzvos*, and constantly review them"), but they were reluctant to fix their signature to the paper....Somehow the crowd seemed to thin out at such times.

❦ ❦ ❦

"Learn with joy," the Chofetz Chaim would say. "Despair should have no place in your life. The way you fulfill your *mitzvos* here is the way you'll have it there [in the World-to-Come]. *Besimcha!*"

◌§ The Glow Afterward

After the Chofetz Chaim was *niftar*, Reb Sholom Aishishok said that he was then permitted to relate an incident that he had been asked not to reveal beforehand....When the Chofetz Chaim was a fifteen-year-old boy, he became very attached to Reb Nochum Horodner, a *tzaddik nistar* who served as the *shamash* for the *beis din* in Vilna. Evenings, after the people left the *shul*, Reb Nochum would lock the door from within...The Chofetz Chaim was curious to see what Reb Nochum did then, so he once hid under one of the benches and waited. At midnight, Reb Nochum took out a *sefer Kabbala* (a mystical text), lit a candle, and started to study — and the room was aglow with light!

When Reb Boruch Ber Leibowitz, Rosh Yeshivah of Kamenitz, heard this, he commented, "That a light should glow when Reb Nochum learned is not surprising, but that the Chofetz Chaim at fifteen saw the light is truly amazing."

Introducing Daf Hayomi to Klal Yisrael

*His youth was no
obstacle to his
introducing a bold
plan that changed the
format of Talmud
study for thousands of
Jews*

On the third of Elul, 5683 (August 15, 1923), while the normal
[night] life... went on in Austria's capital city of Vienna, the
first Knessia Gedolah ("Great Assembly") of Agudas Yisroel
opened at the glittering, elegant Royal Theater building, with some
six hundred delegates in attendance. It was to last for seven days,
with such luminaries in attendance as the venerable (octogenarian)
Chofetz Chaim, the *Rebbe* of Tchortkov, and the *Rebbe* of Ger.

Quite certainly, the greatest Torah authorities were there—
the most renowned Torah scholars and the revered masters of
Chassidic learning and piety—to thrash through the various
grave and weighty problems which faced... Torah Jewry in the
European diaspora.

This account is excerpted from a biography of Rabbi Meir Shapiro by one of his most gifted *talmidim*, Rabbi Yehoshua Baumol הי"ד who was martyed by the Nazis י"ש. The book
has been translated into English by Rabbi Charles Wengrov and Martin H. Stern and has
been published by Feldheim Publications under the title, "A Blaze in the Darkening
Storm: The Life and Legacy of Rav Meir Shapiro."

...Among them was the effervescent Rav Meir Shapiro, still looking, irrepressibly, for ways to promote and launch his *Daf Hayomi* program. Then the Knessia Gedolah... did it for him: It put him on the program to present the idea at one of the formal, plenary sessions. And he spoke:

> *If the entire observant community everywhere, in every single location where our observant Jews exist on this earth, will study the same daf of Talmud on the same day, could we have any better, more palpable expression of the sublime eternal unity between the Holy One, His Torah, and His people?*
>
> *How splendid this could be! A man goes sailing across the sea, and he carries a volume of Maseches (Tractate) Berachos. He is traveling from the Holy Land to America—and every day, with the setting of the sun, he opens the volume and studies the daf. Arriving in New York, he enters a beis midrash, and to his amazement, he finds a group at work on the very page of Talmud that he has reached in his own private learning program. Delighted, he sits down and joins them. He gets into Talmudic debate with them, and is answered back. The net result is that the Glory of Heaven has become greater, mightier, more holy.*
>
> *Suppose someone migrates from North America to Brazil, or to far-off Japan. Having arrived and settled, he will head for the beis midrash and find there, what? A group [occupied] with the very part of the Talmud that he has been studying. Could we have a better way of bringing Jewish hearts into one great, harmonious union?*
>
> *Nor is this all. Until now, thanks to the traditions of the yeshivah world, where every young learner is initiated into the Talmud, only certain masechtos are studied, while others are left to a select few learners and scholars to take pity on them and open their pages. The Daf Hayomi program will put all that right!*
>
> *One further point: Our youth, the future of the Jewish people—it is they above all who must begin this great mitzvah of "wholesale study"!*

...Amid thundering applause, the whole assembly of some 600 delegates rose and stood to attention; and with a fiery holy fervor, with emotions that rose to fever pitch..., [they] accepted the obligation to participate in the program that was now scheduled to begin with the new Jewish year: on Rosh Hashanah, 5684 (September 11, 1923).

At the same time, the convention called on Jewish communities everywhere to adopt the program and proclaim it throughout the world. And thus it was born into the world "in a fortunate hour," to be welcomed and absorbed as an unforgettable and unrepealable part of religious Jewry's way in the world: a global daily study portion.

> *After Rosh Hashanah he received a letter from his only sister, who lived in a far-off village in the region of Bukovina, in northern Rumania, and knew nothing whatever of his activities: "On the night of Rosh Hashanah," she wrote, "I had a dream: I saw you in Heaven, dear brother, surrounded by a great mass of angels with striking figures, all radiant as the light of the firmament; and you, my brother, were standing in their midst, your face alight like the sun it its full strength; and they were all smiling to you, as they thanked you and rejoiced with you very, very greatly.... Please, dearest brother: let me know what the dream means...."*

The reactions to the program, as the Jewish people learned of it far and wide, made the meaning of the dream quite clear to him. Echoes and reverberations of response came, clearly and unmistakably, from all over the world. There was no doubt that the idea took hold, and in scores of far-flung locations... people were taking to studying the Talmud almost in unison—the same leaf, the same two pages, in the same tractate.... And quite certainly the numbers of participants kept growing as the new Jewish year progressed....

When he saw how well the idea had been received, how vigorously the novel learning program was thriving, Rav Meir once gave a most interesting reason for it, in his own characteristic way:

> *We read in the Talmud that when man (Adam) was created, his body came from Babylonia, his head from the Land of Israel, and his limbs from other lands (Sanhedrin 38a-b). This indicates that if there is a wish that an important creation should exist as a permanent, stable entity and be able to spread through the world,*

everywhere—then the component parts that comprise the material for it should be varied, from a variety of places. Then it will belong everywhere; it will find its place everywhere.

Now let us have a look at a page in the Talmud: the Mishnah, the earlier part, was given its redacted form by Rabbi Yehudah haNassi in the Land of Israel; so we have a parallel to Adam, the first, created man: the head derived from the Land of Israel. Now, the Gemora, the later, major part of the Talmud, was put together by the Babylonian Sage, Rav Ashi; again we have a parallel: Adam's body came from Babylonia.

Now further: the commentaries of Rashi and Tosefos, printed with the text, derive from France. [In the back of]... a printed tractate in a volume of Talmud, we have more commentaries: Rabbeinu Asher, from Germany; Rambam on the Mishnah, from Egypt; and then the last ones: Maharshal, Maharsha, Maharam, and so forth—all produced in Poland. Thus the analogy continues: Adam's limbs came from other lands.

Hence, (said Rav Meir) when we read in... Bereishis, "This is the book of the developments of man...," we can apply the words to the Book of the Talmud: it was composed and formed in the same way as Adam. And that is the reason why the Daf Hayomi program has found such a warm reception everywhere among our devout people of the Torah: because there is such a close parallel between a page of Talmud and the human being that the Almighty created.

The success of the idea brought a series of other learning programs in its wake, either for people who would find two pages of Talmud a day too taxing or too time-consuming, or for those who wanted supplementary programs for daily learning. Soon enough, printed schedules appeared for *Mishnah Yomis*, ongoing sections or paragraphs of the *Mishnah* for study day by day; *Nach Yomi*, a daily study portion in the *Neviim* (Prophets) and *Kesuvim* (Writings); *Mussar Yomi*, a daily portion for study in the sacred literature of ethics and morality; and so on.

So the man who yearned and dreamed of achieving major goals in Torah education for his people found himself the founding father and the inspiration for a sound new system of continual daily study by old and young, amid the Jewish people worldwide.

Rabbi Boruch Ber Leibowitz
זכר צדיק לברכה

Fifty Years Since His Passing

His profundity in Talmudic analysis was matched by his unimpeachable temimus (sincerity) and love for Torah and its students

⇜ Reinforcing the Impressions

The close of a fifty-year period is marked by *Yovel* — the Jubilee Year. In his commentary on *Chumash, Haamek Davar,* the *Netziv* discusses the *Yovel* directive, "And you shall return, every man to his possessions, and every man to his family shall you return" (*Vayikra* 25,10). Even if a person does not have any property, he returns to his family roots, as all the family members gather together. The final word in this *Yovel* command, "*toshuvu* — you shall return," appears to be redundant for the opening word — *veshavtem* — already calls for a return home. But of course, it does have a message: One might apply the first command to the *Yovel* year alone. Each and every man should return to his ancestral possessions and his family for the duration of the *Yovel*, and then go back to his previous place of alienation. Thus the repetition: Bringing together all family members to their root place will correct the cause for their being scattered all over, and they will henceforth remain permanently connected with their families.

The fifth of Kislev 5750/1989 marked fifty years since the *petira* (passing) of Reb Boruch Ber Leibowitz, the late *Rosh Yeshivah* of Yeshivah Knesses Beis Yitzchok of Slobodka and then Kamenitz, whose *shiurim* are recorded in the classic *Birkas Shmuel*. Ideally, a convention of all his *talmidim* should have been convened, to re-unite us all. But if a physical convention is impossible, then every *talmid* should at least endeavor to live through a spiritual get-together in his mind: With eyes shut in a secluded room, he should relive his memories of basking in the glow of the *Rebbi* when he achieved an understanding of *amito shel Torah* (the true meaning of a Torah thought), when his shining face expressed the joy of perfecting a clear, deep *sevora* (explanation of a concept).

Remember his delight when, in great excitement, he expressed his feelings over a commentary on the *Gemara*, with: "What a delicious *Rashba!*" Then, immediately correcting himself: "It is Ellul, and I must do *teshuvah*! The entire Torah is so *geshmak* (delicious)! How did I dare single out one *Rashba*?" Remembering that, the *talmidim* might permit their minds to dwell on those *"heilige* words."

But do the *talmidim* transmit these feelings of awe to their children? — to their *talmidim*? Do they realize that there is almost no one left who remembers those precious impressions? — No one who relives those experiences, those feelings?

The vagaries of life take their toll, separating *chaveirim*, disassociating friends, cooling off old warm ties. Thus the binding theme of *Yovel* is relevant even in our days — *especially* in our days, when there are so few of us left. To draw on the *Netziv's* interpretation — "that they shall return permanently to their family, to correct the causes that separated us" — let us reinforce the deep impressions our *Rebbi* made on us.

✺ The Personification of *Temimus*

Does anyone remember the *temimus shel kedushah* of the *Rosh Yeshivah* — his unimpeachable sincerity?

Rabbi Moshe Dovid Danishevski had been *Rav* and *Rosh Yeshivah* in Slobodka, but when he became deaf and dim of vision in his old age, he invited Reb Boruch Ber to succeed him as *Rosh Yeshivah*. Slobodka was a suburb of Kovno, which in those days boasted a population of *talmidei chachamim, baalei battim lomdim,* and *geonim* (a highly educated lay population). They all flocked to Slobodka to hear the first *shiur* of the famous Reb Boruch Ber'l, *talmid muvhok* (prime disciple) of Reb Chaim Brisker. They had expected a profoundly deep lecture, and the *shiur* proved disappointing to them. They registered their complaint with Rav Danishevski, who was a giant in Torah in his own right. "Whom did you select as a *Rosh Yeshivah*? — a mediocrity?"

The *Rav* went directly to Reb Boruch Ber to convey to him the disappointment of the Kovno *lomdim*: this was not what they had expected.

Reb Boruch Ber in his *temimus* replied, "I don't understand. Do you expect me to violate *halachah*? The *halachah* states quite clearly that a merchant should not display the better quality merchandise up front, while hiding the goods of lesser quality underneath. This would be *ona'a* (cheating). *Rashi* quotes the *Midrash* to this effect (*Bamidbar* 13:17). You surely don't expect me to cheat the public!"

Some would dismiss this as naivete, but to us it demonstrated our *Rebbi's* perfect *emunah* in the words of *Chazal* (Rabbis of the Talmud), and complete subservience to *halachah*.

✺ A Matter of Justice

When Reb Moshe Danishevski was *niftar,* a meeting was called in the Yeshivah building to choose another *Rav*. Reb Chaik'l the *shochet* ascended the *bima* and forcefully presented his case: "What are we looking for? For whom are we searching? We have with us the *gaon* and *tzaddik* Reb Boruch Ber. Let him be our *Rav!*"

The crowd backed his proposal unanimously. This suggestion was not as spontaneous as it seemed, however, for on the spot, a completed *ksav rabbanus* (contract) was presented to him! Reb Boruch Ber asked the assembly for time to think over the offer. He then whispered to the *bachur* accompanying him, Koppel Kelmer, "Please take me to Reb Moshe Mordechai's house." Reb Moshe Mordechai Epstein, an undisputed *gadol*, was the *dayan* of Slobodka, and Reb Boruch Ber considered him as having first claim to the position: so he personally delivered the contract to him.

"You are the *bar metzra* (next in line)," said Reb Boruch Ber to Reb Moshe Mordechai. "You are entitled to the *Rabbanus* of Slobodka more than I. So here is the *ksav rabbanus*. It is yours even though it carries my name."

Reb Boruch Ber then returned to the assembly, and announced in a booming voice, "Mazel Tov! We have a new *Rav*! *Moreinu Verabeinu Harav* Reb Moshe Mordechai Epstein! Mazel Tov!"

◆§ Depth of Character — *Middos*

Reb Boruch Ber's daughter became engaged to a young man from Kremenchug, who was considered one of the best *bachurim* in the Yeshivah. As was the custom in those days, the *kalla's* father presented the *chassan* with a new suit, a new hat and a *"tzibbale watch"* (literally, "an onion watch" — a large pocket watch attached by a gold chain to a vest button). Since it was not considered proper for an engaged couple to stay together in the same town, the *chassan* transferred to the Yeshivah in Volozhin until their projected wedding date. But after several weeks, the *chassan* sent back the watch, suit, and hat, and broke the engagement.

Some time later, the *Rosh Yeshivah* received a letter from the young man relating that he had a possibility of entering into another *shidduch* and receiving a *Rabbanus*, but he was in need of a letter of recommendation from the *Rosh Yeshivah*. Would he comply with this request? Without hesitation, Reb Boruch Ber wrote a letter praising the *chassan* as a potential Rabbi Akiva Eiger, and then dispatched Koppel Kelmer to call at once Reb Moshe Perkovitz, the *Mashgiach* of the Yeshivah, Reb Shlomo

Paretzer (Heiman — later *Rosh Yeshivah* of Mesivta Torah Vodaath), Label Slonimer, and Yisroel Filipover (Goldman — known in the Yeshivah as "the junior Ohr Somayach" for his brilliance; he later served as *Rav* in Wilkes Barre, Pennsylvania).

Reb Boruch Ber explained to them that his letter of recommendation may not have been written as well as it should have been since the young man had hurt his daughter, and the letter might be tainted with prejudice. He therefore asked them to approve the letter. He read it aloud to them and they all agreed that it was free of any ill feelings; only then did he send it off. (The young man eventually became a famous *Rav*, wrote a commentary on *Talmud Yerushalmi*, but never had children.)

◆§ Exaggeration in Titles

Some people faulted the *Rosh Yeshivah* for exaggerating in his letters of recommendation and in his *semichah* certifications. If someone were something of a *lamdon*, Reb Boruch Ber would describe him as a *gaon*; the more accomplished in learning, the more grandiose the title. Reb Chaim Ozer Grodzenski once explained this tendency: "To Reb Boruch Ber, Torah is as overwhelmingly important as money is to others."

For instance, when a person has a half-million rubles, people will call him a millionaire. And should he possess a million, people will describe him as a multi-millionaire. It is human nature to exaggerate in regard to items that people admire and value. Reb Boruch Ber valued Torah above all else, and thus, a person who had even a small measure of Torah was fortunate beyond any reckoning in the eyes of the *Rosh Yeshivah*.

◆§ Calculations

Traditionally, *semichah* was only conferred by *Rabbanim*, never by a *Rosh Yeshivah*, for the *halachah* prescribes that only a person who has *semichah* can give *semichah*. Just as a professor in medical school may teach medicine without being qualified to write a prescription, so, too, did many a *Rosh Yeshivah* lack *semichah*, without in any way reflecting on his ability to teach Torah. Thus, when the Chofetz Chaim was preparing for his trip to Vienna to take part in the Knessia Gedolah (World Congress) of

Agudath Israel, he could not get a passport, for he had no *semichah* to back his claim that he was traveling on a religious mission. How could one explain to a Polish non-Jew that the leader and mentor of all rabbis never "graduated" rabbinical school, was never ordained as a rabbi, and had no piece of paper to show for his accomplishments? The organizers of the Knessia Gedolah rushed to Vilna, where Reb Chaim Ozer wrote out a *semichah* for him...Similarly, when the *Ridvaz* left Slutsk for America, the townspeople invited Reb Isser Zalman Meltzer, the *Rosh Yeshivah* of Slutsk, to become their *Rav*. He protested that he did not have *semichah*; so Reb Chaim Brisker wired him *semichah* by telegram.

Reb Boruch Ber was one of the few *Roshei Yeshiva* who did have *semichah*, for he had served as a *Rav*. When he was in Holusk, in 1900, a former *talmid* — whose parents were divorced — asked him for *semichah*. As was his custom, Reb Boruch Ber wrote out a document for him, full of exceptional praises, but in referring to the applicant's father, who was one of the great *Rabbanim* in Russia, he merely said, "*Harav*." The applicant was deeply disappointed. "*Rebbi*," he pleaded, "I wish that I knew half the Torah that my father knows, and you title him merely 'Harav,' while you lavish so much praise on me!"

Replied the *Rebbi*, "You'll surely show this document to your mother. Ordinarily, she would have loads of *nachas*, but also loads of pain. The way I wrote it, she'll have loads of *nachas*, but very little pain."

His concern for the sensitive feelings of a *Bas Yisrael* was truly phenomenal.

✑ Ahavas HaTorah and Modesty in Torah

Reb Boruch Ber had such boundless love for *talmidei chachamim* that he would embrace and kiss each one he met. He even extended this love to their sons and grandchildren. On one particular occasion, a modern-dressed, clean-shaven man with a modish hat, looking far from the typical *ben Torah*, paid him a visit. The *Rosh Yeshivah* welcomed him with great love and affection, to the puzzlement of everyone in the house. It turned out that he was the grandson of the *Rav* in Ozevitz. This *Rav* once had erred in a *psak halachah*, so he decided to leave his position to return to his studies in yeshivah for twelve years, plus one year of practical *halachah (shimush)* under Reb Binyamin Diskin. During all the years of his absence, the town kept the *rabbanus* open for him, until his return! In admiration for this amazing *Rav* and the most remarkable town, Reb Boruch Ber showered love and affection on this *Rav's* grandchild.

❀ ❀ ❀

Reb Boruch Ber once said in a shiur: "Reb Isser Zalman learns pshat in Rambam this way. I learn pshat in another way. And even Reb Isser Zalman himself admitted that his pshat is the better one."

ᵔᔆ The Rebbi — and *His* Rebbi

Reb Shalom Leibowitz, the *Rebbi's* nephew, also served as his right hand. He would review the *Rosh Yeshivah's shiur* for the public; he helped prepare the *Rebbi's sefarim* for publication; he was also the *Rosh Yeshivah's* companion whenever he had to travel somewhere. Once, on the way to a *Siyum Hashas* celebration, the *Rebbi* complained, "*Gevalt*, I have nothing to say!"

At the *simcha*, Reb Boruch Ber delivered an extraordinary *Dvar Torah*. Reb Shalom, who was accustomed to his uncle's greatness, was awe struck. Asked Reb Shalom, "The *Rebbi* was worried that he had nothing to say, and he said such marvelous Torah!"

"Ay, Shalom, Shalom," the *Rebbi* replied, "usually I am *metzamtzem* (take pains) to say precisely what the *Rabbi* [Reb Chaim] would find acceptable, and eliminate the rest. This time, I did not have a chance to select and reject, so I could say wagon loads of Torah."

❀ ❀ ❀

He was a gifted baal menagen. When he davened Musafim on the Yamim Noraim, the sweetness of his voice and his tearful rendition combined to make an unforgettable experience. One Purim, a bachur remarked to him that Reb Chaim Brisker could not carry a tune. Reb Boruch Ber's intense love and respect for Torah extended to his father and his Rebbi. And now someone had insulted his Rebbi! He became ghostly pale. After a tense five minutes, which seemed more like an hour, he broke out in a smile and commented, "A person is created with maalos and chesronos, positive and negative attributes. When Heaven gave my Rebbi his vast koach haTorah — his unusual abilities in understanding Torah — there was a necessity to give him a chisaron, too, so he wasn't able to sing. As for me, I have no maalos. Heaven had to grant me something...so I can sing."

❧ ❧ ❧

It seemed as though Reb Boruch Ber actually succeeded in emulating his *Rebbi's* way of thinking. When still a *bachur* in the Yeshivah of Volozhin, Reb Boruch Ber learned *bechavrusa* (in partnership) with Reb Zelig Reuvain Benges — eventually the *Rav* of the *Eida Hachareidis* in Jerusalem. Once, their voices thundered in sharp disagreement over how to interpret a passage in the *Rashba*. Reb Chaim passed by, listened to both sides and gave the final verdict: "One should say the *Rashba* like Reb Reuvain, but one should learn it like the Slutzker" — a reference to Reb Boruch Ber who was from Slutzk.

❧ ❧ ❧

Reb Boruch Ber once saw a talmid reading an article in Moment Magazine, a Warsaw-based publication that ridiculed religious concepts. He reprimanded the young man, and was visibly upset for the following week. Someone attempted to console the Rosh Yeshivah, arguing that Torah protects its students from harm.

"Torah, yes," responded Reb Boruch Ber. "But my Rebbi [Reb Chaim] said that when someone reads sifrei minnus [heretical works], his Torah-study is not Torah."

❧ ❧ ❧

Reb Yona Minsker, a *talmid* of Reb Boruch Ber and *chaver* of his son-in-law and successor, Reb Reuvain Grozovsky, had emerged as one of the *gedolim* in Mir. At the outbreak of World War II, when the *yeshivos* of Poland took refuge in Vilna, Reb Yona would discuss topics in Talmud with Reb Boruch Ber. (During this period of time, Reb Boruch Ber davened in a small, obscure *shtiebel* in deference to Reb Lazar Yudel Finkel, *Rosh Yeshivah* of Mir, whose group occupied an imposing *shul* in Vilna.) Reb Boruch Ber listed to Reb Yona, offered his own approach, but admitted that he had heard yet a different approach to the contested topic in the name of the Brisker *Rav*, son of his revered *Rebbi*, Reb Chaim. Reb Boruch Ber added, "I'll have to figure out some way to reconcile our views" — even though the Brisker *Rav* was his junior by a dozen years.

"Why?" asked Reb Yona. "So you disagree with the Brisker *Rav*. Is that so terrible?"

To which Reb Boruch Ber commented, "I pity you *bnei Torah* that you take me to be the *bar plugta* (an equal disputant) of the Brisker *Rav!*"

◄§ Ahavas Yisrael

Reb Boruch Ber judged himself quite critically — "When I will stand before the Heavenly Court, and they will ask me, 'What merit have you brought with you?' what shall I answer — Torah? Is my Torah knowledge worthy enough to be mentioned? — Fear of Heaven? Are my deeds worthy of that description? There is only one thing I could possibly claim — that I loved every Jew with all my heart. Whenever I walk in the street and I see a Jew, one thought comes to me — 'a blessing on his head!' " (quoted in *Marbitzei Torah Umussar*, by Aaron Surasky)

❀ ❀ ❀

In those days every baal agala (wagon driver) carried along a "fut-ter" — pieces of hide for the passengers to wrap themselves, for protection from the elements. Once a bachur came to say goodbye before going home for Pesach. Asked the Rebbi, "Do you have a coat?"

"No," was the reply.

"Then take my fur coat, it will keep you warm."

The boy refused, knowing well that a chassan receives a peltz fur coat for a wedding gift, expecting it to last a lifetime. He wouldn't dare think of taking the Rosh Yeshivah's coat.

Grunem Landau was present, and he could not understand the Rosh Yeshivah's insistence that the young fellow take the peltz, and not make do with the pieces of hide in the wagon.

"What's my yichus (special status) over the young man?" asked Reb Boruch Ber. "The fact that I study Torah? — So does he! I am not superior to him!"

Most every kitchen in Eastern Europe had a clay oven. The maintenance trade was mostly in non-Jewish hands, but there were a few Jewish clay-oven masters. Once, when her oven broke, the *Rebbetzin* called in a Jewish tradesman to fix it. The next morning, when the *Rebbi* entered the kitchen, he noticed a man on the floor fixing the oven. He greeted him in Polish: "*Dzien dorbry panie* (Good morning, sir).*"

The man replied, "*Gutt morgen, Rebbi.*"

The *Rebbi* turned white. Imagine robbing a man of his birthright as a Jew! He lowered himself to the floor, kissed the man, and begged his forgiveness a thousand times.

❧ ❧ ❧

Reb Koppel Kelmer recalls how a man came to Reb Boruch Ber with a chicken she'eila (a question regarding its kashrus). There were several dayanim in Slobokda, and since Reb Boruch Ber served exclusively as Rosh Yeshivah, he thought it improper to encroach on the domain of others. So he asked, "Why did you come to me? We have dayanim for your purpose."

Answered the man, "I went to Reb Moshe Mordechai Epstein, and he wasn't home. I went to another dayan — also not home. Rebbi, your psak is good enough for me."

Reb Boruch Ber asked the man to sit down and then whispered to Koppel, "Take the chicken and we'll cross the bridge to Kovno, to the dayan, Reb Lazer Lerner."

The dayan was overwhelmed by the visitor. They embraced, kissed, and began to discuss Torah topics, forgetting about the chicken — until Koppel finally tugged on his Rebbi's sleeve and quietly asked, "What about the chicken?"

The Rebbi placed the chicken on the table, and after a quick glance, the dayan pronounced it treif. On the walk home, Reb Boruch Ber was almost in tears, mumbling, "What are we going to do now? The poor man has one little chicken for Shabbos, and we have to inform him that it's treif!"

As they entered the house, the man fidgeted, and asked nervously, "Rebbi, where have you been? And what about the chicken?"

With a broken heart, Reb Boruch Ber asked, "Do you perhaps have another chicken?"

"No, Rebbi. I spent my last ruble for that chicken."

The Rebbi went into the kitchen, removed a chicken from the boiling pot, wrapped it up and handed it to the man. "Here is a chicken for you, and have a gut'n Shabbos. As for the other chicken, feed it to your dog."

When the Rebbetzin returned from the market, she checked the pot on the stove and found it empty. She knocked gently on the door of her husband's room so as not to disturb him from learning. "Boruch Ber'l," she said, "I know it's very hard to catch a live chicken — she flies, she jumps. But how did a dead chicken ever fly out of a boiling pot?"

From within, the Rosh Yeshivah's voice said, "Get another chicken. I'll tell you the rest later."

Of Love, Pain and Eternity

Reb Boruch Ber was strongly opposed to reading newspapers; in fact, their secular, anti-religious editorial slant made their mere presence repulsive. During Hitler's early years, he was seen scanning a newspaper. When asked about that in view of his rejection of papers, he said, "Jews are suffering. I must read about their problems so I can share their pain."[*]

Several years later, the same *talmid* saw him push a newspaper off his table with the back of his arm, avoiding direct contact out of abhorrence of its contents. "But *Rebbi*," asked the *talmid*, "don't you care to find out about Jewish suffering?"

He responded, "One must share in every individual's pain. If we deal in the suffering of such large numbers, however, it becomes impossible to relate to the individuals, and we become numb, indifferent, and callous."

❧ ❧ ❧

Reb Boruch Ber often expressed his vast love for his children and grandchildren. Of course, he had boundless nachas whenever one of them asked a kushya, or gave a good teretz. And what did this loving Zeide give his grandson in honor of his Bar Mitzvah? Money? — He

---

[*] His son-in-law, Reb Reuvain Grozovsky, carried on Reb Boruch Ber's concern to share in the *tzores* of his fellow Jews, and from the late '30's through the war years, Reb Reuvain was immersed in *hatzalah* (rescue) efforts — especially through the Vaad Hatzala, and later as head of *Moetzes Gedolei HaTorah* (Council of Torah Sages) of Agudath Israel of America.

had none. Sefarim? — *Impossible to buy. According to Rabbi Chaim Grozovsky, his grandson, for his Bar Mitzvah his grandfather gave him a kiss, a brachah, and advice: to cry when he says: "Atta chonein le'adam daas"* — *the prayer for wisdom.*

❧ ❧ ❧

Among the many hundreds of *talmidim* of the Yeshivah of Volozhin were some who later turned to *Haskalah* (such as the poet Chaim Nachman Bialik). In regard to those of his former classmates who specialized in the "scientific study of Judaism," Reb Boruch Ber said, "The *Maskilim* know when and where Abaye was born, and when and where Abaye died. We know where the *heilige Abaye* lives! Right before our eyes in the *heilige Gemara!*"

Reb Isser Zalman used to say, "Reb Boruch Ber is the *Rebbi* of our generation. And his Torah will live and be studied until *Moshiach* will come."

We know where our *Rebbi* lives — in his *heilige sefarim* and in *yeshivos* around the world where they are studied with great effort, awe, and joy.

Reb Boruch Ber
A Paradigm of Wisdom and Piety
collected and translated by Tzvi Zev Arem

Although Reb Boruch Ber is known best for his scholarly *shiurim,* other facets of his gemlike personality are equally deserving of study and emulation. Following is a selection of comments, said or written by the Kamenitzer *Rosh Yeshivah* on a variety of subjects, in which his many attributes come shining through.

◄§ Torah Study

■ Reb Boruch Ber was once traveling with family members and *talmidim,* when they were attacked by armed bandits who beat them severely and tore off their clothing. Though their lives hung by a thread, the *Rosh Yeshivah's* reaction was: "Now we can understand with what joy one must recite the blessing, *'Who has chosen us from among all the nations and given us His Torah.'* Look how low a person can sink if he has no Torah. Who knows? Perhaps without Torah, we too would murder and loot!"

■ After being told that a particular *shiur* of his contained no *chiddushim* (novel explanations), but merely explained the plain *p'shat* (meaning) of the passage, Reb Boruch Ber exclaimed: "That is really what I wanted to hear! Is this not the reward for all our toil — *ah bissele p'shat?*"   (cited in *Reb Elchonon*, by Aaron Surasky)

■ He once observed: "What can compare to my situation? When I wake up in the morning, it's as if I have the *Rambam*, the Vilna Gaon, and the *Nesivos* at my bedside, waiting for me to wash my hands and delve into their words!"

Someone once asked him what kind of dreams he had at night. Replied Reb Boruch Ber: "I go to sleep thinking about some comment of the *Rambam*, and wake up thinking about that *Rambam*. What can I possibly dream about? Either an explanation of the *Rambam* or a question on it!"

◄§ Being a *Mechanech*

■ "Each day we praise *Hashem* Himself as being the *'Melamed* of Torah to *Yisrael*, His people.' " Could one possibly strive for anything higher? Reb Chaim Volozhiner would sign all his correspondence with the appellation: 'Chaim the *melamed*, with the help of G-d, in Volozhin.' "   (Rabbi Yitzchak Edelstein ל״ז)

◄§ Mussar

■ "I exhort every Yeshivah student...to study *Mussar* before all other subjects, for it is the beginning of wisdom."

(*Chayei HaMussar, Birkas Shmuel*)

◄§ Trusting a Fellow Jew

■ A rumor once circulated in Kamenitz that a certain *shochet* had committed a grave sin, and consequently, the *bnei Torah* avoided eating the meat that he sold. Reb Boruch Ber, however, continued to use his meat.

The *yeshivaleit,* convinced that the *Rosh Yeshivah* must not have heard about the rumor, apprised him of it. Reb Baruch Ber's face turned red. He walked over to a solid wall nearby and banged on it.

"Do you see this wall?" he asked. "Can you knock it down? The same is true of a *chazaka* (presumed status). Every Jew who is known to be righteous has a *chezkas kashrus*; we assume that he has not sinned unless proven otherwise. What evidence do you have that the allegations are true? Rumors? They mean nothing! Many people have enemies who wish to destroy their reputations."

(Rabbi Shmuel Berenbaum, שליט"א)

ᴥᔑ Newspapers

■ "If a publication would defame your father, would you read it or allow it into your home? Well, the newspapers write against our Father in Heaven!"

Reb Boruch Ber considered the secular press so repulsive that he avoided even touching them. If he found a newspaper on a table, and he needed to use the table, he would pull his sleeve over his hand before brushing the paper away.

ᴥᔑ "B'li Neder"

■ Fear of sin was a constant companion of the Kamenitzer *Rosh Yeshivah.* He would shudder at the mere thought of doing something that even resembled the slightest transgression. He was literally obsessed with the worry that he might say or do something that might take on the power of a *neder* (vow). Thus, he would often perform *hataras nedarim* to annul any possible vow he may have inadvertently made, and the words *b'li neder* were constantly on his lips.

He once was about to sit down on a chair, when someone warned him that it was shaky.

"I won't fall," Reb Boruch Ber answered, *"b'li neder!"*

ᴥᔑ Agudath Israel

■ "My *rebbi,* the great *gaon*...Reb Chaim ז"ל...proclaimed with great fervor that we should support the Agudah, asserting that we could not possibly manage without the organization. I believe that every Jew is obligated to help these warriors, who are waging *Hashem's* battles, and that we should honor and bless the leaders of Agudath Israel. After all, this is the movement founded by the *geonim* and *tzaddikim* of the previous generations."

(cited in the Hebrew biography *Reb Boruch Ber*)

50 Years Since His Passing — 5 Av 5750

Reb Chaim Ozer Grodzensky, זצ״ל

He personified the marriage of greatness in Torah with leadership on a global scale

◆§ Can We Relate to a Gadol?

Over the past few years, much has been written in The Jewish Observer regarding the literary and educational value of the ever-growing volume of Torah literature in English. In discussing books on *gedolei Yisrael,* one writer contended that all the biographies sound the same: All *gedolim* seem to be born geniuses and are launched almost from birth on a meteoric rise to greatness. How can we relate to such people?

Nowhere does this argument seem more pronounced than with regard to the life of Rabbi Chaim Ozer Grodzensky, legendary head of the *beis din* of Vilna and acclaimed giant of his generation. Reb Chaim Ozer was the genius among geniuses, a man whose breadth and depth of knowledge seemed limitless, whose comprehension was characterized as indescribable by his nephew, Rabbi Eliyahu Eliezer Dessler, and who possessed the ability to pursue three or four unrelated trains of thoughts simultaneously, without losing track or confusing any of them. Rabbi Dessler related to his son, Reb Nochum Zev (currently of Cleveland), that he had seen Reb Chaim Ozer writing with both hands at the same time! He had also seen him write a halachic responsum, compute charity amounts and discuss Torah with someone simultaneously.

Another nephew of Reb Chaim Ozer, Rabbi Yehuda Leib Kagan, was present when Reb Chaim Ozer received the newly published volume one of *Shaarei Yosher*, a 320 page analytical work on Talmudic themes by Rabbi Shimon Shkop. He began leafing through the *sefer* during breakfast and continued to do so for about an hour-and-a-half after his meal. Then he closed the work and immediately proceeded to analyze and discuss various concepts scattered throughout its pages. He had obviously digested all its contents.

⋖§ How Can We Mere Mortals Relate to This?

The answer to this question can be found in the first chapter to *Mesilas Yesharim*:

Man is placed in the thick of a raging battle; all matters of this world, both for bad and for good, are actually tests. On the one hand there is poverty, on the other there is wealth, as Shlomo [HaMelech] said, "Lest I become satiated and deny, and say, 'Who is Hashem?'; and lest I become impoverished and then steal..." (Mishlei 30:9). On the one hand there is tranquility, while on the other there is suffering — the battle, then, is on all sides.

Reb Chaim Ozer was born an intellectual billionaire. Physically, he was quite poor, a frail, sick individual. He died quite wealthy—spiritually; but this he earned by overcoming, time and again, the tests that Providence sent his way. Let us look at some of those tests and see how this *gaon* and *tzaddik* dealt with them.

⋖§ The Pitfalls of Wealth

Along with mental genius come three possible pitfalls: the dangers of arrogance or at least some degree of pride; laziness, since scholastic achievement comes so easily to the genius; and an inability to properly relate to the vast majority of people whose thinking is on a different plane entirely.

Rabbi Dessler saw Reb Chaim Ozer as the epitome of humility, a rare portrait of self-effacement. Toward the very end of his life, when he was deathly ill, Reb Chaim Ozer was unable to read the scores of letters that arrived at his door each day; it was necessary to have his mail read to him. One particular letter opened with an array of sublime descriptions of Reb Chaim Ozer's greatness. By the time the reader had completed relating the salutation, Reb Chaim Ozer was laughing aloud. He explained, "In the days of the Russian revolution, the value of currency plummeted and it became virtually worthless; for a dollar, one could get a million rubles. A poor, downtrodden fellow had no difficulty becoming a millionaire. Judging from this letter, it seems that our spiritual world is experiencing this kind of gross inflation!"

Reb Chaim Ozer's brother-in-law, Reb Elchonon Wasserman,[1] once asked him how he had fasted on Yom Kippur. Reb Chaim Ozer replied, "The physical strain does not particularly affect me, but from where do I draw the spiritual strength to bear the distress of confessing my sins?"

True humility is manifested in one's *savlanus* (tolerance) of the iniquities done him. His confidants would say that no one ever saw him exhibit even a trace of anger. His *savlanus* became apparent early on in his career. He became *av beis din* of Vilna when still in his twenties. Only nine years later, with the passing of the Kovno *Rav*, Rabbi Yitzchok Elchonon Spector, Reb Chaim Ozer's address became the center for all of Lithuanian Jewry. At that time, some *maskillim* in Vilna began to vilify the young *Rav*, whom they viewed as a threat to their own activities. Placards were posted ridiculing the activities of Reb Chaim Ozer, who was referred to as "the new general of the black army."

Reb Chaim Ozer responded with total silence. He forbade anyone from voicing any protests or defense. He said simply, "Their arrows have missed their mark."

---

1. In the mid-1920's, after his first *Rebbetzin* died, Reb Chaim Ozer married a widow, Yacha Kahana. She was a daughter of the famed *Rav* of Shavli, Rabbi Meir Atlas, and a sister to the wife of Reb Elchonon.

In 1928, by which time Reb Chaim Ozer had long been acclaimed as *poseik hador* and a leader of world Jewry, the modern element in Vilna's Jewish community challenged his leadership of their city. They attempted to curtail Reb Chaim Ozer's incredible accomplishments and effectiveness as leader by having one of their own become the government-recognized *Rav* of Vilna. The Torah community, most notably the Chofetz Chaim and the Chazon Ish (who then resided in Vilna), reacted swiftly to this challenge to the honor of Torah, which Reb Chaim Ozer embodied. Outrage was heard also from as far away as *Eretz Yisrael,* where Rabbi Yosef Chaim Sonnenfeld and other notables issued their own letter of protest. Only Reb Chaim Ozer's serenity was not shattered. Not once did he attempt to defend himself or expose the true intent of his attackers. Moreover, he went to great lengths to demonstrate that the dispute was one of principle and was not personal.

A Shabbos afternoon walk took Reb Chaim Ozer past the home of his challenger. Reb Chaim Ozer excused himself to his company and went inside for a moment to wish the Rav "Gut Shabbos." That Reb Chaim Ozer harbored no ill feelings could not have been more obvious.[2]

◅§ Antithesis of Lethargy

Reb Chaim Ozer utilized his G-d-given mental abilities to the fullest as he guided and advised upon an incredible array of public and private endeavors. Nothing of significance was undertaken by Vilna's Torah community without his approval. No *shtadlan* (intercessor) representing a Torah constituency in Lithuania — and to a certain degree, anywhere in the world — ever embarked upon an important mission without first securing Reb Chaim Ozer's approval and receiving his guidance. He was

---

2. Those who knew Reb Chaim Ozer's challenger relate that he was in fact a decent man and a scholar, but he allowed himself to be misled by those whose true intent was to wrest authority away from Reb Chaim Ozer and oppose the ideas that he represented. On the day that Reb Chaim Ozer died, this Rav requested permission to enter the room where the body lay and beg forgiveness of the deceased. Reb Chaim Ozer's confidants discussed the request. One of them said, "Reb Chaim Ozer would not be pleased if someone sought to beg forgiveness and his request was denied." The Rav then entered the room and, with his head bowed submissively, wept before Reb Chaim Ozer's lifeless body and asked that he be forgiven.

consulted on virtually every major rabbinic appointment — even in Jerusalem and Constantinople. He was involved in the founding of every new Lithuanian Torah institution and in the functioning of those already in existence. He headed the *Va'ad HaYeshivos*, the organization that helped sustain the great Torah centers between the wars. He was among the founders of Agudath Israel and served as chairman of its original *Moetzes Gedolei HaTorah* (Council of Torah Sages).

Rabbi Moshe Blau, leader of Agudath Israel in *Eretz Yisrael* until 1946, commented, "If Agudath Israel is defined as a union of a significant portion of *Klal Yisrael*, then Reb Chaim Ozer is its unifying force." The Chofetz Chaim put it more succinctly: "Reb Chaim Ozer is *Klal Yisrael*."

He was the acclaimed *poseik hador*. The Chazon Ish referred to him as *Rabbeinu* (our teacher). In discussing the opinions of a number of *gedolei Torah* regarding a given matter, Reb Aharon Kotler referred only to Reb Chaim Ozer as "*gaon ha'amiti* (the quintessential *gaon*), *meor hagola* (light of the Diaspora)."

To his door, sacks of mail arrived each week, containing letters from all across the globe. Who knows how many thousands of halachic queries came before Reb Chaim Ozer during his more than fifty-year tenure as head of Vilna's *beis din*!

When traveling to a summer resort, he never took along more than a handful of *seforim*. Thus he writes in one responsum (*Achiezer* I:32-33), "I have no *seforim* with me," and then goes on to cite numerous sources, from *Tosafos* to *Nesivos HaMishpat* (nineteenth-century *Acharon*). One *sefer* that always accompanied him was *Mesilas Yesharim*, the classic ethical work by Rabbi Moshe Chaim Luzzatto.

⋅⋅§ Great Accomplishments

It is said that there is a fifth section of *Shulchan Aruch*, in addition to the standard four—that of insight and sensitivity; to decide matters of *halachah* one must be as proficient in this area as in the actual *Shulchan Aruch*. Reb Chaim Ozer's fluency in this fifth section was on a par with his incredible command of the other four.

In Druskenik, there lived an old man with no family. One of his ways of keeping busy was to arrange a private minyan of his own, though the town had no need for it. Reb Chaim Ozer never once refused the man's invitation that he join the minyan for davening. Some wondered about this, as there were minyanim closer to Reb Chaim Ozer's lodging that were certainly more to his liking. Reb Chaim Ozer explained, "Davening with a minyan is a Rabbinic obligation; performing chessed for another Jew is mandated by the Torah."

As Reb Chaim Ozer's halachic proficiency in expertise grew from his Torah, so did his sense of priorities. In a conversation with Rabbi Mendel Zaks, late son-in-law of the Chofetz Chaim, he said, "When I was young, I learned that it was a great accomplishment to propound an original Torah thought. Now I see that it is also a great accomplishment to make an elderly woman happy." In this regard, his compassion and sense of purpose were complemented by rare insight.

Reb Chaim Ozer's dining room was crowded with petitioners. In a corner stood a widow, a Vilna resident. Her husband had been a man of wealth and a supporter of the local Rameilles Yeshivah. When he died, his business collapsed and his family was cast into poverty. Ever since then, his widow was too ashamed to cross the threshold of the Yeshivah where, for years, she and her husband had always been welcomed and honored visitors.

Earlier that day, she told Reb Chaim Ozer that she had felt compelled to enter the Yeshivah. She was devastated by what she saw. The students' straw mattresses were torn and the straw had turned rotten and hard.

"Can the Rav do something about this?" the woman asked Reb Chaim Ozer.

He replied softly, "I believe that you are at fault here. As long as you and your husband supported the Yeshivah, you always kept a watchful eye over the students' needs. Why have you given this up? One can help a Yeshivah in ways other than monetary contributions. Effort and toil are more precious to Hashem than money."

He withdrew some money from a chest. "Here," he said. "This is for new straw; you can surely acquire sacks for the straw free of charge. If you need more money, you know my address. The main thing is that you become involved once again with the Yeshivah — its students, its kitchen, dormitory facilities, everything! Recruit other women to join you in this great work. May the merit of Torah shield you and earn you long life."

The woman took leave of Reb Chaim Ozer with an immense burden lifted from her broken heart.

His genuine love of his fellow Jew was almost tangible, and it had the power to bring those distant closer to Torah.

🍃 *When rescue efforts for European Jewry began with the outbreak of World War II, Rabbi Eliezer Silver decided to send an emissary from America to Vilna, which Reb Chaim Ozer had turned into the rescue center for the yeshivos of war-torn Poland. For this role, Rabbi Silver chose Doctor Samuel Schmidt, who had been an ardent secular Zionist-Socialist. At the time of his journey to Vilna, Dr. Schmidt had already gained an appreciation for Torah and had adopted certain religious practices. His visit to Reb Chaim Ozer transformed him into a complete baal teshuva. As Dr. Schmidt related, he and Reb Chaim Ozer had a very friendly, lengthy discussion during their first meeting.*

"...Then, Reb Chaim Ozer, the genius among geniuses, asked me some very personal questions about myself. He listened with rapt attention, and then, with a look of true friendship, said, 'Allow me, Dr. Schmidt, to address you in a familiar manner, by your first name —Reb Shmuel.'

"His words touched my heart and my tears flowed freely. 'I am not worthy of this!' I protested. He replied, 'Heaven forfend! For a Jew living in the security of America, to undertake a dangerous mission and travel under wartime conditions to a far- away land in order to assist his fellow Jews and rescue the yeshivos — this is proof of his worth.'

"He continued to offer me encouragement. The next morning, I donned tallis and tefillin for the first time...and became observant in Torah and mitzvos in all their fine details."

⸙ Strength and Suffering

The Chofetz Chaim once said that Reb Chaim Ozer's genius overshadowed his great *tzidkus* (righteousness).[3] His sublime attributes were likewise hidden by his very congenial, down-to-earth nature. Reb Chaim Ozer would make his company feel so

---

3. Of the Chofetz Chaim, the converse was said: His incredible piety overshadowed his genius in Torah.

at ease and comfortable that it was difficult to perceive that this man was actually head and shoulders above his generation in virtually every respect. Certain episodes, however, brought to light some of his exceptional qualities.

❧ He and his wife had an only child, Malka. She was a modest, gentle, and good-hearted girl, the apple of her father's eye. It is related that Reb Chaim Ozer considered Reb Chaim Soloveitchik's son Reb Yitzchok Zev (later famous as the Brisker Rav) as a possible match for his daughter. Then, in 1907, when just sixteen years old, she was stricken with a debilitating disease. Her illness was to last four years, during which time Reb Chaim Ozer tried desperately but fruitlessly to locate a doctor who could cure her.

Throughout this trying period, Reb Chaim Ozer's activities — both on the communal and individual level — did not wane. He continued to commit his chiddushei Torah to writing. He attended and presided over major conferences of Torah leaders.

When, in the winter of 1911, his daughter's end drew near, Reb Chaim Ozer hastened to answer all correspondence and halachic inquiries that were of a pressing nature—he would not be permitted to engage in such activities during the week of shiva—writing eighty halachic responsa during the week prior to his daughter's death!

Reb Chaim Ozer was deeply grieved by his daughter's passing, but he would not allow his spirit to be broken. He once told his brother-in-law, Rabbi Yitzchok Kosowsky, that his incessant efforts on behalf of others did much to quell any despondent thoughts.

◆§ The Source of It All

Rabbi Yerucham Levovitz, the legendary Mirrer Mashgiach, once traveled to the mineral baths in Marienbad, where he found himself in the company of an assimilated Jewish professor. Reb Yerucham tried to convince the fellow to return to the ways of his forefathers. The professor, however, was unimpressed.

He challenged Reb Yerucham, "Tell me, Rabbi, have you ever studied the works of Kant or other renowned philosophers?"

Reb Yerucham replied that he had not.

"If so," the man went on, "how can you be certain that your way is the correct one? Perhaps had you studied these works you would

become convinced of their philosophies — which my way of life embodies!"

Reb Yerucham replied, "I know one thing: The Torah way of life has produced such men as the Chofetz Chaim and Reb Chaim Ozer Grodzensky, not to mention the giants of previous generations. They are veritable angels. Does your camp boast such men? No, it does not. That is sufficient proof for me."

To Reb Chaim Ozer, Torah study was not an exercise in dry, cold, mental gymnastics. It was life. It permeated his being, it flowed through his veins. It was in recognition of this fact that the Chazon Ish once declared with certainty that Reb Chaim Ozer never ceased from pondering Torah thoughts.

Some would note the appearance of red streaks on Reb Chaim Ozer's forehead as he prayed the *Shemoneh Esrei*...thought to result from his intense mental strain to banish from his mind all thoughts other than those directed toward his Maker.

In his later years, Reb Chaim Ozer was forced to undergo delicate surgery without the aid of anesthesia. Before the surgery was to begin, Reb Chaim Ozer requested a certain *sefer*. Throughout the surgery, he remained immersed in study, seemingly oblivious to the pain. As his *Rebbetzin* later related to Rabbi Shimon Schwab (currently *Rav* of K'hal Adath Jeshurun, New York), the doctors could not believe that such power of concentration was humanly possible. They could not know that the source of Reb Chaim Ozer's concentration was his being bound up firmly and eternally with the Torah and its Giver.

⋖§ More than a Genius

Clearly, Reb Chaim Ozer was far more than a genius. And though he left behind no children, his legacy is a glorious one, as he played a major role in the survival of Torah during the post-World War I years, as well as in the escape of hundreds of yeshivah students during the early period of World War II. The thriving Torah world that we are witness to today may justly be considered Reb Chaim Ozer's legacy.

His other legacy is the written word, his classic collection of halachic responsa, *Achiezer*. The first volume of *Achiezer* was published soon after the end of the First World War, a time when Reb Chaim Ozer was leading the rebuilding of Torah life in a decimated Lithuania and guiding efforts on behalf of the millions of Jews trapped within Communist Russia. His preface to that volume is highly instructive:

* *Turbulent thoughts pound within one's heart — Is this dire hour appropriate for publishing seforim? Will not people wonder: "The nation of Israel is drowning in a sea of tears and you are singing shirah? Our enemies from within and without are attempting to undermine the foundations of Torah...the sanctuary of Hashem is ablaze, the flames are consuming the Aron HaKodesh, the Tablets and parchments are afire — and you occupy yourself with adornments?!"*

However, this is the power of ancient Israel, in every generation and epoch....Even when the sword was at his neck, the Torah was the Jew's delight all through the day. Even during the destruction of the Second Beis HaMikdash, when the nation's very existence was threatened and the heretics were gaining strength, the faithful never diverted their minds for a moment from Torah....From the day that Israel was exiled from its land, the everlasting and unbroken chain of Gaonim, Rishonim, and Acharonim was never broken — and so, the ancient edifice of Toras Yisroel was preserved through them....

To those who merited it, the study of Torah was always a potion of life. The spreading of Torah study is a shield in the face of retribution, a defense against those who stray and cause others to stray. The Torah and the light within her will eventually return them to the good path and it is Torah that has stood by us to this day, strengthening us so that we do not become lost among the nations.

∘§ Postscript

After Reb Chaim Ozer's death in 1940, a list of ten personal resolutions was found among his possessions, dated *Erev Yom Kippur* 5694 (1934). The resolutions reveal much about the man. The second resolution reads:

To spend at least a short time each day studying *mussar* works, such as *Sha'arei Teshuva, Mesilas Yesharim* and the like; and to make a spiritual accounting every day.

Rabbi Yitzchok Kosowsky commented: "This resolution

came as a complete surprise to many of those close to him, for no one ever saw him studying works of *mussar*....We thought that this was not his way, but we were obviously mistaken. Though he was so preoccupied, he set aside time for this and made the study of *mussar* a statute not to be ignored.

"In essence, his spiritual accounting was revealed to all, for his entire day was one continuous flow of mighty deeds and acts of benevolence. His was a life of Torah, and assistance to everyone who appeared at his door."

In commenting on another resolution, Rabbi Kosowsky wrote how the flourishing of Torah before the war and its subsequent survival is his doing:

"He worked for the strengthening and support of Torah study until his very last breath, literally."

יהא זכרו ברוך.

Rabbi Elchonon Wasserman זצ"ל

Teacher of Torah Perspective
On His 50th Yahrzeit

*His Talmudic insights
and dedication to
Torah principles
continue to guide Jews
in their Torah study
and the conduct of
Jewish communal and
national affairs*

I. Teacher to His Generation— And Ours

Rabbi Elchonon Bunim Wasserman was, by the testimony of his peers and disciples, a "Rebbi's Rebbi," an absolute master at the study of *Gemara* and its commentaries. While he was certainly capable of composing intricate, hair-splitting *pilpulim* (in which a wide range of sources are woven together to produce new insights or solutions), Reb Elchonon always concerned himself with uncovering the *p'shat*, the plain meaning and implication of the text. In one of his first positions, as a *rosh yeshivah* in Brisk in 1910, he was referred to by his students as "Reb Elchonon *baal* (master of) *hap'shat*." They would say: "Every word he uttered was clear and completely lucid, every idea as keen as a well-honed knife."

From 1929, when he was already world renowned as head of the Baranovich Yeshivah, until his death by a Nazi bullet on 13 Tammuz, 5701 (as given in *Kovna HaYehudis Bechurbana*—there is some doubt regarding the exact date) Reb Elchonon was recognized as teacher of his entire generation. In public addresses and through written essays, he articulated the Torah outlook on current events and problems in a period when the Jewish people was plagued by ideological confusion and distortion from within its ranks and anti-Semitism and persecution from its enemies. As with his lectures in *Gemara*, his presentations on Torah perspective were always lucid, uncomplicated, and ringing of truth.

Reb Elchonon was also recognized as the prime disciple of the greatest Torah personality of his time, the Chofetz Chaim. In 1907, at thirty-two years of age and already a successful disseminator of Torah, Reb Elchonon went to Radin to study in the Chofetz Chaim's *Kodashim Kollel*. [1] Until the Chofetz Chaim's death in 1933, Reb Elchonon clung to him in an extraordinary manner. He studied in Radin for three consecutive years and returned there each year to spend the Days of Awe in his *Rebbi's* presence. To Reb Elchonon, every word uttered by the Chofetz Chaim was *kodesh kodoshim,* holiest of holies, and deserved careful scrutiny and reflection.[2] Toward the end of his life, the Chofetz Chaim made plans to settle in *Eretz Yisrael,* a dream that he would never fulfill. When the Chofetz Chaim's plans became known, he was beseeched from all sides not to abandon his brethren in Eastern Europe. Reb Mendel Goldberg, a prominent Baranovich community member, asked the Chofetz Chaim, "To whom have you abandoned your sheep?" to which the *tzaddik* replied, "But Reb Elchonon is staying behind with you!"

At that year's *Simchas Torah* celebration in Baranovich, Mr. Goldberg repeated the Chofetz Chaim's words to Reb Elchonon and implored him to act upon them. That very day, Reb Elchonon delivered a public address of practical substance—the first such

---

1. The order of *Kodashim* deals with the laws of the service in the *Beis Hamikdash*. The Chofetz Chaim revived the study of this order as a preparation for the arrival of *Moshiach,* when the *Beis Hamikdash* will be rebuilt.

2. One Rosh Hashanah, after the Chofetz Chaim concluded his address, someone remarked that he had delivered the same address, word for word, the previous year. Said Reb Elchonon, "This time he added eight new words."

address of his life. From then on, he never hesitated to speak out on the issues of the day, and even published his views in Orthodox newspapers and periodicals. Indeed, Reb Elchonon had so become involved in Agudath Israel as the movement representing organized Torah Jewry, that he was recognized as one of the towering figures at the third Knessia Gedolah (International Congress) of Agudath Israel, at Marienbad in 1937.

◂§ Forever the Disciple

His collected essays, published posthumously under the title of *Kovetz Ma'amarim*, bear the qualities that so deeply characterized their author. While a *gadol* of towering stature, Reb Elchonon was forever the disciple, frequently citing the interpretations and insights of the Chofetz Chaim. Reb Elchonon's words, full of power and intensity, reflect the pure and almost tangible faith for which the Chofetz Chaim was famous. The late Rabbi Moshe Schonfeld (an Orthodox journalist in *Eretz Yisrael*) wrote:

"The holy gaon and tzaddik, Rabbi Elchonon Wasserman, זצ״ל was unique among the gedolei Torah who illuminated the firmament of Judaism (during his era). Like a perfect mirror, his personality reflected the image of his rebbi, the venerable and holy sage, the Chofetz Chaim. Pure awe of Heaven, humility, wholesomeness, and a simplicity that was sublime; a boundless love of Torah and a sense of responsibility for all of Klal Yisrael. Above all was his clinging to the seal of HaKadosh Baruch Hu—truth, and making it known to the masses, without the slightest fear of any man.

"These, and many more characteristics, were shared by the teacher [i.e. the Chofetz Chaim], who was akin to an angel, and his disciple, who perpetuated his legacy. As long as Reb Elchonon was alive, it seemed almost as if the Chofetz Chaim walked this earth, his voice emanated from the mouth of his choicest disciple. Never did Reb Elchonon speak or write without mentioning the Chofetz Chaim and adducing support from his teachings."

The style of Reb Elchonon's essays follows a principle that he would frequently explain with the following comment of the Chofetz Chaim:

When a person is faced with a major decision, one that may even affect the course of his entire life, he must seek the advice of Hashem Himself. Indeed, we are all capable of accomplishing this, for the Torah contains the solution to every possible problem. The Torah is called tushiah—counsel[3] because it is the sole counsel for the Jewish nation, and for every individual Jew, in every situation. One must search the Torah for the advice he needs; of course, to do this, one must be knowledgeable in Torah, know how to interpret it, and where in it to search for any given problem.

Thus, Reb Elchonon's essays and addresses followed a pattern very much like the one he employed in teaching *Gemara*: to cite the relevant sources in the Written and Oral Law and elucidate them with the utmost clarity so that their application to the matter under discussion was perfectly clear. Once, he opened an address in the Great Synagogue of Baranovich by saying, "...Insofar as I am concerned, the question cannot be asked, 'Who appointed you to offer reproof to the Jews of Baranovich?' I tell you nothing of my own; whatever I shall say is written explicitly in the Torah."

Reb Elchonon's essays set forth basic principles of Judaism; they are as relevant now as they were when they were written, during the decade that preceded the Second World War.

II. His Message For Our Times

◆§ Economic Woes and Their Source

The 1930's were a time of world economic turmoil. As with the current recession, it was not drought or other natural phenomena that precipitated the startling decline in world markets. As Reb Elchonon put it, "What is lacking in G-d's world?....Is there any lack of food? In Canada, wheat is being dumped into the sea to prevent prices from falling. The same applies to Brazilian coffee. Is there any scarcity of money? The Swiss banks complain that their coffers are full of gold, but there is no place to invest and no one wants to lend...."

---

3. *Mishlei* 8,14.

Reb Elchonon offered the following explanation: Commerce and industry are based on mutual confidence and trust between parties. When trust has been destroyed, the economy comes to a standstill. G-d is privy to man's innermost thoughts and can direct them at will, and deals with man *midah keneged midah*, measure for measure. When man's faith in G-d wanes, *Hashem* responds by causing man's faith in his fellow to weaken. Neighbors become distrustful of one another; businesses become distrustful of one another; nations become distrustful of one another. An economic downturn is set in motion.[4]

◈ The Antidote

The *mitzvah* of Torah study was a prime focus of Reb Elchonon's essays. Torah study and *emuna* are interrelated and affect one another. Just as belief in G-d leads to belief in the Divinity of Torah and the observance of its laws, so does the study of Torah bring with it a strengthening and clarity of faith.

The Torah tells of the struggle between Yaakov *Avinu* and the Angel of Eisav, who is Satan. Why did Satan choose to do battle with Yaakov and not with Avraham and Yitzchak, who preceded him? Reb Elchonon cites the prophet's cry, "Why was the Land destroyed? Because they forsook My Torah" (*Yirmiyahu* 9,11-12), on which the Sages commented (*Yerushalmi, Chagiga* 1:7) "*Hakadosh Baruch Hu* overlooked the sins of idolatry, adultery and murder, but He would not overlook the sin of *bittul Torah* (disruption of Torah study)." Reb Elchonon explained this by way of a parable: In war, even a great victory cannot be considered decisive so long as the losing army still retains its arms. However, when one side has been disarmed, then the war is surely over. There is only one weapon with which to fight the ways and wiles of the *yeitzer hora*: "I have created the *yeitzer hara*, and I have created Torah as its antidote" (*Kiddushin* 30b). Even when the Jewish people are guilty of serious sins, as was the case prior

---

4. In an essay, Reb Elchonon quoted the verse: "By the sword they shall die, all the sinners of my nation" (*Amos* 9,10). The Chofetz Chaim, citing the *Zohar*, said that the punishment of poverty is a substitute for the sword, and that prior to *Moshiach's* coming, poverty would be rampant among the Jews. The Chofetz Chaim added that those who still held to their wealth would be wise to invest it in worthy causes, lest it become lost to them without having benefited from it.

to the destruction of the First Temple, there is still hope that they will repent as long as they cling to the study of Torah. "If only they would forsake Me but still observe [the study of] My Torah, for its light would return them to the good" (*Yerushalmi Chagiga ad loc.*). However, when the study of Torah has been abandoned, the sole weapon against the *yeitzer hara* has been lost. Faith without Torah is fragile, because man's passions will dominate his heart and pervert his mind. The battle is lost.

Reb Elchonon quoted the Chofetz Chaim, "The *yeitzer hara* does not mind if a Jew fasts and sheds tears and prays all day long—as long as he doesn't study Torah!"

Avraham *Avinu* was the "pillar of *chessed*" in this world; Yitzchak was the "pillar of service to G-d"; Yaakov was the "pillar of Torah." Following the rule that the happenings of the Patriarchs are a portent for their descendants (see *Ramban, Bereishis* 12,6), the struggle between Satan and Yaakov foretold that Satan's primary efforts against the Jewish people would always be directed at weakening their study of Torah.

Reb Elchonon cited the Vilna Gaon's statement that the journey of Yaakov from the house of Lavan, in which he encountered the angel of Eisav and ultimately Eisav himself, alludes to *Ikvesa D'Meshicha*, the period of history preceding the arrival of *Moshiach*. Thus, the struggle between Yaakov and the Angel of Eisav alludes to the attack on Torah study by forces of impurity in the pre-Messianic era. In the end, Yaakov prevailed, but the angel did succeed in dislodging "the sinew of Yaakov's thigh" (i.e. the *gid hanasheh*). The thigh, writes Reb Elchonon, alludes to the support upon which the collective body of *Klal Yisrael* rests. Reb Elchonon identifies two such supports: children who study Torah[5], and the financial supporters of Torah education; Satan will influence those who have the means to support Torah to direct their money elsewhere, so that "even in countries where there is still money to contribute, they will give for all sorts of charitable causes, and leave only pennies for Torah."

---

5. The *Gemara* (*Shabbos* 119b) states: "The world is sustained only in the merit of the breadth [of Torah study] of children." The *Gemara* goes on to explain that their study is particularly potent because it is untainted by sin.

⋙ Fear of Hashem

Reb Elchonon wrote a commentary on selected Aggadic passages, which he entitled, "Expositions of Aggados in Accordance with Their Plain Meaning."[6] In one piece, he cites the teaching of Zohar, that when Hashem said, "Let us make man" (*Bereishis* 1,26), He invited all of creation to contribute something to man's essence. The lion contributed some of its nature, the ox something of its own, and so on. Man, then, is truly a "miniature world," for he has within himself something of all that exists in heaven and earth. Since man's nature contains some of the nature of every wild beast, there is surely no more potentially wild and dangerous creature than man. Moreover, man is endowed with intellect and the power of speech, two potentially lethal weapons that no other creature possesses. Now, if a single beast of prey must be restrained by an iron chain, how many iron chains must be required to restrain the beast in man! In creating man, Hashem surely provided the means through which his nature can be harnessed and directed toward good.

Man's "iron chain," says Reb Elchonon, is *yiras Hashem*, fear of G-d. "Only *yiras Hashem* has the power to restrain man so that he will not be like a beast that tears apart its prey. Nothing else in the world can guard man from causing harm (to others as well as to himself)—even if he is wise and a philosopher of the stature of Aristotle—when he becomes overwhelmed by base inclinations." Thus does Shlomo *Hamelech* conclude *Koheles* with, "The sum of the matter when all has been considered: Fear G-d and observe His commandments, for that is the whole of man." *Koheles* teaches that *yiras Hashem* is not merely one more virtue; it is the totality of man. Without *yiras Hashem*, man is just another beast; he is not a man at all. Conversely, the greater the degree of one's *yiras Hashem*, the greater the man he is.

Reb Elchonon's own *yiras Hashem* was manifest in his avoidance of any taint of sin. Once, a visiting student asked to purchase a copy of Reb Elchonon's *Kovetz He'aros*. Reb Elchonon handed the volume to the student and said, "I do not accept payment for the *sefer* from a *ben Torah*." When the student persisted,

6. *Kovetz Ma'amorim* p. 31-52.

Reb Elchonon said, "If you insist on paying, then please let me examine the *sefer* for any possible defect or omission. I am not obliged to do this when giving a gift, but I must do so when a sale is involved. Otherwise, there would be the possibility of theft."

✑ The Visit to America

In the fall of 1937, Reb Elchonon arrived in the United States for a visit that lasted sixteen months. The decision to separate himself from his beloved *talmidim* for so long a period was heartrending, but there was no other choice. Reb Elchonon's yeshivah was in deep financial straits; at times, there was barely any food to serve the students.[7]

The trip was a success in several ways. In advance of Reb Elchonon's departure, Reb Chaim Ozer Grodzensky[8] wrote letters to leading *rabbanim* in the U.S., urging them to assist Reb Elchonon in his mission. Reb Chaim Ozer had high hopes that Reb Elchonon's visit would have a great impact on the Orthodox community in America, a spiritual wilderness at that time. Reb Elchonon visited many American cities,[9] delivering impassioned addresses to huge crowds wherever he went. His effect on the American scene was profound, both on a communal and individual level. Some became complete *baalei teshuvah* as a result of their encounters with him. It was Reb Elchonon who prevailed upon Mr. Elimelech ("Mike") Tress, a young Zeirei Agudath Israel activist, to relinquish his promising business career and devote himself totally to the *Klal*. Mr. Tress, who later became the president of Agudath Israel of America, was bound heart and soul to Reb Elchonon, as were other Zeirei members. To quote

---

7. When the *talmidim* learned of Reb Elchonon's planned trip, they sent a delegation to him, saying that all would willingly forgo a meal a day rather than have Reb Elchonon leave them. While touched by his students' *mesiras nefesh*, Reb Elchonon felt that the trip was absolutely necessary.

8. Head of Vilna's *beis din* and recognized Torah leader of world Jewry. After his first wife died, Reb Chaim Ozer married the sister of Reb Elchonon's *rebbetzin*, making them brothers-in-law.

9. Reb Shraga Block would call himself, "*Dem Rebbin's baal agalah*" (the rabbi's wagon-driver), during Reb Elchonon's stay in New York. One day, Reb Shraga drove their car across a Times Square intersection. Reb Elchonon, who always looked toward the ground when outdoors and who was totally unfamiliar with the section, called out, "A stench rises from this place. Where are you taking me? The *tumah* (impurity) breaks out here." Reb Elchonon did not relax until their car left the area.

Rabbi Moshe Sherer, "In Reb Elchonon, we saw how a great personage regarded the work of Agudath Israel as an integral part of the 613 *mitzvos*."

Reb Elchonon was still in the U.S. as winter ended in 1939. By that time, Hitler had already seized Czechoslovakia and conquered Austria; ominous storm clouds hung over Poland. Those who had been drawn close to Reb Elchonon pleaded with him to remain in America and send for his two sons who were in Europe.[10] Reb Elchonon replied, "I don't have only two sons; I have four hundred—the yeshivah *bachurim*. How can I leave them?"

When asked what justification there was for returning to a danger zone, Reb Elchonon answered unequivocally, "I am a soldier; I have to go to the front."

To Rabbi Shimon Schwab (*Rav* of K'hal Adath Jeshurun)— then *Rav* in Baltimore— he quoted R' Meir of Rothenberg[11]: "When someone makes up his mind to sacrifice his life for the sake of Heaven, then no matter what is done to him—stoning, burning, burial alive, hanging—he feels no pain. There is no one alive who would not cry out if his finger touched fire....Yet, many commit themselves to the flames or execution for the sake of *Hashem*, may He be blessed, without uttering a word."

He would not delay his departure by even a day. On March 24, 1939, the Jews of America bid Reb Elchonon a sad farewell. On the return trip home, he stopped off in England; and there, too, he was implored not to leave. To Mrs. Sternbuch of London, he said, "These are the birth pangs of *Moshiach* and it has been decreed upon us to bear them. No one can escape or avoid his assigned portion of the birth pangs of *Moshiach*."[12]

---

10. His son Reb Simcha, today *Rosh Yeshivah* at Yeshiva Ohr Elchonon in Jerusalem, was already in America at that time.

11. Cited by *Tashbatz* 415.

12. It should be noted that Reb Elchonon did attempt to escape to Sweden in June of 1941, after his yeshiva had been forced to disband. His bags were packed and a wagon came to fetch him and his family. As his son Reb Naftali was loading his bag, it fell and broke his leg. The escape was rescheduled for a few days later. Meanwhile the Germans drove the Russians from Lithuania, ending Reb Elchonon's plans.

III. Ikvesa D'Meshicha

While in America, Reb Elchonon published a Yiddish monograph entitled *Ikvesa D'Meshicha* (Footsteps of Moshiach), in which he employed an array of Scriptural and Talmudic sources to interpret the frightening events that had occurred and were unfolding. Additional sources elucidated the proper course for a Torah Jew to follow at that critical hour.

Ikvesa D'Meshicha had a major impact on Torah Jews around the world. When a copy reached the *Chazon Ish* in Bnei Brak, he sent it to Rabbi Schonfeld for translation into Hebrew. An English translation (entitled *Epoch of the Messiah*) was prepared by Rabbi Cooper of London.

There were those who, after a cursory reading of the work, contended that Reb Elchonon's interest in writing it was to predict the impending catastrophe. But that was not so. Always the *ba'al hap'shat*, Reb Elchonon's interest was to show how current events and their causes were found quite clearly in the Torah—if one knew how to look for them.[13] Out of deep love and concern for his brethren, he strove to show what *Hashem* was demanding of them at that time.

To this day, the essay has remained a prime source for the Torah outlook on how a Jew is to conduct himself in *golus,* and what the ramifications might be, G-d forbid, when he pursues the wrong goals and aspirations. Some of the observations found in the essay were only comprehensible decades after they were written, for they were written by a man who saw past, present and future in the Torah's holy words.[14]

A full discussion of the essay is not within the purview of this article. A few of its points, however, merit particular attention.

---

13. Reb Elchonon cited the comment of *Ramban* (*Devarim* 32,40) that the Torah anticipates all future events to the extent that, "even if it were merely a document left behind by a star-gazer who predicted future events, it would command our acceptance...because all its predictions have come true and nothing has been omitted."

14. During his stay in the U.S., Reb Elchonon was asked what he thought would be the ultimate fate of Russian Jewry. Reb Elchonon replied, "Originally, I entertained a certain theory, but then reconsidered and reached a new conclusion. First, I thought that Heaven had despaired of Russian Jewry [for their having embraced Socialism in the pre-Communist era], and would not restore them to their roots; eventually, they would disappear from the community of Israel like the ten lost tribes. However, upon reflection, I felt that of the Russian Jews it is certainly said, "The time will yet come. The day will come when they will return to their roots."

◆§ The Wheels of Time

The Torah refers to the very last period in Jewish history as the End of Days; *Chazal* (*Mishnah Sota* 9:15) refer to it as *Ikvesa D'Meshicha*. *Acharis Hayamim* encompasses both the pre-Messianic and Messianic periods, while *Ikvesa D'Meshicha* refers only to the period preceding Moshiach's arrival. Both the *Tanach* and the *Gemara* speak of the awesome difficulties that *Klal Yisrael* will face during that period. Chapter Twelve in the Book of *Daniel* states that the sufferings of that period will surpass anything that the Jewish people has ever experienced. Of that period, a Sage of the Talmud said, "Let him [*Moshiach*] come, but let me not see him (i.e. let me not witness that which must precede his arrival)" (*Sanhedrin* 98b).

Yeshayahu *Hanavi* refers to the Redemption as a rebirth of the Jewish people (*Yeshayahu* 66:8). Thus did *Chazal* refer to the events that would precede the Redemption as *Chevlei Moshiach*, the birth pangs of *Moshiach*. The *Vilna Gaon* elucidated this term: Just as a woman's birth pains become increasingly strong as the actual birth nears, so will the travails of *Ikvesa D'Meshicha* increase as time goes on. And just as the birth pangs herald the birth—and cease once the baby is born—so will it be with *Chevlei Moshiach*. In this, the final Redemption parallels the redemption from Egypt, where the persecution increased shortly before the redemption process began (*Shemos* 5,9) but later ceased entirely.

Reb Elchonon cites the following observation of the Chofetz Chaim: "Today, within a short period of time, the world is undergoing major changes which, in earlier generations, would have occurred over the course of centuries. We see that the wheels of time are turning with lightning speed. 'What has *Hashem* done to us?' Why are conditions affecting us undergoing such rapid changes?" The Chofetz Chaim explained: "In Heaven, countless accounts have accumulated from the time of Creation until today. Before *Moshiach* can arrive, these accounts must be settled, for the Redemption will bring with it an end to the *yeitzer hara*, and all matters of this world relating to man's struggle with his *yeitzer hara* shall cease. Therefore, every soul must now pay the debt which it owes to Heaven (for past sins), for the days of *Moshiach* are very near."[15]

Reb Elchonon noted that since the end of the First World War, when the above observation was made, the pace of history had quickened even more: "Literally overnight, events are occurring which in earlier times would have happened over a period of generations....Every intelligent person understands that we are living in a unique period, one that is destined to change the entire world order."

✑§ A Nation Apart

To the events of his time, Reb Elchonon applied the verses found in the *Tochachah* (Reproof), "You shall be mad from the sight of your eyes" (*Devarim* 28,34). This punishment, he explained, applies only to those who attempt to understand the happenings around them through human reasoning, but it does not apply to one who delves into the Torah for understanding. Then, "all is clear and understandable."

Reb Elchonon observed that certain verses of *Parshas Ha'azinu* (*Devarim* ch. 32), which foretells all that will transpire with the Jewish nation until the Final Redemption, deal specifically with the period of *Ikvesa D'Meshicha*. "For *Hashem* will judge His nation; He will relent concerning His servants" (*Devarim* 32,36). *Hashem* will "judge" His nation with suffering and affliction, but in the end, He will redeem them from exile. The source of their affliction is found there as well, as *Hashem* demands of His people, "Where are their gods, the rock in whom they trusted? [Where are the gods] which ate the fat of their sacrifices, and drank the wine of their libations? Let them rise up and assist you, let them serve as your protection" (*Devarim* 32, 36-38). Reb Elchonon defines *avodah zara*, idolatry, as any factor that one erroneously believes can cause benefit or harm, independent of *Hashem's* will. Included, then, under false gods, are the Enlightenment, which emanated from Berlin, Liberalism, Socialism, Nationalism and a host of other "isms." There is a single underlying purpose behind the Jews' embracing these false

---

15. *Kovetz Ma'amorim.*

ideals, and this is mentioned explicitly in the Book of *Yechezkel* (ch. 20), "Let us be like all the nations."

In the end, says Reb Elchonon, all these ideologies will disintegrate into nothingness (as we are witnessing in our day with the fall of Communism). Reb Elchonon finds a source of this phenomenon in Yechezkel *Hanavi*'s prophecy regarding the punishment to be visited upon Egypt, "because it was a staff of support for Israel," meaning that Israel had at one point placed its faith in Egypt. The "false gods" to which the Jewish people turned at any point in history will ultimately disappear from the face of the earth. "And against all deities of Egypt I shall execute judgments; I am *Hashem*" (*Shemos* 12,12).

◆§ The Wrong Response

The last *Mishnah* in *Sotah* (9:15) details the signs of *Ikvesa D'Meshicha*, one of them being, "The face of the generation will be like the face of a dog." The Chofetz Chaim would repeat the following explanation in the name of Rabbi Yitzchak of Volozhin: When a stone is hurled from behind at a dog, the dog pounces upon the stone, not realizing that someone hurled the stone. Similarly, in the time of *Ikvesa D'Meshicha*, there will be Jews who will attempt to challenge those who threaten their people, failing to realize that they are merely rods in the hands of *Hashem*. Reb Elchonon decried the actions of those Jews who promoted the boycott of German goods in the 1930's, which accomplished nothing, save to enrage Hitler and his cohorts. Our self-appointed leaders, who see only the stick and refuse to acknowledge Who is yielding it, have declared war on mighty states. "What strength, what might do we have? Our bullets are articles in Jewish newspapers, and what is the result? We only provoke the anger and fury of snakes against us."

He cited a number of Aggadic teachings, all of which underscore the same principle: in *golus*, a Jew should avoid confrontation with his enemies. "If you see a wicked man enjoying success, do not antagonize him" (*Berachos* 7b). Also: "R' Chiya said, 'If you see that Eisav seeks to antagonize you, do not oppose him; rather conceal yourself from him until his moment has passed.'"

When famine struck the Land of Canaan and only Yaakov

Avinu's household remained with an ample supply of food, Yaakov instructed his sons to behave as their neighbors did and journey to Egypt to purchase food. Yaakov said, "Why show yourselves [i.e. why attract attention?] before your neighbors, the sons of Eisav and Yishmael?" (see *Rashi* to *Bereishis* 42,1). Reb Elchonon commented, "This is a clear admonition that we not afford the nations an opportunity to notice us and to speak of us. The less other nations think and talk about us, the better our lot. Only when other nations issue decrees against *mitzvah* observance are we to be firm and unyielding."

✑§ Escaping the Birth Pangs

What is a person to do at so difficult a time? The *Gemara* (*Sanhedrin* 98b) provides the answer: "R' Elazar's disciples asked of him, 'What can a person do to be saved from the birthpangs of *Moshiach*?' He told them, 'Let him toil in Torah [study] and *gemilas chassodim* (acts of benevolence).'" The Chofetz Chaim observed that R' Elazar used the term *"ya'asok*—let him toil," which is related to the word *"eisek*—business." To be saved from *Chevlei Moshiach*, one must dedicate himself to Torah and *chessed* as one would to a business enterprise.

Reb Elchonon lamented the weakened state of Torah study in his generation. For thousands of years, the dreams and hopes of Jewish fathers and mothers had always been that their children grow up to become great in Torah and *yiras Shamayim*. As for education as preparation for earning a livelihood, the Jewish parent had always believed faithfully that "He who provides life, provides sustenance." In recent generations, however, a weakening of *emunah* (faith) has brought with it a weakening in *bitachon* (trust in *Hashem*). Many parents, said Reb Elchonon, believe that a complete secular education will guarantee their children all their material needs for the rest of their lives.

To the adult population, Reb Elchonon addressed the verse, "Do not rejoice, Israel, with the joy of the nations." A Jew's recreation must not mirror that of non-Jews. To them, time not spent at work is best spent in self-indulgence. The Torah demands of a Jew, "You shall be holy" (*Vayikra* 19,2): his home must be holy, his heart must be holy. The Torah tells us, "And I will separate you from the nations to be Mine" (ibid. 20,26)—"If you will remain apart from the nations, then you are Mine" (*Rashi* ad loc). When a Jew finishes his day's work, he must immerse himself in Torah study. One who is not capable of studying on his own should attend *shiurim*. And one must dedicate time for the performance of acts of *chessed* and other good deeds" (*Kovetz Ma'amorim*, p. 118).

"What shall we do with our sister on the day when she is spoken of?" (*Shir HaShirim* 8,8). *Klal Yisrael* in *golus* is likened to a lone lamb among seventy wolves. In such a situation, it is best for the lamb to be ignored by the wolves. The more the wolves occupy themselves with the lamb, the greater the dangers. Reb Elchonon wrote his essay at a time when the Jews were a prime topic of discussion—a situation in which we find ourselves today. It is regarding those times that the Heavenly angels ask, "What shall we do for our sister—the Jewish nation—on the day when other nations do not cease from discussing her?"

To this, *Hakadosh Baruch Hu* answers, "If she is a wall, we shall build for her a palace of silver; but if she is a door, we shall enclose her with panels of cedar" (ibid v. 9). If the Jewish nation will remain rock-firm in its faith, and, like a wall, not allow itself to be swayed by foreign winds, then it shall be deserving of a palace of silver. "Just as silver is exposed to fire and remains intact, so does Israel enter foreign kingdoms and emerge intact." If, however, the Jewish nation is, G-d forbid, like a door that sways on its hinges, if it allows itself to be influenced by the winds of secular ideologies, then it will be like wood, which when left in dampness turns rotten.

This solution is an eternal one. We must remain firm in our *emunah* and not be influenced by external forces. And how is this accomplished? "I am a wall—this refers to Torah" (*Midrash Shir HaShirim*). Only through Torah can we remain strong in faith and unyielding in the face of all trial and adversity.

ᨳ Pioneers on the American Scene

Torah takes root in barren—even hostile—terrain, thanks to prescient, uncompromising leadership

Dr. Gershon Kranzler

Elimelech Gavriel Tress, זצ"ל

A Hero in Our Time

Fired by the charge of Reb Elchonon הי"ד, inspired by the unforgettable classes of Reb Shraga Feivel זצ"ל, he rose to the challenge of transform- ing a rag-tag group of youths into a major force of rescue and spiritual uplift

I t is now over a quarter-century since Divine Providence saw fit to take you unto Him, leaving our world bereft of one of its most dynamic movers and builders. Yet, to all who had the privilege of growing under your guidance, of walking and working with you, of acquiring a sense of mission and a heightened awareness of the challenge ahead, you will always remain a powerful, motivating presence. For your enthusiasm, your strong faith, and your con- stant concern for others sparked them at a crucial time of their being and coming. They readily accepted your challenge to grow beyond the limits and limitations of their personal ambitions and goals to assume responsibilities far beyond their age.

❅   ❅   ❅

The youth of today may recognize your name, but they can not possibly know you the way we do. They never witnessed the singular role you played in making Agudath Israel a powerful reality, a movement that under your direction waged a ceaseless battle on behalf of the needs and concerns of Torah Jews and Yiddishkeit. To the young, as well as to the adults, Agudath Israel is an accepted fact whose glorious functions they are enjoying. For it gives broader meaning and an extra dimension to their being, their learning, and thinking, when they attend the mass gatherings, and join the ranks of Orthodox world Jewry as a movement reckoned with by those in power. The youngsters proudly partake in the regional and national learning contests, and they and their elders appreciate the Mishnayos and Shas Siyumim that provide them with renewed incentives to future growth. Similarly, thousands are privileged to attend the annual conventions of Agudath Israel, when outstanding Gedolim, Roshei Yeshivah, Rabbonim and Rebbeiim, scholars, professionals, and laymen gather to take stock and to evaluate the historical dimensions of the challenges that face our time. Yet, neither the youngsters nor most of the adults can realize how you gave your very heart and soul (until the last breath of your all-too-short life) to make Agudath Israel a vital factor of Jewish life in this country. I will attempt to share my memories — so very alive even now — with those who were not privileged to know you firsthand.

◆§ Breaking Through the Walls of Indifference

We were all with him — his *chaveirim*, the Pirchim, Zeirim, and adult members of Agudath Israel — as we struggled to break through the walls of indifference, if not outright animosity, to reach out and to extend a helping hand to the growing masses of Jews who turned to us in desperate search for affidavits of sponsorship as means of escape from the countries darkened by the sinister clouds of the gathering storm. I remember how a group of the listeners of our first mass meeting chased us down Bedford Avenue, enraged by his attempt to awaken their sleeping conscience! Yet only months later, they were among the hundreds that flocked to the doors of our modest offices which he had established in our then-proud building at 616 Bedford Avenue, pleading for counsel and assistance to help their relatives and whole communities caught in a maelstrom of evil that was systemically destroying the very heartland of intensive Jewish life and scholarship in Eastern Europe.

It was then that Reb Elimelech almost singlehandedly made Agudath Israel a beacon of hope in a world confronting the raging fires of the Holocaust. Indefatigably, he worked day and night, knowing neither rest nor sleep, fearing lest the next moment might prove to be a moment too late to save a handful of victims...to rescue some of the *Gedolim*, the *Roshei Yeshivah*, the foremost *Rebbeiim*, scholars and leaders whom the *Hashgacha* had chosen to escape and continue their work in this country. A flood of desperate telegrams, calls, and letters inundated our offices as he turned our *chaveirim*, young and old, into his most effective assistants, his associates in his heroic struggle for rescue...while the large and powerful organizations, with the means and contacts that were necessary to open doors and channels of effective help, were standing idly by.

The stories and facts, the records that could fill rooms, are now being gathered, and soon, a comprehensive, full portrayal of how he wrought near-miracles with the limited resources at his disposal will be published. Then our present-day youth and adults — and the world — will learn how one courageous young man gave up his thriving business career, used up his personal fortune, plunging himself and his growing family into poverty, while he transformed all those about him into a strike force for the salvation of our people.

Yet, this moment is too precious. As the twenty-fifth *Yahrtzeit* of his *petirah* and the seventieth anniversary of the founding of Agudath Israel coincide, the flow of memories and images open once more, so I share them, 'ere time and distance make them fade'— so that the credit that is due Reb Elimelech (or "Mike," as we called him in those early years) will not be lost on the youngsters and the parents of today who are now enjoying the fruits of his labor.

✑§ Reb Elchonon Wasserman's Final Message

People who know of Reb Elimelech's work ask: How did he grow in stature and effectiveness to become a hero of rescue, a veritable giant to the masses who turned to him for help and direction?

What and who were the main influences that motivated Reb Elimelech Gavriel Tress to grow beyond himself and transform all those with him into an effective organization that stepped in where other, more powerful movements remained inactive when the challenge for emergency help was greatest?

Can anyone unravel the complex web of strains and strands that produce such an unusual persona, or as he would rather have had it, a precious *neshamah* so rare, so imbued with *bitachon* and *mesiras nefesh*? Yet, as the memories reach back across the decades, there is one scene, one experience, that stands out as perhaps the most significant that can help us explain what turned him into the leader the *Hashgachah* had chosen to accept a challenge that dwarfed the potential and inner strength of anyone of lesser stature and personality.

It happened at the very time when the foundations of the world were shaking under the impact of the tragic events that were beginning to undermine and destroy the pillars of society, of morality, and human decency. We had brought Reb Elchonon Wasserman ל"יצז, one of the world's foremost Torah sages, to the boat, after he had spent a few months in this country to gather the urgently needed funds to carry on his work in his yeshivah in Baranovich.

We, and so many others, had tried to dissuade the great scholar from returning to Europe, from going knowingly to the lands threatened by the fires that were to consume the most important bastions of Torah and Torah study, the mighty communities that had blossomed for centuries. Yet, all our efforts of impressing him with the importance of what he could achieve here, if he remained to transplant his inexhaustible storehouse of knowledge and insight into a fountainhead of renewed scholarship, were in vain. His tired, yet clear eyes in that worry-drawn face turned to Reb Elimelech, and with determination he looked into his face, and in his succinct, pithy Yiddish, he said:

> "Stop pleading with me, I do not count. I have to go back to my yeshivah, to my talmidim and share with them whatever Divine

Hashgacha has in store for us. But remember, you young people here in America have personally a tremendous task, a challenge that you must heed, come what may. This is no time to live for yourself. You must act now so that you will be ready when the opportunity for decisive action will come. Hashem will be with you. He will give you the strength and will guide you and show you what must be done!"

After this final exhortation and desperate charge to him, the gentle giant of Torah scholarship, with the slightly rounded back, bent from years of incessant study, turned, and impervious to our last attempts of holding him back, walked up the plank into the ship that was to take him to London. From there he went back to his yeshivah in Baranovich, to share the fate of his *talmidim, al Kiddush Hashem.*

Reb Elimelech Tress, as Reb Elchonon had called him, was never to be the same after this personal, emotional appeal. Those words had forever changed him and — through him — those with him. That final charge had imparted to him the huge responsibility, the urgency of the time and the challenge to devote all his efforts to prepare himself and his organization of young people into a ready strike force. This became uppermost in his mind and motivated everything he was.

◄§ Other Major Influences

There had, of course, been other important influences that helped to mold him, his thinking and his work, for Reb Elimelech had already proven his leadership in fusing the sundry groups of Zeirei and Bnos Agudath Israel in the various Jewish neighborhoods of New York into a functional organization. There was first and foremost our *chaveir,* Reb Gedalya Schorr צז״ל. Ever since his return from the Knessia Gedolah, the World Conference of Agudath Israel in Vienna, in 1929, as the representative of the American Agudah Youth, he had devoted much of his time to learning, teaching, and guiding the discussions of Zeirei Agudath Israel — even before he went to spend those precious years as a *yungerman* in Kletzk, under the guidance of Rabbi Aaron Kotler זצ״ל — to transmit to the Zeirim the inspiration and Torah ideology of Agudath Israel. And when he came back to us from Kletzk, at the very last moment before the war broke out, at the very time when we had moved into our own building at 616 Bedford Avenue, he again became our *Rebbe*, and *chaveir*, teaching *shiurim*, and directing our education and personal growth, together with "Mike," until his growing responsibilities as *Rosh Yeshivah* at Mesifta Torah Vodaath demanded all of his time and energies. Under his guidance and urging, Reb Elimelech became active and assumed leadership in our movement; and as ever more newcomers joined our ranks, he made them feel welcome and at home, and helped them adjust to the requirements of a new world and strange life styles.

Then, of course, there was Reb Shraga Feivel Mendelowitz ז״ל, the great sage and educator of generations of *bnei Torah*, of professional and lay leaders..., all of whom came under the spell of his extraordinary personality in and around Mesifta Torah Vodaath. Reb Elimelech and we all were deeply influenced by his unforgettable classes, his *shiurim* in *Pirkei Avos*, in *Biur Tefillah*; his teaching of *Derech Hashem* turned into masterful lectures on *Galus* and *Geulah*, through which he gave us a sense of understanding of the history of the Jewish people. Every one of us — even the well-known industrialists, professionals and intellectuals, who sat at his feet during their visits to Camp Mesivta — drew inspiration and love for Torah for the People, and the Land of Israel, from him. With tears in his eyes, and with enthusiasm and sagacity, he gave us insight and understanding of the work of Divine Providence in the midst of the great catastrophes of *Yisrael* in *Galus*.

Reb Elimelech became one of the close co-workers of Reb Shraga Feivel, who had long before realized his great potential for leadership. Like so many of the high and mighty, as well as the ordinary men and women and children, he too turned to Reb Elimelech for help, when the requests for aid and means of rescue flooded his office. He guided and advised Reb Elimelech as his work for *hatzalah* broadened, and he brought some of the world's most famous *Roshei Yeshivah* and *Chassidic Rebbe*s to this country. Through Reb Shraga Feivel, he was able to call on the wealthy and powerful who had become the admirers and disciples of Reb Shraga Feivel, and who gladly opened their hearts and pockets to Mr. Tress, when their help was needed most.

And then, there were so many others, especially among the newcomers, who turned to him for help, but who became important co-workers, guides and conscience to him because of their knowledge, experiences, and insight into what were the most urgent of the constant calls for help. He was able to work with all of them, giving all of them their due respect, the *Rebbes, Roshei Yeshivah*, and famous heads of organizations and institutions and of the world of Torah scholarship.

We remember how Moreinu Yaakov Rosenheim זצ״ל, the World President of Agudath Israel since its founding in Kattowitz, moved his office to this country, for the war years, until he settled in the Holy Land. And we remember the delegations of the great scholars and leaders of Agudath Israel who came to us to America to enlist Reb Elimelech's help and cooperation for their projects. There was Reb Moshe Blau, and Reb Itche Meyer Levin, the brother-in-law of the saintly Gerer *Rebbe*, זכרונם לברכה, who became a member of the Knesset and holder of a cabinet post in the State of Israel. Dr. Yitzchok Breuer זצ״ל, the brilliant ideologue of Agudath Israel, and Rabbi Meir Karelitz, זצ״ל the brother-in-law of the *Chazon Ish* — they all came, worked with him, guided him, and in turn received the help they required; he became their confidant easily, as he had worked so successfully with the Pirchim and Zeirim, to whom he had been "Mike"...., and whom he molded into active members of our movement.

Then, of course, there arrived *Gedolim* whom the *Hashgachah* had spared to continue their great tradition, which eventually blossomed into the vaunted Renaissance of Torah and of Orthodoxy in this once "treifene medina." There were Reb Elya Meir Bloch and Reb Mottel Katz, זכרונם לברכה, carriers of the proud Telshe tradition and scholarship, who had always been active in Agudath Israel, and who, with Mr. Tress's help, reestablished their *Yeshivah Gedolah* in Cleveland. There was the unforgettable Reb Michoel Ber Weissmandl, the noted scholar who became one of the foremost leaders of rescue efforts, plotting to destroy the railroad tracks that brought trainloads of victims to Auschwitz. After he had pleaded in vain with the mighty and the great of the free countries, he came here to continue his desperate efforts to help the unfortunate victims of Nazi brutality. He became their voice as he traveled around, addressing our mass meetings, and shaking the listeners' conscience into action. Even as he reestablished the Nitra Yeshivah in Mt. Kisco, New York, he continued his intense efforts to direct Agudath Israel and other organizations in the listeners' efforts to help the survivors of the concentration camps and of the DP camps, until the very end of his life, of his pain-racked body and soul.

And then there was, of course, Rabbi Avraham Kalmanowitz ז״ל, the founder of the Mirrer Yeshivah in America and head of Vaad Hatzalah, the master orator and scholar who could move mountains, and who with cries, pleas and fainting was able to open the closed doors of the hostile State Department so that Reb Elimelech, Rabbi Schorr, and their co-workers were able to pry open the sorely needed avenues of help.

And, lastly, there was, of course, the dynamic, spiritually towering personality, Rabbi Aaron Kotler ז״ל, with whom we had been in touch when he was still in Kobe, Japan, and whom we brought to this country, early during the war. His *talmidim* and the large group of the outstanding scholars from the Mirrer Yeshivah, came here and to the Holy Land from Shanghai, where one of our *chaveirim*, Frank Newman, hired a ship to take many of them to America. Here and in Israel they became the foremost *Roshei Yeshivah*, educators, *rabbonim*, and heads of institutions and organizations — in great measure due to Mr. Tress's untiring efforts. But it was Reb Aaron ז״ל, more than anyone else, who threw himself into feverish activities, to establish his *kollel* in Lakewood, which became the model for so many others. Some of his main efforts were devoted to working with Reb Elimelech, and to become the guiding force in the vast networks of *rabbanim* and *Roshei Yeshivah* who were devoting themselves to the ever-growing needs of the *hatzalah* work. Equally important, he joined Rabbi Reuvain Grozovsky ז״ל in enlisting other *Roshei Yeshivah*, including Rabbi Yaakov Kamenetzky and Rabbi Moshe Feinstein, to form the *Moetzes Gedolei HaTorah*, the supreme institution of authority in all matters of policy and *halachah* of Agudath Israel.

✑ The Myriad Of Accomplishments From Which We Are Benefiting

It would take many more pages to do justice to all that Reb Elimelech Tress achieved over the years, benchmark accomplishments from which we all are benefiting. One has only to think of the time and effort it took him to make Camp Agudah a reality — from the ranks of whose campers, waiters, counselors, and directors have come some of the foremost leaders of the Jewish Day School movement, and other vital institutions and organizations that transformed Jewish life in this country. One has only to think how he established the one and only Refugee Home in Brooklyn at the very beginning of the war, whose residents he guided, supported, and provided with the means of sustenance, with education, with the opportunities to establish themselves in some realm of business in this country. Under his guidance, Mr. Josef Rosenberger was able to break through the ignorance and disinterest of the American Jewish community and to establish the Shatnes Laboratory, making a forgotten mitzvah an integral part of Orthodox Jewish life in this country.

Would that this were the time and place to sketch some of the most valuable contributions you made in the few decades of your life as a leader, innovator, creative organizer and director of people and projects in this country, and war-torn Europe during and after World War II. This will have to be left to those researchers who will make the portrayal of your life and work as comprehensive as possible, for the benefit of the generations of today and tomorrow. May they, too, draw inspiration and strength from it to confront the challenges that are lying ahead of them, with the help of the L-rd, as we did in our time.

Lynn M. Berkowitz

"A Preacher of the Word of G-D"
Rev. Isaac Leeser ז״ל
(5566/1806-5628/1868)

*He battled for the
integrity of true
Judaism in Kashrus,
education of the young,
and the printed word*

❧ Youth On The Rhine

There is a popular misconception among many American
Orthodox Jews that Torah-observance was virtually
unknown in this country prior to the great mass migration from
Eastern Europe that began in the 1880's, and that even those few
who remained strictly observant were not acknowledged or
respected by their contemporaries or by the outside, non-Jewish
world. Yet there arose, during the so-called "German period" of
American Jewry (1830-1880), a leader of such dynamic energy,
enormous talent, unshakable devotion to Torah, extraordinary
yiras Shamayim and diligence of character that he has been called
the most outstanding American Jew of the nineteenth century. He

was a teacher, a preacher, a writer, a newspaper editor, an outspoken champion of Jewish rights and a firm and faithful believer of *Torah min haShamayim*: Isaac Leeser.

Isaac Leeser was born on December 12, 1806 (5566) in the town of Dulmen on the Rhine, near Neuenkirchen, Westphalia, the son of Uri ben Eliezer, a butcher, and his wife Sarah. (The name of Leeser derives from the grandfather Eliezer.) Isaac's mother passed away when he was six years old, and Uri Leeser then moved with his three small children into the home of his parents. Isaac fondly remembered his grandmother, Gitla, "a sage among women," pious, intelligent, modest, and loved by all who knew her. Isaac and his younger brother Jacob attended *cheder* in Dulmen, taught by Rabbi Benjamin Jacob Cohen, and later on Isaac studied with Rabbi Abraham Sutro, Chief Rabbi of Munster, a fierce opponent of the new Reform ideology that was just then beginning to spread among German Jewry. Isaac absorbed his teacher's fiery zeal for traditional Torah Judaism from which he never swerved. He completed the study of several volumes of *Shas* under the instruction of Rabbi Sutro, and also studied for a short time in a secular *gymnasium*, but did not go on to attend university.

≥§ Farewell to Dulmen

With the death of Uri Leeser, followed a short time later by grandfather Eliezer and grandmother Gitla, the three young Leeser children, Leah, Isaac and Jacob, were left destitute.

For a time, family members in Dulmen supported the orphaned Leeser children until they received an invitation to join their uncle, Solomon Isaac Cohen, the brother of their mother, Sarah. Cohen had emigrated to America in 1789 and was a successful merchant in Richmond, Virginia. In America, he had changed his name to Zalma Rehine (pronounced *Rhine*), after the town of his birth, and was married to Rachel Judah, a Sephardic Jewess with family connections to the well-known Seixas family. When Issac and his younger brother Jacob arrived in America — their older sister, Leah, remained behind — Zalma Rehine enrolled them in a (non-Jewish) private grammar school. At age eighteen, Isaac Leeser became a clerk in his uncle's store, but he continued to study both Torah and secular subjects on his own.

Zalma Rehine took his two German nephews to Richmond's Sephardic congregation *Beth Shalome*, where his brother-in-law Isaac B. Seixas was *chazzan*. Young Isaac Leeser assisted him in teaching young children, and from time to time officiated as reader during services. He adopted the Sephardic *minhag* and cantillation. While in Richmond, Isaac also made the acquaintance of Israel Ber Kursheedt, the son-in-law of the venerated Rev. Gershom Mendes Seixas. Kursheedt had studied in the yeshivah of Frankfurt-on-the-Main, and was recognized as the most accomplished Talmudic scholar in America, although he had never received *semichah*. Shortly after Isaac's arrival in Richmond, Kursheedt moved to New York, where he helped to found that city's first Ashkenazi synagogue, Congregation *B'nai Jeshurun*.

✒ With Pen In Hand

Within a few years, Isaac Leeser had so completely mastered the English language that he was able to write a passionate and eloquent defense of the Jewish people in response to a ferociously anti-Semitic article that had appeared in the *London Quarterly Review* and reprinted in a New York periodical. He submitted this article to John Pleasants, editor of the *Richmond Whig*, who published the response. Thus was launched the journalistic career of Isaac Leeser.

This fervent defense of traditional Judaism, appearing in a major secular publication over the byline "A Native of Germany," attracted the attention of Jews and gentiles alike. The Sephardic Congregation *Mikveh Israel* of Philadelphia learned the identity of "A Native of Germany" and invited the young man to serve the Jewish community as a *chazzan*. Isaac was at first reluctant to accept such a prestigious position, but as he later explained, "Knowing my own want of proper qualification, I would never have consented to serve, if others more fitting in point of standing, information or other qualities had been here; but this not being the case (as is proved by there being yet two other congregations at least in this country without a regular *chazzan*) I consented to serve."[1]

1.Letter from Issac Leeser to Chief Rabbi Solomon Hirschell of England, 1834.

Leeser became, by default, the virtual *mara d'asra* of the Jewish community of Philadelphia. Besides teaching Hebrew to private pupils, he officiated at weddings and at funerals, convened a *beis din* to admit converts, and rendered decisions on matters of *halachah* as far as his knowledge permitted. In more complicated halachic matters, he referred *she'eilos* to Israel Ber Kursheedt or to Chief Rabbi Solomon Hirschell of England. In addition, he may have referred *she'eilos* to the only other rabbis in America during that early period: the itinerant *meshulachim* who came from the Holy Land to raise funds for the poor Jews of *Eretz Yisrael*.

Leeser continued his literary activity, in 1833 publishing his first major work, *Jews and the Mosaic Law*, an expansion of his original defense of Judaism in the *Richmond Whig*. He recognized the need to educate American Jews in their own religion using the language of the country, and to strengthen Jewish observance generally. To further this objective, he introduced what was considered a radical innovation at the time: the delivery, in English, of lectures and discourses during the Sabbath morning service.

In 1834, tragedy struck. A smallpox epidemic swept Philadelphia, and Isaac became infected by the deadly disease. Jacob Leeser, coming up from Richmond to nurse his brother, was also taken ill and passed away. Isaac eventually recovered, but was left nearly blind and facially disfigured by the disease. The young woman he had been courting broke off their engagement, and after this heartbreak, Isaac Leeser remained a lifelong bachelor.[2]

He threw himself back into his work of furthering Jewish education. In 1837, together with Rebecca Gratz, of *Ivanhoe* fame, Leeser established the Hebrew Education Society of Philadelphia. It was Leeser's original intention to organize a Jewish all-day school, but as not enough students could be enrolled for such an

---

2. Whiteman, Maxwell, "The Legacy of Isaac Leeser," *Jewish Life in Philadelphia 1830-1940*, Philadelphia: Ishi Publications, 1983. It is not known whether she broke the engagement because of Leeser's disfigurement, or because her father, a wealthy Sephardic aristocrat, objected to his daughter's marriage to a lowly "Tedesco" (Ashkenazi). She remained a spinster, teaching at the Hebrew Education Society under the direction of Rebecca Gratz, and writing books for Jewish children.

ambitious venture, Leeser settled for a Sunday School. At first, the only Bible available for instructing English-speaking American Jewish children was the King James version. Rebecca Gratz and her staff of young women teachers used glue pots and scraps of paper to paste over non-Jewish concepts, while Leeser began working on an English translation of the *Tanach* according to the traditional authorities, a project that would take him almost two decades to complete.

In the meantime, he realized that American Jews were desperately in need of other inspirational and instructional material in English. In 1837, he published a collection of his addresses and discourses (he refrained from calling his English lectures "sermons"), in 1838 a Hebrew primer in both Sephardic and Ashkenazic versions, and a year later his *Catechism for Jewish Children*. This unpretentious little book, dedicated to Rebecca Gratz, presented the basic concepts, obligations, customs and practices of Torah Judaism in a simple, question-and-answer format that could be used by educators even today. In 1850, he published *Descriptive Geography and Brief Historical Sketch of Palestine*, an English translation of the work by the Jerusalem *gaon* Rabbi Joseph Schwarz. Leeser saw the urgent need for a publication society that could publish quality Jewish literature in English for both adults and children. He established a Jewish publishing house in 1845 that produced a number of works, but the warehouse burned down in 1851 and virtually all production was halted.

✍ Launching *The Occident*

In 1843, Leeser embarked on what is considered by many to be his major contribution to American Jewish life: an English journal of Jewish thought called *The Occident and American Jewish Advocate*. This monthly magazine, which he continued to edit throughout his life, was the first Anglo-Jewish paper to be published in America, and the only one published during the nineteenth century to remain consistently loyal to the standards of Torah and *halachah* throughout its entire publication.

The Occident went to subscribers throughout the Western hemisphere and Europe. Jewish emigrants in remote outposts on the frontier were delighted with a journal that encouraged them in their region, though they may have neglected their observance for years. Wrote an enthusiastic reader in Belton, Texas:

"I am sorry to say that I am a Poor Scholar I cane not express my feeling with the Pen — when I accidently came in Posession of such valuable inphomation as containing in Your valuable Occident...I am sorry to say that I was ignorent...I am in this countiry 15 Years. But nearly all that Time was spent hear & in mexico & California. I am happy were happy Indeed to see that our True riligion has a Publick advocate. I cane not findwords to express my feelings...belive me to be a True Jew a Friend to our Caus."[3]

This Jew, isolated on the Texas frontier, asked to subscribe to *The Occident* and also ordered Leeser's English *Tanach* translation and a *machzor*. Other readers wrote to Leeser for advice in finding work that would allow them to observe Shabbat.

Leeser himself frequently traveled around the country and visited most of the Jewish communities east of the Mississippi River, reporting his visits in *The Occident*. On one trip to his "home town" of Richmond, in 1859, he was pleased to write: "Rev. Mr. Bermann, of the Polish *Kahal Knesseth Israel*, has established a *mikveh*, which has long since been a desideratum in Richmond. We also learn that it does not remain unused..."[4]

The Occident usually contained an editorial as its leading article, followed by a sermon that had been recently delivered in one of the congregations. For the first few issues, Leeser supplied his own sermons, and later featured sermons of other Rabbis, especially Rabbi Abraham Rice of Baltimore.[5] Book reviews, historical sketches, poetry, news items and an occasional piece for children filled out the pages. Although the magazine was in English, occasional letters appeared in German, written for the benefit of recent immigrants, and some scholarly, rabbinic articles and poetry were printed in Hebrew. As *The Occident* became popular, an advertising section was included. In 1859, Leeser turned

---

3. Letter to Isaac Leeser from Isaac Jalonick, Belton, Bell Co. Texas, May 28, 1853. Document on file in American Jewish Archives.
4. *The Occident*, May, 1859, vol. XVII.
5. *The Jewish Observer*, January 1975.

his magazine into a weekly newspaper, but the outbreak of the Civil War and the loss of his Southern readership as a result of the Union blockade put an end to this experiment and *The Occident* resumed its monthly format.

⤳ Controversy, Advocacy, and Literary Showcase

The pages of *The Occident* are a treasure-chest of American Jewish life in the mid-nineteenth century, filtered through the eyes of a committed, traditional Jew. In the very first issue, Leeser solicited congregational histories from his readers, so the journal is a valuable document of early American Jewish history.

Aware of the use of his journal as a learning tool, especially for women and girls, he encouraged talented women to submit articles, stories and poetry for publication. In this manner, he acquainted the public with the works of Grace Aguilar, Celia Moss, and Rebekah Hyneman.

Leeser did not shrink from controversy, and very early on made it clear that *The Occident* stood on the side of traditional Torah Judaism, and in opposition to Reform, which was just beginning to sprout in the New World. Most of the polemics in *The Occident* were directed against Reform leaders who had claimed some Orthodox credentials for themselves. Even as early as 1843, there were other Reform clergymen in Europe who had already gone the full gamut of radicalism, even to the extreme of the present day, by advocating interfaith marriage and the absolution of circumcision. Such men were virtually out of the fold of Judaism, and Leeser felt that there was little to be gained from any controversy with them. This was not the case with such men as Isaac Mayer Wise, Max Lilienthal, and Gustavus Posnanski, who demanded recognition from the Orthodox community and introduced their reforms into what were strictly Orthodox congregations. The Cincinnati temple where Isaac M. Wise functioned as minister contained a *mechitzah* until 1866, and the men prayed wearing *talleisim* and with covered heads. Even after the adoption of the Reform "Minhag America" prayer book for Sabbath and weekday services, Wise's congregation continued to use the Orthodox Roedelheim *machzor* on *Rosh Hashanah* and *Yom Kippur*. Commented a European visitor to Cincinnati in 1859:

"Perhaps they were afraid that G-d was awake on those days and they might be the worse for it in G-d's judgment."[6]

In those days, the Trojan horse used to transform an Orthodox synagogue into a Reform temple was the organ. Many German emigrants who clamored for organ music and a choir of mixed voices to enhance the service did not understand the reason for the prohibition of instrumental music, or *kol isha*, and even the most sincere Orthodox opponents were unable to articulate the *halachah*. Leeser, in *The Occident*, attempted to clarify the issue, and solicited the opinion of Rabbi Abraham Rice, who was then the only ordained Orthodox Rabbi in North America. The Reform craze for organ music and soprano voices caught on and spread like wildfire. Other innovations quickly followed. In the words of one historian:

> "*Reform, for the sake of Reform, was totally unrabbinic, but it created an excitement; its innovations held a feeling of modernism and convinced many [Orthodox Jews] that deviation was permitted and progressive.... Congregations learned that they could get the answer they desired to their inquiries by asking the right person; in common law this is called 'forum shopping'; in Jewish life this is called hefkeirus [a free-for-all]."*[7]

Leeser would allow the advocates of Reform to state their position in articles for *The Occident*, and then he, or other readers, would controvert their views. But under no circumstances would he permit personal attacks or name-calling. When Max Lilienthal, angry because his attempts to introduce Reform Judaism and secular education into the *yeshivos* of Russia had been thwarted by the firm opposition of the *Tzemach Tzeddek* and his *Chassidim*, referred to the Lubavitcher Rebbe and his followers as "fanatics," Leeser chided him: "...we do not approve altogether of the tone with which Dr. Lilienthal expresses himself of the Russian rabbis...one can have no cause to accuse the other of fanaticism, any more than he ought to be charged with too much liberality. It is

---

6. Benjamin, Israel J., *Three Years in America, 1859-1862*, Jewish Publication Society, 1956, vol.I, p.310.
7. Sharfman, I. Harold, *The First Rabbi*, Malibu: Pangloss Press, 1988, p.393; used with permission.

unfortunately this want of toleration...which works so much mischief among our people."[8]

✍§ Expanding the Orthodox Agenda

Leeser bemoaned the lack of Jewish education as the primary cause of confusion and non-observance. No *yeshivos* existed in the Western hemisphere, and the few day schools that had been established in the larger cities were sparsely attended. Most of the formal instruction was conducted in congregational Sunday schools. He was seconded in this by Reverend Samuel Myer Isaacs, the minister of *B'nai Jeshurun* in New York, and by Major Mordechai Manuel Noah, who was the first to urge, through the pages of *The Occident,* the establishment of a "Hebrew College," where Jewish young men could receive a classical education without being forced to submit to Christian practices then required at other colleges and universities. The need for academies for girls and young women was another urgent priority. The establishment of an American yeshivah was a goal that Leeser struggled for all his life.

Kashrus was another problem facing American Jews in the mid 1800's. Apart from flour and oil, few products that required special supervision were manufactured commercially. Major Noah was the first to inform the readers of *The Occident* that a scientific method had been devised to test the purity of olive oil, which unscrupulous importers were mixing with lard and selling to Jewish consumers. Leeser recommended that *mashgichim* be appointed to supervise the production of oil, and to place their seal on each bottle: the first *kashrus* labeling in America.[9]

The urgency of establishing a local source for ritual objects such as kosher *esrogim* led to a lively discussion in *The Occident* as to the validity of the West Indian citron for use in *arba minim.* To enhance his slipping reputation as a halachic authority, Dr. Max Lilienthal was *machmir* in this one instance: he *paskened* that the West Indian esrog was *pasul* for ritual use, on the grounds that these citrons were grafted from lemon stock. Leeser solicited the opinion of Rabbi Abraham Rice, whose authority he revered, and

---

8. *The Occident,* 1843, vol.I, p.142.
9. *The Occident,* October 1844, vol. II, pp.347-349.

the Baltimore sage ruled that the West Indian *esrog* was kosher for *arba minim*. Other readers of *The Occident* joined in the esrog controversy, each one expressing his learned opinion. One enthusiastic subscriber, signing his letter *Emeth* [Truth], thought that Leeser should dedicate *The Occident* to nothing else but discussions of halachic topics. Isaac M. Wise, recently arrived from Bohemia and already flexing his Reform muscle, thought such hairsplitting a waste of time: "[Emeth]... wishes a journal of this enlightened age shall fill up its pages with discussions about *esrogim murkavim* and lard oil!...Are we *Chabotnic* [Lubavitcher] *Chassidim*?"[10]

To Leeser and his audience, discussion of such minutiae was essential to the proper observance of Judaism in America: "If the public were not constantly educated and made aware of the importance of these *mitzvot* by concentrating on the details of their observance, not only the entire festival of Succos but eventually all the rituals, all the *Yomim Tovim* would be neglected and forgotten."

❧ Concerns at Home and Abroad

Civil liberties were important topics in *The Occident*. While human rights were taken for granted in America, there was a great concern for the plight of Jews in other parts of the world, particularly in Russia and Poland. In 1858, when Edgar Mortara, a 6-year-old Italian Jewish boy, was taken away from his parents after being secretly baptized by his Catholic nurse, the Jewish world erupted in protest. At a mass meeting in New York, Samuel Myer Isaacs called for the formation of an organization to protect the religious liberty of the Jews in America and abroad, a call which was seconded by Leeser in *The Occident*. A year later, the Board of Delegates of American Israelites was established, with Leeser as its vice-president.

In addition to protesting the Mortara kidnapping and the American treaty with Switzerland, which upheld a Swiss law that banned Jews from living in certain Swiss cantons, the Board of Delegates also worked for Jewish rights in America, in 1861

---

10. Sharfman, *op. cit.*, p.225.

selecting a Rabbi, Dr. Arnold Fischel, to serve as a civilian chaplain for Jewish soldiers in the Union Army.[11]

✑ The Battles Continue

Back in Philadelphia, trouble was brewing between Leeser and Congregation *Mikveh Israel*. He was at times difficult to get along with, and his sermons were long-winded and tedious. In 1850, matters came to a head. A vicious canard, anonymously circulated, cast aspersions upon Leeser's mode of living alone in a boarding house owned by a Christian woman. Although no one implied that Leeser ate non-kosher food or violated the Sabbath, he was required by the board of trustees to sign a document promising that he would conduct himself "in strict accordance with Jewish law" as a condition for renewing his contract. Leeser, feeling that his integrity had been wrongfully impugned, refused to sign. That *Rosh Hashanah*, after conducting the service with great devotion, he stepped down from the pulpit and never returned to *Mikveh Israel*.

He threw himself into his work for *The Occident* and his publishing activities. Six years later, a group of his friends founded the Congregation *Beth El-Emeth* and invited him to become its minister. He accepted, and served this congregation faithfully until the end of his life.

During this time, the polemic warfare against the forces of assimilation continued in the pages of *The Occident*. Isaac Mayer Wise established his own journal, dedicated to the dissemination of progress, enlightenment, and reform, and to dispel the "forces of darkness" represented by his arch enemies, the "hyper-Orthodox," led by Leeser, Rice, Raphall and Illowy. He assembled unto himself a crowd of followers, empty men, who were, according to the son of Rabbi Illowy:

"*Hazanim, ex-shochatim*, teachers, young men who had looked in upon a yeshivah but found the acquisition of knowledge of the Torah too onerous a task, and even laymen who for some reason or other sought these positions rather than follow the vocations they were trained to or take up a peddler's pack as

---

11. *The Jewish Observer*, November 1992.

did or had done most of their co-religionists. These gentlemen quickly assumed the title of Reverend and ere long the Reverend Doctor. Wise — with his geniality, generous disposition and eagerness to make friends, adherents, followers, for his cause — was very liberal in bestowing the degree of Doctor (which was not specified) upon the few who were too modest or too timid to assume it themselves. An article reviling Orthodoxy and its defenders was sure to be so rewarded."[12]

Wise had called for the establishment of a Rabbinical Conference, to be held in Cleveland in 1855, which Leeser and Illowy at first applauded. Illowy soon realized Wise's true intentions, and withdrew his support for the function, and warned Leeser not to attend. Leeser argued that he was required to attend as a journalist. Perhaps to pacify his Orthodox opponent, Wise proposed the first and second plank of the Cleveland platform: that the Bible which was received at Sinai is the revealed word of G-d, and that the Talmud contains the logical and legal developments of the Holy Scriptures, and that its decisions must guide Jews in all matters of practice and duty.

Satisfied that the Conference was under control, and that the Reform tendencies of Wise were not as radical as he had feared, Leeser returned to Philadelphia. As soon as he was out of sight, the Conference got down to business: a vote was taken to abolish *chalitzah; mezuzah, tzitzis* and *tefillin* were likewise sacrificed to the Moloch of assimilation. Leeser, outraged at this treachery, rebuked Wise and his cohorts:

> "*Reformers! Why did you deceive us when we wanted to be one again with you?...to please us or to deceive us, you adopted our platform, but in your hearts you sneer at it. You do not believe in ceremonies...Yes, the rising generation, young America is before you. We confess that you will have plenty of followers. We have seen something similar. Eighteen centuries ago there was one Nazarene to one thousand Israelites, and now it is the reverse...*"[13]

---

12. Illowy, Henry, *Sefer Milchamot Elokim*, Berlin: Poppelaur, 1914, pp.5-6.
13. Sharfman, *op. cit.*, pp.324-325.

An American Vision

Even more than the treachery of the Reformers, Isaac Leeser deplored the constant quarreling and disunion that prevailed among the Orthodox congregations. The tendency of emigrants to segregate themselves into minuscule congregations in even the tiniest communities was to him a weakness. He had a vision for American Jewry as forming another Golden Age, as Spanish Jewry had once represented: a synthesis of Sephardic and Ashkenazic, Polish and German culture — uniquely American, and yet still utterly loyal to the standards of the Torah, enjoying justice and prosperity.

Instead, disorder and indifference prevailed. The Reform movement gained adherents by default as new immigrants found that observance of the Sabbath and dietary laws stood in the way of their material success. For many new arrivals, the lavish, magnificent temple, with its trained choir, English-language services, "family" seating and rigidly enforced rules of decorum, represented the very epitome of upward mobility. Leeser advocated enforcing similar decorum in Orthodox congregations — the disorderly behavior, talking during *davening*, arriving late and leaving early, that prevailed in many synagogues appalled and dismayed him as disrespectful in the extreme. There were three remedies to correct the ills that afflicted American Jewish society: education, education, and education.

In the last year of his life, Leeser saw the fulfillment of his fondest dream: the establishment of Maimonides College in Philadelphia, an academy dedicated to the training of young Jewish men as teachers, *chazanim, shochtim,* and *mohelim,* in addition to providing a full curriculum of secular studies. An institution dedicated exclusively to the study of Torah *lishmah* was not on the agenda — American Jewry had far to go to reach such a rarified atmosphere.

Worn out physically, but not spiritually, Leeser never lived to see the flourishing of his dream. Soon after the establishment of Maimonides College, he succumbed to throat cancer and passed away at the age of 62. The final act of his life was to prepare the next issue of *The Occident* and to provide a guide for its final year of publication. Two loyal disciples, Moses Dropsie and Mayer Sulzbacher, edited *The Occident* for one year after Leeser's death, and then the magazine ceased publication. Without Leeser's genius to guide it, Maimonides College soon closed its doors, and Congregation *Beth-El Emeth* also disbanded.

ᴥᔥ Clearing the Wild Prairie So Others Might Plant

Leeser's life may seem like a failure, since none of the institutions that he guided during his lifetime survived long after his death. But what he accomplished during his life was to clear and plow the wild prairie, so that others might plant and reap the fruit. *The Occident* was to many Jews a pillar of fire in the wilderness of the New World, guiding them in the steps of their ancestors, and his English translations provided many with Jewish books that they could read in no other language.

Leeser's grave is in the cemetery of *Beth El-Emeth* on Market Street at 55th in West Philadelphia. His congregation erected a lavish monument, a bit too grand perhaps, for a man known in life for his modest ways. The white marble obelisk contains four inscriptions, two in Hebrew and two in English. The main English inscription reads:

> THE REVEREND
> ISAAC LEESER
> FIRST MINISTER OF THE
> KAHAL KADOSH BETH EL EMETH
> FOR FORTY YEARS A PREACHER OF
> THE WORD OF G-D
> BORN AT NEUENKIRCHEN PRUSSIA
> DECEMBER 12TH 1805[14]
> DIED AT PHILADELPHIA
> FEBRUARY 1ST 1868
> MAY HIS SOUL REST IN PEACE

The *Gemara* relates in *Yoma*: When the poor man, the wealthy man, and the wicked man appear before the Heavenly Court,

---

14. The date on the monument is incorrect. Leeser was born in 1806.

they are each asked why they did not occupy themselves in Torah. If they use their personal status as an excuse, they will be challenged by three *tzaddikim* — Hillel, Rabbi Ben Harsum and Yoseif — respectively. Yet another person with an excuse too frequently heard is the immigrant to America: "I came to a foreign country, not speaking the language. There were no yeshivos, no Torah teachers, no jobs to be had without working on the Sabbath. I was a victim of circumstances."

Isaac Leeser will come forward to challenge the American immigrant.

Lynn M. Berkowitz

The Rabbi of the Potomac
Rev. Dr. Arnold Fischel ז"ל

He tended to the spiritual needs of the troops of the Union Army with stirring pride and warm compassion

*I*expected to have gone home for "New Year" but could not get a furlough, so must content myself with the prospect of visiting home very
soon, hoping and trusting in the One Above that the coming year may
be one of health not only to my dear family, but of peace to us all and
also to our distracted country.[1]

With these words, a young Jewish cavalry officer in the
Union Army expressed his hopes and fears on the eve of Rosh
Hashanah, 1861 (5622). This officer — Michael M. (Meir) Allen, of
Philadelphia — in civilian life was a Hebrew school teacher and
assistant *chazzan* at Rev. Isaac Leeser's Orthodox congregation
Beth El-Emeth. Allen was of Sefardic descent — his ancestors had

---

1. De Sola Pool, David, *The Diary of Chaplain Michael M. Allen, September 1861,*
Publications of American Jewish Historical Society, vol. 39, 1948.

been living in America since the time of the American Revolution. Although strictly observant, young Michael Allen volunteered for service in the Civil War, becoming a Captain in the 5th Pennsylvania Cavalry, or "Cameron Dragoons," a regiment assembled in Philadelphia by Col. Max Friedman. This regiment, which contained a significant proportion of Jewish volunteers, had elected Allen as regimental chaplain, the first Jew to serve in this capacity in the United States Armed Services.

Michael M. Allen was a non-denominational chaplain for all the soldiers of his regiment. Allen was not an ordained Rabbi, but neither was Rev. Isaac Leeser, the leading Orthodox spokesman of that period, nor Isaac Mayer Wise, the champion of Reform; nor were most of the Jews who functioned as congregational leaders in American synagogues. *Chazzan* and *shochet* were requirements demanded by American congregations far more often than formal rabbinic ordination. The few qualified ordained rabbis in North America at that time included Rabbi Abraham Rice[2] of Baltimore, Rabbi Morris Jacob Raphall of New York City, and Rabbi Ber Illowy[3] of New Orleans, all ordained in European yeshivos — none existed in the United States at that time. Michael Allen had studied *Shulchan Aruch* with Isaac Leeser, in particular *halachos* of *tefillah*, and in 1850 had been *farherred* by Dr. Max Lilienthal, who at that time was still accepted as an Orthodox Rabbi practicing in New York City, although his credentials were suspect.[4] Lilienthal gave Allen a certificate naming him *chaver*,[5] which meant that he was an observant Jew who understood the commandments but needed to consult with an ordained Rabbi for implementing the laws.

As regimental chaplain, Michael Allen did nothing specifically Jewish to meet the spiritual needs of his comrades. He obtained permission for himself to attend Rosh Hashanah services at the *Washington Hebrew Congregation*, a half hour's walk

2. For more details, see Rabbi Shmuel Singer's "From Germany to Baltimore," *The Jewish Observer*, January 1975.
3. See Singer's "Rabbi of the Rebels," *The Jewish Observer*, May 1976.
4. Schneerson, Rabbi Joseph I., *The "Tzemach Tzedek" and the Haskalah Movement*, translated by Zalman Posner, New York, Kehot Publications, 1969.
5. Hebrew document identifying Meir ben Yehudah, a *talmid* of Issac Leeser, as *chaver*, on file in the American Jewish Archives, Cincinnati, Ohio.

from the 5th Pennsylvania's bivouac at "Camp Stoneman." On Yom Kippur he was granted a furlough to go home, where he led the Franklin Street synagogue *Beth El-Emeth* in *Shacharis* and *Minchah*. For *Shabbos* and *Yom Tov* meals, he was a guest in the home of Washington photographer and Jewish activist Adolphus S. Solomons. On Sundays, he held a non-denominational service and preached an inspirational sermon, usually dedicated to some patriotic theme or the importance of brotherly love, carefully avoiding any sectarian topics so as not to offend anyone. Ever the teacher, Allen also offered to tutor those recruits who were immigrants and needed instruction in the English language.

◆§ Chaver, Yes; Christian, No

Chaplains in Civil War times were not appointed directly by the government, but were elected by vote of the officers of the regiment; in the 5th Pennsylvania Cavalry the majority were Jewish. Chaplains did not enjoy the loftiest of reputations in the Union Army. Wrote one Maine officer: "Our chaplain...drives a fast horse, has never spoken of religion...since he has been in the army." Wrote a private: "I have lost all confidence in the chaplain. He lied to me about carrying the mail & does nothing at all but hang around his tent & sort the mail. He never goes around any amongst the men & I think he is nothing but a confounded humbug and nuisance." Another complained: "The people at home have an idea that the soldiers cannot appreciate a good chaplain so the scum is sent to the army."[6] One regiment, the 48th New York, carried a special privilege of sanctity because so many of its officers were ministers. It fell from grace, however, when a brigadier general asked the lieutenant colonel if he really was a preacher. He replied apologetically, "Well, no, General, I can't say I'm a regularly ordained minister. I'm just one of those — local preachers."[7]

Despite being a modest, devout young man, Allen — more than any of these others — was disqualified for the chaplaincy: On July 22, 1861, Congress had enacted a law which required that

6. Wiley, Bell Irvin, *The Life of Billy Yank: The Common Soldier of the Union*, Garden City, New York, Doubleday & Company, 1971, pp. 263-265.

7. Catton, Bruce, *Mr. Lincoln's Army*, Garden City, New York, Doubleday & Co., 1962, p. 176.

every chaplain appointed "by the vote of the field officers and company commanders, must be a regular ordained minister of some *Christian* denomination." Allen's *chaver* certificate and ministerial experience as a *chazzan* might have been "proof" of ordination, but he certainly did not meet the denominational requirement. A representative of the Young Men's Christian Association of Philadelphia, visiting the encampments in the Washington, D.C. area to check out the qualifications of chaplains, was appalled to discover that the spiritual leader of the 5th Pennsylvania Cavalry was a *Jew*! Despite the scandalous antics of the other reverend gentlemen, the Y.M.C.A. agent immediately publicized Allen's religion and the young officer was ordered to disqualify himself from the regiment or face suspension without pay. Rather than subject his family to the humiliating ordeal of his dismissal, Allen turned in his resignation on Sept. 23, 1861 (5th day of *Chol Hamoed Sukkos*), citing poor health as the reason. Thus ended the brief career of the first Jewish chaplain in United States military history.

⋘ Rejection by the Secretary of War

Colonel Friedman was outraged. The forced resignation of Michael Allen, when so many unqualified chaplains professing Christianity went unchastised, was to him an act of anti-Jewish bigotry that should not go unanswered. Friedman was determined to appoint a Jewish chaplain for his regiment, but he wanted to have a man of impeccable credentials, whose rejection by the government could be for no other reason than religious prejudice. He turned to the Board of Delegates of American Israelites — a body that had been established two years earlier to safeguard the civil rights of the Jewish community, both in the United States and abroad — to recommend a suitable candidate.

The man selected was a civilian, Reverend Dr. Arnold Fischel, a Dutch Jew educated in England, who had recently resigned as Rabbi of New York's Sefardic Congregation *Shearith Israel*, after having occupied that position for five years. Fischel was an enthusiastic student of American Jewish history, having delivered two lectures on the subject at the New York Historical Society, and was preparing a manuscript on "The History of the

Israelites in America." He was about to embark on a tour of the United States, to continue his research and to accept invitations for speaking engagements in various cities. Prior to his coming to the United States, he had been Rabbi in two congregations in England—in Portsmouth and in Liverpool. Like most nineteenth-century American Jewish personalities, the details of his early life, his education and credentials, are hard to pin down, but he apparently enjoyed a reputation as a scholar while still in England, although the source of his doctorate and his *semichah* is not known. What is known is that on October 17, 1861, Dr. Fischel wrote to the War Department, at the request of Col. Friedman, applying for a commission for the chaplaincy office vacated by Michael M. Allen. In reply, he received the following communication from the Secretary of War, Simon Cameron:

> *War Department, October 23, 1861.*
> *Rev. A. Fischel, Rabbi, Jewish Synagogue, No. 5 Carroll Place, New York:*
> *Sir, — Your communication of the 17th inst., enclosing a letter from the Honorable F.A. Conkling, in reference to the Chaplaincy of the Cameron Dragoons, has been received.*
> *In reply, you are respectfully informed that by the 9th section of the act of Congress, approved July 22, 1861, it is provided that the Chaplain appointed by "the vote of the field officers and company commanders, must be a regular ordained minister of some Christian denomination." A like provision, also, is made in the 7th section of the act of Congress, approved August 3, 1861. Were it not for the impediments thus directly created by the provisions of these two acts, the Department would have taken your application into its favorable consideration.*
>
>
> *I have the honor to be,*
> *Very respectfully,*
> SIMON CAMERON,
> *Secretary of War*
>

This rejection, signed by none other than the Pennsylvania Cabinet member for whom the "Cameron Dragoons" was named, caused an uproar when released to the press. There could be no question now that this was an issue of civil rights, and a case of clear-cut religious discrimination. The Jews, it was argued, were loyal citizens, paid taxes, volunteered to defend the Union and the Flag, paid with their blood, and were therefore entitled to a minister of their own fatih. Others defended the Congressional act. *The Presbyter,* an Evangelical Christian periodical published in Cincinnati, voiced its objection to the concept of Jewish chaplains: although they had a profound interest in the "spiritual welfare" of the Jews, there was no reason why the government should "foster their prejudices" and "harden them in unbelief" by allowing chaplains of the Jewish faith to minister to Jewish soldiers. The notion that all religious groups in America should be equal before the law was "as broad and universal, as it is wicked and pernicious."[8]

✑ Bringing the Case to President Lincoln

The Board of Delegates realized that Rabbi Fischel's responsibility to the Jewish soldiers went far beyond those who enlisted in the 5th Pennsylvania Cavalry. On Dec. 5, 1861, the ex-minister of *Shearith Israel* was appointed to supervise "the general spiritual welfare of the Israelites in the camps and military hospitals attached to the Department of the Potomac."[9]

Arnold Fischel wasted no time in embarking on what he now saw as a holy mission to all the Jewish soldiers in the Army of the Potomac. He obtained letters of reference from a number of prominent individuals in New York, and stopped in Philadelphia only long enough to collect more petitions, letters of introduction to the President, and the blessing of Rev. Isaac Leeser in his endeavor. His mission was to be twofold: to work for the elimination of the requirement that Chaplains must be "of some Christian denomination," and to serve as an unofficial, civilian chaplain for the Jewish soldiers until he obtain a government commission.

Upon arriving in Washington, Fischel established his "command headquarters" in the photographic studio of Philp & Solomons and immediately went to the White House to seek an interview with President Lincoln. He wrote:

---

8. Korn, Bertram W., *American Jewry and the Civil War,* Philadelphia, Jewish Publication Society, 1950, p. 64.
9. Letter dated December 6, 1861, from Myer S. Isaacs, secretary of the Board of Delegates of American Israelites, to Dr. Arnold Fischel, on file at the American Jewish Historical Society.

"All the influential gentlemen, with whom I spoke on the subject, assured me that it would be impossible for me to get an audience, as the President's time was altogether taken up with public business."[10]

Fischel was not discouraged, however, and gained the attention of the President, but his letters do not reveal what resourceful means he employed. His letter states:

"Seeing that I could not obtain admission by the usual process, I had to devise a plan whereby the subject could be at once brought under the notice of the President, and in this I was perfectly successful. I called this morning at ten o'clock at the White House where hundreds of people were anxiously waiting for admission, some of whom told me that they had been for three days awaiting their turn. I was, nevertheless, at once invited to his room and was received with marked courtesy."[11]

President Lincoln listened to Rabbi Fischel's petition, asked for additional details and then assured Fischel that he believed the exclusion of Jewish chaplains had been altogether unintentional on the part of Congress, that this was the first time that the subject had been brought to his attention, and that he would give it his serious consideration.

The Rabbi thanked Lincoln for the interview, and assured the President that he had come to contend for the principle of religious liberty, as guaranteed by the Constitution.

◆§ Headquarters in Washington

Washington, D.C., at the end of 1861, was home to about 2,000 Jewish civilians and an equal number of Jewish military personnel. There were six kosher restaurants, two kosher boarding homes, and one synagogue, the *Washington Hebrew Congregation*, which boasted twenty-nine paying members and gathered for worship in a second-story room of a commercial building at D Street and 12th.[12] Dr. Fischel rented a room in a more central section of the city, and had his meals at one of the kosher restaurants.[13]

---

10. Letter from Arnold Fischel to Henry Hart, dated December 11, 1861, on file at the American Jewish Historical Society.
11. *Ibid.*
12. *The Jewish Messenger,* January 24, 1862.
13. Letter from Arnold Fischel to Henry Hart, December 13, 1861, on file at the American Jewish Historical Society.

Having met with the President and established his influence with the congressmen on the Military Affairs Committee, who had the power to amend the Volunteer Act regarding chaplains, Dr. Fischel now set out on his primary activity, visiting the Jewish soldiers in all the hospitals, forts and encampments of the Army of the Potomac, to strengthen them in their *Yiddishkeit*.

Fischel had no difficulty obtaining the passes required, as a civilian, to gain entry to the various forts, hospitals and army camps. He wrote:

"The number of Jews in the army is very large, I found some even among Berdan's Sharpshooters...They are not known as Jews, but hundreds with whom I have conversed express their anxiety and hope that some provision may be made for them, so that in case of sickness or death, they not be left to the mercy of strangers. This was more forcibly impressed upon my mind by the numerous Jewish patients I visited in the hospitals, nearly all of whom complained that they had not seen a 'Yehudee' since they entered the hospitals, that they have in addition to the sufferings of disease, to submit to the torture of religious controversy, forced upon them by Christian clergymen, who are anxious 'to save their souls'(!), and all expressed the wish to be interred in a Jewish burial ground."[14]

At the outbreak of the war, the idea of establishing a military hospital for Jewish soldiers was suggested, modeled after the Jews' Hospital of New York City, "where Jewish *nurses* can moisten the parched lips, bathe the fevered brow, and smile and breathe words of comfort to the suffering patient; where nutritious *food,* cooked under the prescribed Laws of our Faith, can be administered; where experienced *medical and surgical attendance* will do all that science and kind treatment can accomplish, and where the last moments of the *dying* can be soothed by the שמע ישראל of the attending Hazan."[15] Dorothea Dix, the superintendent of nursing services, was consulted and promised to give such a hospital her best services, and her support in its establishment. Unfortunately, a similar interest was not found among the Jewish community, and the project was abandoned for lack of funding.

14. Letter from Arnold Fischel to Henry Hart, dated December 20, 1861, on file at the American Jewish Historical Society.
15. *The Jewish Messenger*, letter from "Semi Occasional," dated May 26, 1861.

◦§ Tending the Needs of the Troops

While many Jews chose to conceal their identity, others did not wait for Dr. Fischel to remind them of their heritage. One unidentified young recruit in the Army of the Potomac, who wrote a series of letters to *The Jewish Messenger* signed only "A Jewish Soldier," described the activities of his comrades:

> *It is quite common for Jewish soldiers belonging to the same company to meet together for worship on Sabbath....The character of these devotions is not the less interesting from the fact that they are always performed in solemn silence, and in some secluded spot, where the noise of the camp cannot penetrate....When looking on those groups, I cannot help reflecting on the remarkable history of our race. Here are the descendants of the Hebrew patriarch who smote the confederated kings near Damascus, the descendants of those who overthrew the colossal hosts of proud Egypt, and conquered the powerful nations of Philistea, who, under the Maccabees, triumphed over the Syrian despot, the survivors of all ancient dynasties, the participants in every remarkable event of history, behold them now in the New World, shedding their blood for the maintenance of the liberties secured to them by this Republic. Whilst thus reflecting, I feel most solemnly impressed by hearing in these Virginian forests my brethren utter the Shema Yisrael, which first our great lawgiver proclaimed in the plains of Arabia.*"[16]

Corporal Joseph C. Levi, of the 37th New York, commented on the lack of kosher food:

> *"In the matter of rations, perhaps as a good Orthodox, the less I say on the subject the better. If first our bill of fare was bread, coffee and pork for breakfast, coffee, pork and bread for dinner, and pork, bread and coffee for tea, it has, at all events, improved with time..."*[17]

While Rabbi Fischel encountered no difficulty in gaining access to the encampments and military hospitals, he was forced to pay his expenses out of pocket. The Board of Delegates had promised to reimburse him for his food, lodging and travel, and Fischel was counting on the Board to conduct fund-raising on his

---

16. "Sketches from the Seat of War," by A Jewish Soldier, *The Jewish Messenger*, February 7, 1862.
17. Letter from Joseph C. Levi to *The Jewish Messenger*, June 12, 1862.

behalf, as his own time was completely taken up with his lobbying and *kiruv* work. This could be quite costly. One expedition, to visit Jewish soldiers attached to General N.P. Banks Western Maryland division, took eight hours by railroad car and cost $20, "a journey as expensive as it is disagreeable," Fischel commented.[18] But he added that the trip had been worthwhile: he met some soldiers who belonged to his former congregation who expressed great enthusiasm for his mission.

In those days before dog tags were invented, Fischel had visiting cards made up which he distributed among the Jewish soldiers, so that he could be contacted by anyone needing the attention of a Jewish clergyman. He put *bikur cholim* on a higher priority than *kiruv*, and visited the military hospitals daily, the encampments less frequently. When a Jewish soldier died in one of the military hospitals, Dr. Fischel informed the family and arranged to have the body sent home for Jewish burial. Besides this, he continued to work for an amendment to the law that would modify the exclusion of Jewish clergy from the chaplaincy.

The young Rabbi contracted cholera as a result of his frequent visits to the military hospitals, and he was confined to bed for a week. Dr. Fischel begged the Board of Delegates not to release this information to *The Jewish Messenger*, which had been providing weekly updates of his mission, "as it may alarm my relatives abroad."

When he recovered, he resumed his activities. He asked to have *Siddurim* and *Tehillim* sent, the smallest size available, and reminded the Board of Delegates that he was running low on funds, as his traveling and illness had made a deep hole in his pocket. But he was not about to discontinue his good work.[19]

◄§ The Reform Opposition

Not all Jews were pleased with Rabbi Fischel's chaplaincy. Isaac Mayer Wise, the fiery leader of the Reform movement in America, had castigated the Board of Delegates of American

18. Letter from Arnold Fischel to Henry Hart, dated December 27, 1861, on file at the American Jewish Historical Society.
19. Letter from Arnold Fischel to Henry Hart, dated January 2, 1862, on file at the American Jewish Historical Society.

Israelites and ridiculed Fischel's mission. Although invitations to join the Board had gone out to all parties within American Jewry, the founders were Orthodox and only Orthodox congregations chose to participate. Wise feared that a united Orthodoxy might slow down the momentum of his Reform program, and he therefore denigrated the Board of Delegates from the pages of his weekly newspaper, *The Israelite*.

Wise and his Reform colleagues now tried to undermine the activities of Dr. Fischel. On Jan. 6, 1862, an advertisement appeared in the leading newspapers of Washington, Philadelphia, and New York, issuing a "Protest" against the Board of Delegates for claiming to speak in the name of all American Jewry, signed by Isaac M. Wise, David Einhorn, Samuel Adler, Henry Hochheimer, Bernard Felsenthal and Max Lilienthal.[20] No motive, other than spite, malicious mischief and jealousy of Dr. Fischel's success, has been given for this action on the part of Wise and his colleagues.

Fischel was outraged. "Those Reform Rabbis seem to have no other object than to injure the cause of Judaism both socially and religiously," he wrote angrily in a letter to the Board of Delegates.

In any event, the "Protest" had made no impression on the Military Affairs Committee, and excited ridicule rather than sympathy. So Fischel cautioned *The Jewish Messenger* not to respond to the venomous attack of Wise and his confederates with unseemly invective.

Although Fischel gives no description in his letter of celebrating Purim or Passover among the soldiers, he did accompany the Army of the Potomac into Virginia for part of General McClellan's "Peninsula Campaign." He was traveling with the "left wing" of the army, and was excited and optimistic. He promised to send his next report to the Board of Delegates from Richmond, once it had been captured by Federal troops. We have no more letters from him after that, other than his "Final Report," dated April 3, 1862. In it, he reiterated his conviction for the necessity of a chaplain for the Jewish soldiers, and thanked the

---

20. *Sinai*, February 1862.

Board of Delegates for having given him the opportunity to officiate in that capacity. It is not known if he actually ministered to Jewish soldiers while on the battlefield, although he is thought to be the author of an anonymous article in *The Jewish Messenger*, titled "A National Disgrace," poignantly describing the death of a Jewish soldier at the Battle of Williamsburg, Virginia, whose body could not be recovered for Jewish burial. The article spoke about the Jewish soldiers:

> *Poor fellows — they have risked all — even their lives, to assist in restoring peace and concord to our distracted country. They have displayed bravery worthy of the Maccabees, endurance, and courage befitting heroes — but their brethren have forgotten them, have neglected their silent but powerful appeal — and they are left to die among strangers, their last moments agonized by the attention of ministers and "Sisters of Mercy" — well meant — for who can fail to recognize the kindly, the noble motives by which they are actuated? — but utterly foreign to what they would wish to receive, and so harsh and painful to Israelites looking for the soothing consolations of divines of their faith. They are left to be buried near the field of battle, "unwept, unhallowed and unsung," their graves unmarked — whereas they should be interred in consecrated ground, where rest the bones of their ancestors; and co-religionists should be with them when on their beds of sickness, to administer consolation, and soothe their dying moments, receive their parting requests, and, if death should claim them, bear their bodies tenderly to their former residence, and relieve the anxiety of their distressed families by assurances that they died as Jews in the faith of Israel.[21]*

◆§ Dishearted by Apathy and Indifference

Rabbi Fischel was ultimately forced to give up his activities of strengthening *Yiddishkeit* among the Jewish soldiers in the Army of the Potomac as a result of apathy and indifference on the part of the Jewish community. He commented bitterly that American Jews could contribute ten thousand dollars for the Jews of Morocco, but could not raise one-tenth of that sum for their brethren at home defending their country and liberties.[22]

21. *The Jewish Messenger*, May 30, 1862.
22. Letter from Arnold Fischel to Henry Hart, dated January 2, 1862.

Disheartened, the dedicated young Rabbi returned to New York. When the chaplaincy clause was finally amended, and Jewish clergy given the right to serve as military chaplains, the first appointment, given on Sept. 18, 1862, went to Rev. Jacob Frankel, of Philadelphia, the *chazzan* of *Congregation Mikveh Israel.* Dr. Fischel certainly deserved a commission for his activities, the first such actions on behalf of Jewish soldiers in the United States Armed Services, but he was never honored for his self-sacrifice. He remained in New York for two more years, appearing occasionally at public functions. He was the keynote speaker at the dedication of the Hebrew Orphan Asylum in 1863, at which he spoke most eloquently of the home providing a haven for the orphaned children of Jewish soldiers who fell in the service of their country. Finally, on August 21, 1864, he left the United States to return to England, where his family had remained. He died in Holland in 1894.[23]

Dr. Arnold Fischel was a man who accomplished many firsts: the first permanent minister of the historic *Shearith Israel* congregation, the first serious scholar to write on American Jewish history, and the first Jewish chaplain to United States servicemen. Yet his achievements have been passed over and more credit is given to those who came later.

---

23. Korn, *op. cit.,* p. 77.

Anonymous

Remembering
Rabbi Binyomin Steinberg ע"ה
A Fresh Reaction to his Passing by a Graduate of Bais Yaakov of Baltimore

He strived for the best in himself as an educator, inspiring his students to aspire for no less perfection in themselves

⋙ Overwhelmed With Loss...

I just walked into my apartment in Brooklyn after a four hour drive from Baltimore, Maryland. I am exhausted, hungry, depressed, my nerves on edge because I have to care for my five-month-old baby. And yet, something is compelling me to sit and write. I have been to too many funerals ר"ל and hope this one will be the last. However, this is the first time my emotions are overwhelming me so that I can suppress or control them no longer. My husband, as wonderful a companion as he is, is not able to help me cope or express my feelings at the moment.

Rabbi Steinberg, ע"ה, was the type of person to move and inspire one to such actions. How else can one explain the outpouring of grief where there was not one dry eye in the entire

Bais Yaakov? Where three thousand people from all walks of life, from the entire spectrum of *Yiddishkeit*, who left jobs, children, errands, nursing babies, traveled for hundreds of miles to pay their last respects?

I have been thinking over some of the *hespedim* (eulogies) spoken there, and one common theme was noted. He was a *mechanech* (pedagogue). But not *just* a *mechanech*: one that was supreme, exemplary, brilliant, talented, of finest quality, *par excellence*. He strived for the best in himself as an educator, at the same time inspiring us to strive for no less perfection in ourselves.

◢§ "I Was Not the Best Student"

I can still remember him when I was a tenth-grader. I was not the best student. My home was one beset with marital strife, saturated with hypocrisy, the antithesis of what Bais Yaakov stands for. I have forgotten what infraction I was called into the office about. But I do remember him staying extra late at school to talk to me. Remember, I was the low-achiever, the one who was elated with a 70 in *Chumash!* The one who the teachers prayed to keep out of their classroom. And yet, he took the time to speak to someone like me, who may not accomplish much nor soar to inspiring heights. But I was his student. And I deserved extra attention because I didn't receive it at home. He criticized me in a manner that gave me *chizuk*, uplift. But what struck me most was that ride home.

He took out time to read a Purim newsletter that the seniors had printed in honor of the approaching holiday. He told me, "I said to myself that before I left school I would read this."

And there we were, the two of us sitting in his car in the middle of the Bais Yaakov parking lot, I watching him laughing at the jokes they wrote, wondering the entire time why he did not become enflamed with rage at what I considered the utter *chutzpah* of what the girls wrote about him. And he thought it was funny!

◢§ History Lived in his Lectures

History was his forte. Bais Yaakov girls from Baltimore were known for their vast knowledge and familiarity in history. If I could hope for a good mark in any subject, it was in history. But the way he taught and made the lessons come alive! His class was the one that—if you had a lousy experience at home the night before, and hated the rest of the day, without any hope for the future, you could be assured of excitement—no—entertainment! Where the words of the *gedolim* and (*lehavdil*) the *resha'im* came to life, where you were there at the Damascus Affair, sat next to Rav Shrira Gaon, Rav Hai Gaon, *Rambam, Ramban....* I still have my notes from his classes, now made more priceless with his loss. I always looked forward to his lessons, which consisted of not only *ikrei emunah* (fundamentals of faith) but *ikrei hachaim* (fundamentals of life).

I could not survive as a Jew without his teachings. Why, even my discussions about *Hilchos Melochim* by the *Rambam* make my husband *kvell* (glow with pride).

✑ "I Am Experiencing a Lot of Pain"

But there is something else that I am experiencing now, and that is pain. A lot of pain. I can still hear his sons' *hespedim* ringing in my ears. They described a definitive sweetness when they heard him sing *zemiros*, a *niggun*, when they danced with him. I for one can verify that. I can still picture him walking barefoot across a stream at a nearby state park, or playing baseball at the same place. Which other dean of a school would encourage the girls to challenge him with questions? To *kvetch* to him? He treated us like a father. We were all one big happy family, our Bais Yaakov family. We all felt secure and happy being near him, sitting at his feet.

What most struck me was that no one there could utter a bad word about him. No one! I still remember how the girls who were involved with Bnei Akiva were upset with the school policy of not allowing them to use the Bais Yaakov facilities for their events. I also remember how indignant their parents were about it. My parents davened in the same *shul* as those people. I used to hear them rant and rave about it. In contrast, Bnos was given free access to and use of the facilities. They use to cry in outrage over it: "Bnos can use Bais Yaakov but we can't. Why not? What difference does it make? I'll tell you what it is. It's politics! Pure and simple. How dare they!"

Yes, they were upset over the policy. But one word against Rabbi Steinberg? Never!

A Friend of Mine...Expelled

I remember a friend of mine being expelled. She had gotten involved in some kind of fraud, a type of misdeed that even in today's world would raise more than just a few eyebrows. And I remember how Rabbi Steinberg, ע״ה, literally chased us away from her, forbidding us to talk to her. But not one word could the girl, nor her parents, raise against Rabbi Steinberg. And even though he loudly denounced her actions, discouraged us from even the most minimal contact with her, we — her classmates, the girl herself, and all who were aware of the issue — could not come up with one complaint, one bad word, not a single reproach against Rabbi Steinberg.

Anyone who sent their daughter to Bais Yaakov, taught there, gave money, even just said a mere hello to Rabbi Steinberg, was struck by his warmth, his kindly countenance, his grace even under the most crushing pressure. We all recognized these qualities in him and more, and strove to make them our ideal. This and so much more I want to commit to pen and paper, but only because of the human limitations of attention and the real lack of space or time, do I stop. I was never known for my eloquence of thought or words, though never short of producing both. But at this moment, my emotions so overcome me that it is difficult for me to see my own handwriting through my tears. The enormity of his loss is beyond my powers of description.

I will miss you so very, very much, Rabbi Steinberg.

This volume is part of
THE ARTSCROLLSERIES®
an ongoing project of
translations, commentaries and expositions
on Scripture, Mishnah, Talmud, Halachah,
liturgy, history, the classic Rabbinic writings,
biographies, and thought.

For a brochure of current publications
visit your local Hebrew bookseller
or contact the publisher:

Mesorah Publications, ltd

4401 Second Avenue
Brooklyn, New York 11232
(718) 921-9000